China — The Remembered Life

CHINA

The
Remembered
Life

BY PAUL FRILLMANN
AND GRAHAM PECK

Introduction by
John K. Fairbank

*Illustrated with
photographs and maps*

HOUGHTON MIFFLIN COMPANY · BOSTON

1968

DS
777.53
F73
1968

First Printing c

Printed in the United States of America

712357

Authors' Note

THIS BOOK began about two years ago, in a conversation we had at a party in New York, after not having seen one another for several years. We had been friends in postwar Peking, Shanghai, and Cambridge. During the war, though we never met, our paths had crisscrossed repeatedly.

We were then fellow members of a rather small group of men in the U.S. armed services or civilian agencies who were set off from the majority of Americans in China because our work was with the Chinese and we lived among them, most of us speaking the language to some degree. Because of an active grapevine telegraph within the group, even those of us who did not know one another used to hear much news — most of it fondly derisive — about everyone else.

At the party in New York we found we had both passed fifty and naturally began reminiscing about the interesting and important things we had seen as young men. The idea followed that we should try to record more of this eyewitness history before it all dimmed.

Peck had already published two books about his own experiences in China. While Frillmann had recorded a series of taped interviews for Columbia University's Project on Aviation, he had not succeeded in turning the voluminous typescript of this spoken account into a written narrative. We decided therefore to collaborate on Frillmann's book. Luckily the circumstances of both our lives made this possible.

Frillmann was then working in New York, but spent the weekends with his wife and daughters in Scituate, Massachusetts. Peck was a partner in a silk-screen printing business in South Pomfret, Vermont, about four hours' drive from Scituate. We arranged to spend every other weekend together, in one place or another. We found a full weekend's conversation took at least two weeks to convert into readable prose. The book was finished in a little more than a year.

PAUL FRILLMANN
GRAHAM PECK

Contents

Consul of the United States

Illustrations

Maps

Introduction

HISTORY is made by multitudes, but sometimes it can best be understood through one man's life story. Paul Frillmann is a rather representative American from Illinois who went to China in 1936 as a missionary, stayed on in wartime as a chaplain, got his training and served as a soldier, and went back again in peacetime for the State Department. During fifteen years he changed his role as history unfolded. But all the time his keen interest in the Chinese people represented the American effort to understand them and be of help.

His three careers in China were full of dramatic incident. They transported him from the strictly starched Evangelical Lutheran Mission compound in Japanese-held Hankow to the wet jungle camp of the secret Flying Tigers air force in lower Burma. Then when the Flying Tigers became General Chennault's Fourteenth Air Force, he jumped again to Kunming in southwest China and worked behind the Japanese lines for air force intelligence. After the Japanese war he worked in the American Consulate General in Mukden in the midst of Chinese civil war, and finally, after the Communist conquest of China, he served as Public Affairs Officer at Hong Kong.

Curiously enough, this evolution in Paul Frillmann's experience — from performing good works to waging war as

China's ally and then to being evicted from the mainland — parallels in miniature the national experience of whole countries in their contact with China. Many have been called to be friends of the Chinese people, but few have been chosen permanently. For example, after the Japanese had proved their importance by defeating China in 1895, they became teachers to a whole generation of young Chinese patriots. Tokyo became the seedbed of Sun Yat-sen's 1911 revolution. Not until 1915 did the Japanese become a new menace, which became aggressive in 1931. Similarly, the Soviets in their first decade of contact to 1927 became great friends of the Chinese revolution. Again in the 1950's they functioned as helpful allies, only to become apostate revisionists after 1960. So the American experience has been nothing new. The missionaries, businessmen, consuls, and teachers who assisted the early modernization of China down into the 1930's became the closest allies and the chief support of Chinese nationalism for a time in the 1940's, only to be enshrined by the new regime as "imperialist enemies" from 1950 onward.

The inner logic of this Chinese cycle in which foreign friends are accepted, worked with, and learned from, until they are eventually distrusted, feared, and expelled, is one of the more fascinating features of Chinese history. The pattern is so deeply ingrained from ancient times that the modern-day foreigner should not take his rejection personally, any more than he should attribute his original warm acceptance entirely to the overwhelming effulgence of his own personality. The fact is that, as an outsider in the Middle Kingdom, he has been cast unknowingly in a very old role with a built-in ambiguity.

This role goes back to the basic point that the Chinese have never been able to get rid of foreigners. Partly, China has always been a great lodestone of civilization and trade, drawing the outer peoples in. Partly, the nomadic tribes of the Inner Asian steppe from early times developed cavalry forces that

Chinese peasant armies could not contain. In the result, the Chinese liked to stay at home, and the non-Chinese liked to come into China. Generations of Chinese, from peasant to statesman, thus had to learn how to deal with the foreigner, keep on the good side of his warriors, utilize his power in Chinese politics, and try to avoid his domination. As the Chinese people came into the twentieth century and began to modernize their society through revolutionary changes, foreigners became more useful than ever. But the old syndrome still operated, and the fear of foreign domination, now fueled by nationalism, became stronger than ever.

None of us Americans who were in China in Paul Frillmann's day had this kind of historical perspective, because we had not yet studied Chinese history. This has been studied in the West only in recent decades, a bit late. But now in Paul Frillmann's record of his "remembered life," we can see the recent variations on this old historical theme.

First about Paul himself: born in 1911, he was brought up with the old-time religion in Melrose Park, Illinois, and attended Concordia College, a preparatory school in Milwaukee, from 1925 to 1931. Thence he went to Concordia Seminary in St. Louis, 1931–35, and elected to become a missionary. This took him to China as a young man of twenty-four. After about a year of Chinese studies in Hankow, his story opens in 1937, a few months before the outbreak of Japan's aggression. Paul is a staunchly built, forthright, compellingly friendly man, both sincere and amusing and certainly one of the great raconteurs. Indeed, his conversation has always so fascinated his friends that they have despaired of ever getting it down on paper.

Here enters Graham Peck, an accomplished artist and writer whose picture of wartime China, *Two Kinds of Time,* has already become a classic and recently been reprinted both in hard cover and in paperback. To have Peck write down Frillmann's story is, as the Victorians would say, like piling Pelion

on Ossa, or having Odysseus tell you about Achilles. Graham
Peck, like Paul Frillmann, is a warm personality, naturally in
immediate contact with people round about, and moreover a
disciplined and graphic craftsman with words, who had a very
similar experience in China. Both of them spoke the colloquial
language. Time after time, as Frillmann describes Japanese air
raids or Anna Louise Strong or the inflation or General Claire
Chennault, I think I can see Peck at the typewriter choosing
le mot juste. But the reason for their collaboration is not that
Frillmann can't write. On the contrary. Their collaboration
recreates the past from a common perspective and as a mutual
enthusiasm, each leading the other back to those salient vignettes
that give history significance.

One theme that Frillmann-Peck see again and again is the
clash of cultures. For example, Chinese repeatedly seem callous
toward individual suffering and death, in a land where so many
have always suffered and died, while Americans time after time
seem immersed in their material culture in a way that shuts out
the poverty and pain of the Chinese around them. Surely this
touches on the secret of the Chinese-American emotional involvement, that love-hate relationship that bedevils our diplomatic relations. Here also a syndrome operates: China's state of
suffering evokes American sympathy; the Americans bring to
bear their material resources and know-how; however, these are
not adequate to "save China" but only to demonstrate an American type of superiority. In the resulting situation the Americans
enjoy their own feelings of benevolence and adequacy, being
themselves not stuck in the morass of Chinese life. Meanwhile,
the Chinese with their inbuilt sense of reciprocity, the absolute
duty to repay favors or lose one's moral integrity ("face"), are
by turns thankful and humiliated. For the Americans the relationship is superficial, the experience vicarious. For the
Chinese the foreigner's help may mean eating or not eating, life
or death; the price may be sycophancy or self-abasement, meet-

ing the foreigner's criteria, dancing to his tune. This is the psy-
chological pain of "Westernization" and even of modernization.
One gives up one's old ways under external compulsion. In the
end, one hates the well-intentioned foreigner, and this in turn
hurts the foreigner's feelings. He has meantime been disil-
lusioned and even embittered by the corruption of the old
order and its different standards of personal conduct. The
residue of the Sino-American encounter may thus be mutual
hostility.

Since we see this same syndrome at work again in another
part of the Chinese culture area, Vietnam, the Frillmann-Peck
documentation of it in China of the 1940's is both timely and
provocative.

No "lesson" need be sought from Paul Frillmann's adventure
story, for it has its own fascination. Nevertheless, I think one
point emerges quite clearly: the great solvent of Sino-American
enmity must be person-to-person contact. Only by knowing our
opposite numbers in their lives' daily struggles can we appreci-
ate the heroism of the great majority of good-guys in China, and
only by such contact can we really understand why we dislike
the bad-guys there. Conversely, it will take personal acquaintance to convince the new generation in China that America is
not all bombs and missiles. The kind of participation in the
life of the other people, which took Paul Frillmann and Graham
Peck to China and kept them there for so many years, cannot
be resumed on the old basis. But Sino-American contact in
some form must somehow be resumed in both directions on a
massive scale if we are ever to achieve a tranquil world.

JOHN K. FAIRBANK

China Missionary

CHAPTER I

Hankow Falls 1938

HANKOW in 1938 was surely one of the most exciting cities in the world. From January until October it was the temporary capital of China. The Yangtze beside it and the railways passing through were main channels for the Chinese retreat from the Japanese invasion. Spread on a flat plain beside a navigable river, Hankow had no natural defenses, and I don't think anybody really thought it could be held, but then, few had thought the Chinese Nationalist government could survive its defeats on the coast and move inland. The fact that Chiang Kai-shek was in Hankow and still resisting sent a wave of patriotric pride through China, and the city was a magnet for young volunteers for war work.

Every day the crowded streets resounded with bugles and the stirring songs of marching soldiers. Holidays were celebrated with giant rallies and parades. Banners daubed with war slogans streamed above chanting thousands, while cannons, tanks, and planes made of painted paper and sticks bobbed among waves of raised fists. Despite the increasing number of wounded soldiers unloaded at the railway stations and the hordes of miserable refugees waiting patiently on the waterfront, the atmosphere wasn't just martial; it was giddy. Only

Spain and China held wars in 1938, and in Hankow that year I always felt history was here and now.

For half of the thirty years since then, I have lived in China, first as a missionary, then as chaplain of General Chennault's Flying Tiger volunteer aviators, next as a combat intelligence officer for the 14th U.S. Air Force and later the Office of Strategic Services, finally as an information officer and consul of the U.S. State Department. My experiences were so varied that I often could not put them into any larger context. Looking back I can now see the historical pattern and realize I was witness to one of the major events of our times — the collapse of the old order in China, which opened the way for our problems in Korea and Vietnam and will no doubt continue to shake Asia for years to come.

I had been disappointed when I arrived in Hankow, fifteen months before the Japanese invasion. I was then a twenty-four-year-old missionary, brand-new to China, and I expected that a city deep in the interior would be exotically picturesque: crumbling shrines, quaint bazaars, moon gates. By 1938 I had learned that Hankow showed a truer face of modern China. The customs and attitudes of the world's oldest continuous civilization were there, and — when you knew where to look — so were sturdy traditional buildings and objects, as well as the old handicraft skills which could still make them. But right in the middle of the city, along the Yangtze, were the Foreign Concessions, a jumble of shops, warehouses, and residences in every architecture known to 19th-century Europe and America. Tall new commercial buildings dotted the masses of close-packed Chinese tenements, and the few pagodas stood among smoking factory chimneys.

The Yangtze itself held a great drama of contrasts. It was nearly a mile wide, six hundred miles in from the ocean. In autumn and winter its treacherous brown waters receded for

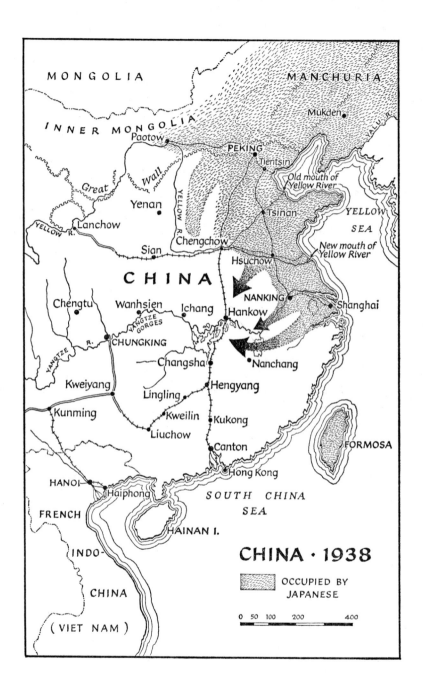

MONGOLIA

MANCHURIA

INNER MONGOLIA

Mukden

Paotow

Great Wall

PEKING

Tientsin

Old mouth of
Yellow River

YELLOW R.

Yenan

Lanchow

Tsinan

YELLOW

YELLOW R.

Sian

Chengchow

SEA

New mouth of
Yellow River

Hsuchow

CHINA

NANKING

Chengtu

Wanhsien

Ichang

Hankow

Shanghai

YANGTZE
GORGES

CHUNGKING

YANGTZE R.

Changsha

Nanchang

Kweiyang

Hengyang

Lingling

Kweilin

Kunming

Kukong

Liuchow

Canton

FORMOSA

HANOI

Hong Kong

Haiphong

SOUTH CHINA
SEA

FRENCH

HAINAN I.

INDO-

CHINA · 1938

CHINA

OCCUPIED BY
JAPANESE

(VIET NAM)

0 50 100   200   400

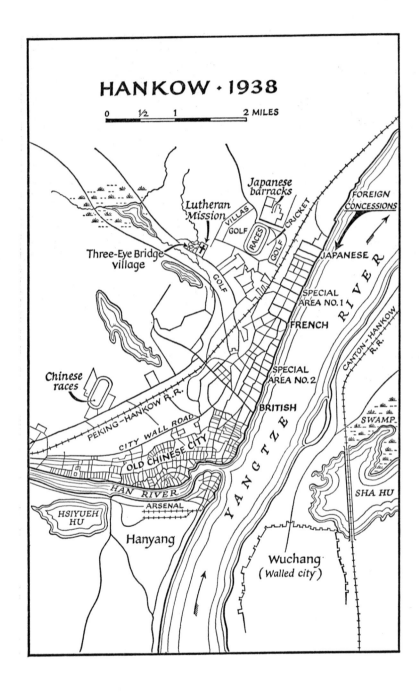

HANKOW · 1938

0   ½   1   2 MILES

Japanese barracks

Lutheran Mission

VILLAS

GOLF

RACES

GOLF

CRICKET

FOREIGN CONCESSIONS

Three-Eye Bridge village

GOLF

JAPANESE

R   I   V   E   R

SPECIAL AREA NO.1

FRENCH

CANTON–HANKOW R.R.

Chinese races

SPECIAL AREA NO.2

PEKING–HANKOW R.R.

CITY WALL ROAD

BRITISH

Y   A   N   G   T   Z   E

SWAMP

SHA HU

OLD CHINESE CITY

HAN   RIVER

HSIYUEH HU

ARSENAL

Hanyang

Wuchang
(Walled city)

hundreds of yards, down steep banks and across wide yellow sandbars. In spring and summer powerful floods with a burden of refuse and corpses swirled up to street level, sometimes over it. Always the river swarmed with motley traffic: ocean-going freighters and tankers moored to floating docks, riverboats for passengers and freight, Chinese and foreign warships, thousands of traditional Chinese craft, from massive wooden junks to tiny sampans — "three planks" is what that name meant, and that's about all they were.

The constant sucking and sighing of the currents mingled with the chants — "Ay-y-y hey, Ay-y-y hey, hey" — of huge gangs of coolies carrying burdens along the waterfront. The whistles from nearby boats, or from distant trains and factories, were mournful, thunderous, or shrill. Often in 1938 air raid sirens howled over all; then the ships moved quickly to shore and everyone crept silently out of sight as this tableau of contemporary China was completed by Japanese bombers sowing death across the city.

When I first came to Hankow on a steamer from Shanghai, another of my illusions began to crack right on the docks. I had assumed a missionary would live simply, perhaps in a native house in a Chinese neighborhood, and would walk or bicycle wherever he went. I was met by fellow missionaries who had a shining new Dodge station wagon parked on the waterfront.

They drove me rapidly away through wide paved streets and out into farming country where radio towers and small factories were scattered among old-fashioned peasant villages. The fields looked wonderfully fresh and green, for it was April Fools' Day, a date on which many important events of my life have occurred. We passed a cricket field, a race course, a golf links, and a luxury suburb with big houses which would have looked all right outside Chicago, if it hadn't been for the high walls around them. On the edge of unspoiled farmland and

half-surrounded by a sprawling peasant village, stood a compound the size of at least one American city block. A moat-like
canal at the foot of its red brick walls made it seem a fortified
point in hostile territory. Inside the walls lines of trees bordered vegetable and flower gardens, a conservatory, play-
grounds including a clay tennis court. A big building for classes
and administration was flanked by long dormitories for Chinese
students. Five large residences for the American staff stood in
their own gardens. This was the quarter-million-dollar home
of the Evangelical Lutheran Mission, which ran an elementary
school in English — it was the best American School in Hankow
— and a seminary in Chinese for the graduates of Chinese high
schools and colleges. I was to teach in the latter as soon as I
learned Chinese.

My early misgivings about mission life were soon submerged
in fascinating language studies. I had two hours a day with
each of four Chinese teachers, one at 8 A.M., the others at
10 A.M., 1 P.M., and 3 P.M.

They were relays of fresh horses, and I'm afraid I started as a
slow cart. I was fluent in German, since many classes in my
seminary in St. Louis had been given in it, and I knew some
Greek, Latin, and Hebrew. Studying each of these languages
had helped with the others, but when I began studying Chinese
nothing familiar or even recognizable could be grasped.

None of the teachers spoke English and their methods were
the simplest. *"Cho-tse, cho-tse,"* one would say, pointing to the
desk and having me repeat it with him until I not only knew
cho-tse was a desk but could pronounce it perfectly. This was
easy enough, but even the first step away from seen objects
brought problems. The teacher who took up pronouns pointed
at himself and said *wo* for I, pointed at me and said *ni* for you,
then gestured over his shoulder and said *ta* for he or she. It was
some days before I realized *ta* was not the door to my study.

Once I had the hang of it, though, it was amazing how easily the teachers could lead me to understand abstract words — not just the easily acted ones like fear, hunger, or love, but conceptual terms like imagination, piety, or politics. This direct method may have been slower than conventional teaching with textbooks, but once I learned something, I didn't forget it, and my fluency was always greater than I could have gained through books.

After a few months the teachers included written Chinese and that ended a time of frustration. On walks and bicycle rides I had been tantalized by the Chinese ideographs which spread their splendid patterns everywhere: huge formal ones of gold on scarlet lacquer boards, hung over the gates of temples, banks, or barracks; violently brush-stroked black ones slashing among the angry cartoons on political wall-newspapers; gay ones of calico scraps sewn on banners advertising a sale of dry goods. It had maddened me not to know what they said, and now the whole language seemed to be opening up. After another slow period while I mastered the Chinese writing brush, I was swept along for a year and more in a frenzy of wanting to know.

Looking back, I think Chinese was the easiest language I learned. Certainly spoken Chinese was. It had little grammar, and once the ears had been taught to keep open for them, the crisp monosyllabic words would bounce through the head like wooden beads, their meaning determined by the rhythm with which whole phrases and sentences were accented. Despite its simplicity, it was expressive and could be beautiful. At that time the population of China was probably little more than half what it is today, but studying Chinese already had the stimulus of knowing this language was spoken by more people than any other on earth.

Without my studies, those pre-invasion months could have ended in discouragement. My fellow missionaries were older, married, and shared few non-parochial interests with me. I was soon chattering with coolies, shopkeepers, and others I met on my walks, or having stilted conversations with the seminary students, but I was so walled away inside a little enclosure of middle-class American comfort that I didn't know how to start making Chinese friends.

I was also shocked to discover how much of the foreign community regarded missionaries as figures of fun, or outcasts little better than the poverty-stricken White Russian refugees. I had grown up among eleven lively brothers and sisters, and my being the only one headed for a religious career had never prevented my joining all the noisy fun of a big family. In Hankow it was a blow to learn that a young bachelor, fond of sports and festivities, could be ignored by the non-missionary foreigners who enjoyed such things.

The first friendly hand was extended by one of the American consuls, John Paton Davies. He was the son of American missionaries in China, had been born and raised there, and was completely at home in the Chinese language. He introduced himself to me at some official function so large that missionaries were invited; I was struck at once by his alert and amused expression. Having known the strains of missionary life, he evidently saw my dilemma, for he began riding out to the Lutheran compound on weekends, bringing another horse so we could make trips into the country. We used to play tennis on the Lutheran court, one of the best in town, and gradually he introduced me to foreigners who could forgive a missionary if he had a good backhand. At meals in his apartment I began to meet interesting Chinese.

Although there have been gaps, I have kept in touch with John ever since. I think the great thing about him is that he always wants to move right in and affect life. There must have been others in Hankow who noticed a lost young missionary easily helped, but John was the only one who bothered. In 1943, while he was General Stilwell's political adviser, he saved some other lives more dramatically when their transport plane went down over the Hump. While the others wasted priceless minutes assuring themselves nothing was wrong, John got into his parachute and helped the crew open the cargo doors. When the sinking plane cleared one mountain ridge by the barest margin he jumped, emboldening the others to follow so quickly that only two were left aboard to be killed when the plane hit the next ridge. He showed another kind of courage still later by writing government reports describing how weak the Chinese Nationalists were growing, and how strong the Communists. He was rewarded for this by being eased out of the State Department soon after rapid Communist victories proved how right he had been.

By the summer of 1937, when the Japanese invasion began near Peking, my Chinese was good enough for me to follow the war news in the one-sheet tabloids hawked on our suburban street. Despite obvious censorship and official optimism, it was easy to see the news was bad for China from the start. In early August Peking fell without a shot fired within its medieval city walls, and the Japanese soon attacked at Shanghai in central China. In the heaviest fighting anywhere since the first World War, Chiang Kai-shek's best troops, including thirty crack German-trained divisions, slowly retreated the hundred and fifty miles from Shanghai to Nanking, then the capital. Nanking fell in mid-December, with massacres, rapings, and pillage which seemed profoundly shocking Asian excesses to a world still ignorant of what modern Europeans could do.

All through the autumn, government bureaus, schools, hospitals, and factories moved upriver to Hankow from Nanking. Judging by the street traffic, the population nearly doubled, with refugees camping in offices, warehouses, garages. No new buildings were attempted, but shantytowns spread on the beaches, in the suburban ricefields and cemeteries, even on the flat roofs of older buildings.

Several hundred foreigners arrived in the refugee wave: gov-

ernment advisers and technicians, doctors and nurses, news-
papermen, the European or American wives of Chinese who
had studied abroad. Two houses between the racecourse and
the Lutheran compound were leased by the German Military
Mission led by General von Falkenhausen, and on trips to town
I would have to veer my bicycle into the ditch when I heard
the horn of one of their big black limousines speeding up from
behind, its Nazi flags flapping.

Though we hardly ever saw them, two or three hundred Soviet Russian aviators were sequestered at the airfield which
had been leveled in the farmland out beyond our compound.
They were said to be active in the air defense of Hankow, but
the Chinese press played them down. All I remember hearing
of them was that they were crazy about American movie magazines and wristwatches, wearing several of the latter at a time,
and were wild on the rare occasions when they were allowed to
visit the bars and nightclubs on "Dump Street" downtown.

We heard more about the little International Squadron of
the Chinese Air Force, which operated under the informal command of Claire Lee Chennault, a retired captain from the U.S.
Air Force who was an adviser to Madame Chiang, with the Chinese rank of colonel. The Squadron numbered only twelve to
twenty pilots, depending on how many were wounded, sick,
hung over, or suspended for infractions. The tough mercenary
fliers were American, French, German, and Dutch. They accounted for more than their share of downed Japanese planes,
but their automatic glamour — at least one had flown for the
Ethiopians, a couple had flown in Spain, on both sides — so
hypnotized the foreign press that it sometimes seemed the sizable Chinese and Russian Air Forces were a sideshow, while
the Squadron was the main event. Several of the Internationals
practically lived on Dump Street and were so indiscreet that
frequent rumors forecast the disbandment of the Squadron for
security leaks.

*

Generalissimo and Madame Chiang Kai-shek spent most of that year in Hankow, but were rarely seen. Their headquarters were in a military compound in Wuchang, across the Yangtze, but they were said to have half a dozen houses elsewhere, and might eat or sleep in any of them to thwart bombers and plotters.

Not long after they arrived, an aide telephoned the Lutheran compound and said they would like to inspect our schools. Naturally there was excitement. On the great afternoon, the students were all drawn up in their Sunday best. The Chiangs came in a cavalcade of cars full of bodyguards and, as I remember, the first moments of the visit were awkward, with the missionaries and the Chinese faculty uncertain whether to bow or shake hands.

The little Generalissimo, in a simple gray uniform, did a great deal of smiling and nodding, mumbling *"Hao, hao, hao"* (Good, good, good). His coolly beautiful Madame in a green silk sheath was gracious in English with a Southern accent and put us nearly at ease.

Then we went inside. Our classrooms had locally-made furnishings and we were proud of them. Suddenly the Generalissimo pointed at the desks and whispered to his wife.

"Is that Ningpo varnish?" she sharply asked the head of the school.

"Yes," he replied with beaming pride. "It is the best varnish in the world."

She reported to her husband. He turned on his heel and fled. She followed. They tumbled into their car and sped away, never to be seen again at the Lutheran compound. We later heard the Generalissimo had a painful skin allergy to Ningpo varnish. He had been born and raised in a small village in the Ningpo district, which certainly made him a country boy with a good reason for going far.

Despite the fiasco, my fellow missionaries were left proud and gratified by the Chiangs' visit. No such politeness had ever been shown by lesser officials, the provincial and municipal nabobs. Not even the American or British heads of the rather piffling Hankow sub-offices of the great oil or tobacco firms had ever honored them with a visit.

In the last years before the Japanese invasion, and for a year or two afterwards, the Chiangs made a point of visiting mission compounds wherever they traveled in China; I've heard this was done at the suggestion of W. H. Donald, the astute Australian who advised them from 1936 to 1938. The adoration their visits aroused in some mission hearts neared the pitch forbidden for images. The missionaries might be making little progress in China, and be regarded as eccentrics by their countrymen there, but through their supporting churches they had immense influence in America. Missionary praise of the Chiangs would later contribute to the fatally unreal picture of China which so many Americans accepted.

The Japanese began bombing Hankow in the late winter, once or twice a week at first. By summer, early afternoon raids by twenty-seven or more planes were daily events in clear weather; so were night raids when the moon was full. Foreign properties were hoped to be neutral, so at the first alarm tens of thousands of people would wedge into the few blocks of the old Foreign Concessions, standing or sitting silently in the streets until the all clear.

Our Lutheran compound was supposed to be neutral too, but it was so near the biggest airfield — a major target in all early raids — that the bombers would circle over it as they went into their target run. Looking straight up we could see the bombs fall out of the bays and arch obliquely down toward the field. The terrible explosions of the first raid panicked me, and I ran outdoors with no thought but to save myself; under the shelter of a tree I found that the only thing I carried was a cracked vase I had bought off a junk stall for a few pennies. But apparently it only takes time to get used to anything. Within a few weeks the raids were part of the routine of the city, and even I found myself cycling off on mission errands before the all clear sounded.

The raids alarmed our Mission Board in America into ordering the evacuation of the seminary and elementary school. All the missionaries except myself were to take them westward to the small river towns of Shasi and Ichang, then up through the Yangtze Gorges to Wanhsien, a big provincial city east of Chungking. As the only bachelor, I was to stay and try to bar the Japanese from our big Hankow compound. We had some small primary schools inside the old Chinese city, taught in Chinese, and I was supposed to keep them running as long as possible.

Through several weeks my colleagues took the schools off piecemeal, with batches of students, books, or furniture going whenever there was an opening on the crowded buses or boats. Then I was left alone, with a servant, a caretaker, and a gardener. I would have been dismally isolated if I hadn't met the daughter of a former Congregational Bishop of Hankow, Pattie Sherman, who had come out from America and started language studies about the time I did. When my teachers began appearing irregularly because the bombings made their trips to the suburbs risky or impossible, she suggested that we study together at the Episcopal mission where she was boarding. This was another big walled compound with a school, a church, several bungalows, and a big residence for the Episcopal Bishop, Logan Roots. I could cycle in before the bombings for a morning of lessons, then we usually had lunch at the Bishop's table, where I met more kinds of people than I had known existed.

Logan Roots went to China in 1898 when it was still the Manchu Empire, hardly out of the Middle Ages. He became Bishop of the Hankow Diocese in 1906, and in the next thirty-two years his benign tolerance helped make friends for him in every faction which briefly held the city: monarchists, warlords, Nationalists, Communists, and Nationalists again. In name at least, 1938 was a year of United Front between the Nationalists and Communists, and on separate occasions the Bishop entertained visitors as far apart as the Generalissimo's brother-in-law, H. H. Kung, and Chou En-lai, head of the Communist Army Headquarters in Hankow.

Such bigwigs didn't appear at his potluck lunch table, but lesser Nationalists in trim uniforms ate and talked peaceably with young Communists in faded cotton tunics. The foreigners who filled out the big table often included missionaries of warring sects — more proof of the United Front effect of the Bishop's benevolence — or traveling Oxford Groupers, another of his interests. Younger diplomatic men, military attachés, and correspondents were also regulars; as I recall, there was an account book to sign, and you settled with the number-one boy about once a week. As China's tragedy unfolded on the front pages of the world, many of the great prima donnas of journalism appeared in Hankow, usually after a stay in Madrid, and found their way to the Bishop's table. It was a fine place to learn the news omitted from the city's censored papers.

In the heat-hazed skies of spring, planes were hard to see, but dogfights between the outnumbered Chinese and the pursuits escorting the Japanese bombers were quite common. In the silence after the final sirens we could hear guns in the sky and sometimes saw parachutes or planes falling in flames. The greatest Chinese victory came on the Japanese Emperor's birthday, April 28, and Colonel Chennault was credited with planning it.

The day before, all fighter planes in the Hankow area were withdrawn far to the west; numbers of planes were secret but the total was believed to be about forty Russian planes with

Russian pilots, and thirty Chinese planes manned by International Volunteers and Chinese. That afternoon the Japanese reconnaissance planes found the airfields empty and the city an irresistible target.

At dusk the defending planes flew back to refuel at small dispersal strips near Hankow and were ready next morning, high in the sky, when forty or more Japanese bombers approached with a large escort of pursuits. The Russian and Chinese planes dived, and in a short time destroyed half the bombers and several pursuits. A Japanese who parachuted from a burning plane and was captured on the roof of the Hankow railroad station proved to be one of Japan's leading aces. Unfortunately a Russian pilot who parachuted into isolated farmland several miles from the city was said to have been massacred by peasants, who thought any foreigner from the sky must be Japanese.

In February the Chinese Air Force raided a Japanese aircraft factory on Formosa, and in May it made a token raid on Japan itself, dropping leaflets instead of bombs. But most of the planes China had when the war began had been destroyed in the defense of Shanghai and Nanking, and replacements were hard to get, as they had to be shipped up on the train from Hong Kong and assembled by overworked mechanics on fields which were frequently bombed. The great achievement of the Chinese Air Force in the Hankow period was its air-warning net, set up with the help of Chennault, who, before his retirement, had vainly tried to persuade the U.S. Air Force of the need for a similar net in America.

In primitive China the net had to be simple. Plane-spotters with small short-wave radios were stationed deep in occupied territory, within sight of the Japanese airfields. Others waited on mountaintops in unoccupied territory. They reported any movement of Japanese planes to an interconnected net of telephone lines radiating out from every major Chinese city. Chen-

nault and the Chinese Air Force had set up this net to help discover and turn back Japanese attacks, but its immense value to
civil defense made the Chinese maintain it carefully through
the long periods when they had virtually no Air Force. In eight
years of invasion, the Japanese made at least twenty thousand
air attacks on Chinese cities, but the net had few major failures. Until the invention of radar it was the best in the world.

By early summer it was grimly evident that Hankow's fate
was to be decided on the ground, and very soon. The best Chinese troops had withdrawn from Shanghai and Nanking to the
neighborhood of Hsuchow, a key railway junction about 250
miles northwest of Nanking and 300 miles northeast of Hankow. Through spring months of stalemate and skirmishing the
Japanese deployed some hundred thousand fresh troops before
Hsuchow. In May the Chinese attacked, and at a small town
called Taierhchwang scored a victory which sent a short-lived
thrill of triumph through the country. In Hankow it set off the
greatest parade of all, with miles of marchers singing through
the streets.

In June the Japanese counterattacked, took Hsuchow after
heavy fighting, and began an inexorable drive toward the temporary capital. Chinese troops retreating west from Hsuchow
blasted the Yellow River dykes and kept the Japanese from
pursuing them into northwest China, but caused one of the
greatest man-made disasters, for the river began emptying into
the ocean hundreds of miles from its old mouth; its new course,
miles wide in places, ran through rich, thickly-populated, farmland.

By July three Japanese drives threatened Hankow. An offensive south of the Yangtze balanced the northern thrust down
from Hsuchow. In the middle, the Japanese navy pressed
slowly upriver through mine fields and booms made of merchant ships scuttled the winter before. Now Japanese pressure

on Nazi Germany caused the withdrawal of von Falkenhausen's Mission. The generals went off to Hong Kong on a special train covered with Nazi flags to keep the Japanese from bombing them.

On July 4 I met Colonel Chennault at an Independence Day jamboree the American Consulate gave at the Race Club. Following a lunch of hot dogs and Cokes, a baseball team of Americans was to play a team of other foreigners, mainly British. John Davies introduced me to Chennault, our pitcher. He was a smallish man, very much the soldier of fortune, as I remember, with a silk aviator's neck-scarf, and other accessories. He was standing with a court of ambiguous-looking men — semi-adventurous, semi-commercial types whom I later found to be his perennial cronies.

By the end of the afternoon I had to admit to myself that he was a lousy pitcher, and a vain one, no matter how much I admired him as an aviator. I was put out in left field, and despite all Chennault's flourishes, windups, spitting on leather, and the rest, the cricket-playing Englishmen lambasted the ball all over the lot, especially into left field. I caught about eighteen flies, putting eighteen men out, then I missed one that was miles over my head. The glare Chennault sent me from his dark hawk face was something I remembered years later when I read that at a wartime conference Churchill had noticed Chennault in a roomful of generals, asked Roosevelt who he was, and said, "I'm glad he's on our side."

After the game he said to me with a condescending laugh, "Well, Frillmann, you're a pretty good player, but if you had caught that ball they wouldn't have got those three runs."

By July the United Front had developed as far as it ever would. The Communists had guerrillas behind the Japanese lines, and limited co-ordination of Nationalist and Communist attacks delayed but could not halt the Japanese advance. In my own small world it was also the peak of United Front time:

Bishop Root's lunch table had become known as the "Moscow-Heaven Axis," and was dominated by four unusual women — Anna, Rolf, Agnes, and Freda. They lived together in the Episcopal compound and were all writing books about China, talking a mile a minute meanwhile. At lunch I felt like a sparrow hunched in a cage full of parrots.

Anna Louise Strong was much the biggest bird. If you didn't know she had gone to Russia during the revolution and ended up editing the Moscow *Daily News*, the English-language propaganda paper mailed all over the world, you might have put her down as an American clubwoman, a chairlady, even a member of the DAR. She was a big, buxom, white-haired woman with piercing baby-blue eyes, conservatively dressed in dark suits with white lace at the neck and black hats clacking with artificial fruit.

We heard she was such a steamroller in search of news that the Chinese she brushed aside called her a "left-wing imperialist." She obviously annoyed the other ladies at table, with her frequent hints that General So-and-so had told her a secret and she would soon break the story of the year. She was writing a book, *China Fights for Freedom,* and later went back to Russia. After the war the Russians deported her for vaguely-stated reasons, but she became a favored visitor to Communist China after the Sino-Russian split. Now in 1967, aged at least eighty-five, she is a vigorous member of the Red Guard youth movement in Peking.

Ilona Rolf Sues was writing *Shark's Fins and Millet* in 1938. She was a slim Swiss girl, not pretty but charming, with a beret, a cigarette holder, and a witty continental manner. After opium-control work with the League of Nations in Geneva, she came to China bringing her big black cat in a basket. On the advice of the Australian, W. H. Donald, Madame Chiang appointed her as a semi-official semi-adviser on publicity in Nanking.

When she criticized cousins of high officials who were writing foreign propaganda in Chinese with no knowledge of foreign countries, she was semi-demoted by Madame Chiang, and in Hankow was broadcasting the news in English and French. She was chaperoned at the lunch table by her black cat, on its seventh or eighth life after bombings and evacuations, and she specialized in catty sidelights on the highly placed. I recall one of her stories because I later worked with other volunteer aviators.

Madame Chiang apparently had a weakness for uplifting speeches when she found a captive audience, and as head of the Nationalist Air Force she was in command of the International Squadron. It was her pleasure to visit their barracks on Sunday mornings, when hangovers were at their worst, for a combined sermon and pep talk.

"The things she said to us," one hard-bitten aviator later marveled to Rolf. "Why, I'd be ashamed to talk like that to a football team of twelve-year-olds."

Agnes Smedley was the self-educated daughter of an impoverished Colorado miner. During the First World War, while putting herself through night college in New York, she was jailed for being secretary to some anti-British Indian revolutionaries. Unknown to her, their Indian friends in Europe were subsidized by the Germans, so the American secret service considered her a German spy. On her release after the Armistice, she worked her way to Germany as a stewardess, and for eight years lived with one of the Indians, involving herself not only with revolution in Asia but with other causes a warmhearted woman in Berlin of the 20's might find appealing — the plight of German workers ruined by inflation, of German women bullied by their husbands. She helped found the first official birth-control clinic in Germany.

She came to China in 1928 as a correspondent for the *Frankfurter Zeitung*, the liberal paper later closed down by the Nazis,

and became an admirer of the Chinese revolutionaries who
even then were mainly Communists. She helped fugitives from
the Nationalist secret police, and smuggled medical supplies
to the Communist armies. Protected by American citizenship
and German credentials, she became a favorite whipping girl
for the Nationalist press. I heard her recalling with laughter a
Shanghai tabloid's story that she had slipped into the Communist areas to attend a Soviet Congress, taking along a case of
whiskey to corrupt semi-indoctrinated students, and then
opened the Congress by singing the "Internationale" in the
nude, except for a Red Army cap.

She turned up in Hankow in the spring of 1938, after months
of hardship with guerrillas behind the Japanese lines. She
looked ill and half-starved, with her cropped sun-bleached hair
and intense blue eyes set off by a faded cotton Communist uniform. When friends pooled some money for a change of clothing, she bought the reddest jacket and skirt she could find in
Hankow. Her stories at the Bishop's table opened windows out
of that comfortable room of cruets and napkin rings onto a
cruel landscape of suffering, atrocities, and starvation.

In Hankow she did foreign publicity for the Medical Corps
of the Chinese Red Cross, and earned another name as a radi-
cal, for she thought that more of the money remitted to China
through the International Red Cross should go to the Medical
Corps which aided wounded soldiers. The International Red
Cross Committees in China were heavy with missionaries who
preferred to send the relief funds to mission hospitals for use
on civilian patients, sometimes at commercial rates.

The heartrending nature of rescue work in a primitive country kept Agnes's emotions always close to the surface. I remember one lunch when she had some photographs from the
front. The cruelest showed a Red Cross truck jammed with
walking wounded who knew the advancing Japanese would
butcher them. Even if the truck hadn't been too overloaded

to drive over the wretched roads, the driver couldn't get into the cab because it, too, was packed with desperately wounded.

"If I should describe things like this abroad," Agnes said bitterly, "the neat little souls of Americans and Englishmen would keep them from giving a cent to China; they'd just go to another movie to watch love solve everything."

She worked for the Red Cross in China until 1941 when she returned to America, publishing *Battle Hymn of China* in 1943. She spent most of the rest of her life in America, lecturing and writing to raise funds for relief and left-wing causes in China. She always claimed she was not a Communist, saying she was too much the individualist to accept party discipline. During the Russo-German Pact she was caustically critical of the American and European Communists who supported it. When she died in England is 1950, she willed her scanty possessions to Chu Teh, head of the Red Army, and asked that her ashes be sent to Communist Peking for burial.

Freda Utley was an Englishwoman who went to Russia in the 20's and married a Russian Communist official. When her husband disappeared in a Stalin purge, she emigrated to Japan. She became anti-Communist, but for years remained more broad-minded than most of the recanted. She wrote *Japan's Feet of Clay*, an analysis of the ways Japan's internal tyranny might weaken its external aggression. In Hankow she seemed anxious to learn from everyone, and as her book *China at War* later showed, she understood that here was a vast country with multiple problems reaching far back into the past, or deep into social and economic ills. She was an admirer of Agnes, who she said reminded her of "the best of the old Bolsheviks." She was an intense brunette, given to slacks and big dark sunglasses.

She was in Hankow for a few months in 1938, and briefly visited China again after the Japanese surrender in 1945. This resulted in an extremely pro-Nationalist book, *China Strikes*

Back. In 1950, not having been back to China in years, she published *The China Story*, a story in the Hans Christian Ander-
sen sense.

From it I learned with surprise that Agnes had sowed the
seeds of Nationalist China's destruction right under my eyes,
at Bishop Root's table. She had fascinated all the gullible correspondents and military and diplomatic men, fooling them
into thinking the Chinese Reds were agrarian reformers, not
really Communists — this reminded me how many times I'd
wanted to nudge Agnes and say "Take it easy," when she waxed
vehement about what dedicated Communists and revolutionaries her Chinese friends were. In *China at War* in 1939, Freda
had described John Davies as one of the "iconoclasts," along
with herself, who bravely declined to join the then-fashionable
leftists. In *The China Story* in 1950, John was the Machiavel-
lian founder of something called the "Davies-Stilwell Axis"
which led to Chiang Kai-shek's rejection by several hundred
million Chinese.

In September, Hankow, the exciting temporary capital, began to fold up and disappear quickly like a circus moving on to
the next stop. The parades tapered off. No new posters or
banners appeared, and the old ones grew torn and dusty. The
writing women in the Episcopal compound — and all the rest
of the traveling international zoo — disappeared by plane or
train to Hong Kong, bus or boat into the interior. One morning
Japanese bombers came over the airfield early, and all the
planes of the International Squadron — filled with gas and
bombs the night before — vanished in one giant explosion. A
final security leak through "Dump Street" was blamed, and
the planeless fliers were out of jobs.

As Japanese naval guns gradually became audible down-
river, the tempo of departure quickened. Heavy machinery had
been moved from the factories since midsummer. Now squads

of soldiers went through town wrenching up everything that could be used as scrap metal — manhole covers, water pipes, ornate iron fences, and gates from 19th-century foreign mansions — and hauling it off to the west. The crowds on the docks spread as people deserted their homes and moved their luggage to the waterfront to wait for ships. Soon many of them desperately abandoned what they couldn't carry and started west on foot. There was bitter cursing at the stories of officials who had commandeered whole ships, or trucks, or ambulances, to salvage their hoards of goods, their furniture, even their next winter's coal or next summer's potted shrubs.

It later became known that much of downtown Hankow was to have been blasted or burned to "scorched earth," but this may have been prevented by Adolf Hitler. His triumph over England at Munich in September encouraged the Japanese into a surprise attack on Canton, which the Nationalists were not prepared to defend because they hoped it was protected by its closeness to British Hong Kong. Canton fell in a few days, and fears that all Nationalist China would collapse confused and paralyzed the officials charged with destroying Hankow.

I bicycled downtown the day before the Japanese came, and though I had heard many Chinese were planning to stay, they were hidden away behind locked doors and shuttered windows. The streets were empty except for long columns of weary Nationalist soldiers, silently dragging their way west. Along the gutters tottered or crawled the dirty delirious wounded, moving more and more slowly. The living ignored the dying except when one collapsed and lay still, then the nearest soldiers would step out of line and squabble about who would take his shoes.

CHAPTER II

Occupied Hankow 1939–41

OUR CONSULATE wanted all Americans to move downtown, where we could take refuge on the gunboats if need be, but I decided I must stay at the Lutheran compound. John Davies advised me to get a hoard of groceries, then keep out of sight until I knew the Japanese controlled the neighborhood without disorder.

Nobody else was left in the compound except one young servant, Liu Wang, and his wife and two small children. Luckily I had a monstrous dog, Sandy, half German shepherd, given to me by some American sailors when he grew too big for their little gunboat. I bought a rickshawful of sugar, coffee, canned milk, and fruit — terribly expensive by then — and asked Liu to get extra bags of rice. We had a flock of chickens in the compound, and the garden was full of cabbage and other autumn vegetables. American flags had been painted on roofs and walls of the mission when the bombings started, and in an attic I found big cloth flags to hang by the gates. Then we barred ourselves in and waited.

For a day or two we heard heavy bombing at the airfield and west of town, then silence. The artillery along the river stopped, so did the city noises. No more train, boat, or factory whistles, not even the growling and klaxoning of buses and cars. The telephone went dead and the electricity failed, silencing the radio. We could have been deep in the country.

The large front gate of the compound was in the center of the western wall — toward Hankow. Across the canal before it was a wooden bridge with three arches, or "eyes" as the Chinese called them, and from this came the name of the mission compound and the peasant village to the north and east. The only other mission gate was a small one in the center of the north wall, leading right into the heart of "Three-Eye-Bridge Village." Only a few steps separated our wide orderly lawns and brick buildings from crooked alleys and crumbling mudbrick houses.

Because the imposing front gate was visible for at least half a mile, down a long stretch of wide motor road, while the little north gate with its screen of crowded houses was invisible from more than a few feet away, the village became my first source of news about the occupation. Since the big flag-bedecked compound right next door offered the villagers a refuge which might prove illusory but was the only one they had, they soon began trying to move into it. As far as I ever learned, my missionary predecessors had ignored the village except as an occasional source of servants, but I was only one man, the villagers many.

After a day or two of silence, Liu learned in the village that all Hankow had fallen without fighting, and a small Japanese garrison already occupied the closest barracks, about a quarter of a mile away. So far the Japanese were under strict discipline, but the villagers were alarmed and wanted to move all their women and animals into my compound, at least during the nights. This was a quandary. I knew the Nanking "Safety Zone," set up by several missionaries and other foreigners, had proved no more than a convenient reservoir of women for the invaders to rape and men for them to work and massacre. I was dubious about the "Safety Zone" the International Red Cross had set up in the Foreign Concessions of Hankow, and had no confidence in my own ability to protect anyone. I suggested that the women would be safer hidden in the village or the fields, but agreed to shelter some livestock. Within a few hours a horde of water buffalo, pigs, and geese were staked out on the carefully raked lawns, and wicker baskets full of chickens and pigs were stowed under the shrubbery. To make this bona fide American property I tried to buy everything at token prices — a nickel for a water buffalo, and so on down. But trying to keep track was hopeless. They just poured in.

That afternoon, and on nearly every day for a couple of weeks afterward, I was visited by junior Japanese officers in twos and threes who came to the front gate and said they wanted to inspect the compound. Most spoke some Chinese, others a little English or German. I had an old .38 Luger with no firing pin and no ammunition, but it looked like a weapon. When I heard beating on the gate, I would take the Luger and Sandy and parley with the visitors through the small, grilled, eye-level door set into the gate-timbers. I don't think any of them had official authority to inspect the compound — just free time and curiosity. When I told them repeatedly that this was neutral territory — "Can't you see the flags?" — and they had seen the gun and Sandy, they went peaceably away.

Sandy was certainly our best defense. He was a good-natured oaf of a dog — a bigger, darker version of Little Orphan Annie's — and he loved to romp with much "Arf! Arf! Arf!" But as some dogs don't like postmen or policemen, he didn't like Japanese. When he sensed them outside the gate he would growl and bark, then stand on his hind legs with his front paws in the grille, putting his head inches higher than mine. A long pink tongue dangled hungrily from his sharp teeth. I had heard that the small Japanese liked big dogs as much as they did outsize horses, and envy as well as alarm seemed to show in my visitors' faces.

*

Before long we heard that Japanese soldiers from the nearest garrison were marauding in the villages at night, stealing food and abusing women. We began to hear nearby rifle fire after dark. Then they came to Three-Eye-Bridge Village, but in their first raids only stole poultry and eggs; the flocks of refugee fowl in the compound doubled. Then came a night of shrieks and sobbing in the village, and half the population — men and grown boys as well as women and children — came up over the compound walls on ladders. Next morning I was a really ugly American, sanctimoniously telling them what I had been taught; they were jeopardizing American property by seeking refuge on it. Then I drove them out.

Later a committee of village elders asked me to see the women who had been raped, the younger ones many times. I saw them and that was enough. I told the men to arrange a warning system so we could get the women into the compound when a raid started. They posted watchers with gongs, but there must have been at least five hundred females between seven and seventy, and it soon proved there wasn't time for all to get in. I had no choice. I said the women could spend their nights in the compound, and opened the empty buildings for them.

They swarmed in with bamboo cots and tons of big blue cotton quilts, cooking utensils and portable stoves. A grandmother, two or three daughters-in-law, and half a dozen girls would crowd into cubicles intended for two bachelor students or a childless couple. Fortunately all floors were tile, so there was little fire hazard in the scores of makeshift kitchens set up in the corridors, the toilets, and on the stairs, each tended by a stoical grandmother patiently fanning the fire. We were without electricity for two or three months, and in the twilight hour of supper-making the crowded dormitories looked like weird campgrounds, lit only by the little stoves and dim oil lamps.

On the first night the women came in, the village elders for-

mally presented me with a bundle of big red ceremonial can-
dles, evidently collected from the cherished hoards of many
households. These were to "help with my studies," but I found
little time for reading at night. The Japanese immediately discovered where the women were, and we had to set up an alarm
system inside the compound. In small gangs — luckily, I don't
think we ever had more than six at once — the soldiers would
come up over the walls and start scouting. Village men with
gongs waited inside each wall and we had a code of beats to
tell where the danger was — front gate, side gate, back wall.
When an alarm sounded, I would run out with the Luger and
Sandy, barking thunderously as he strained at his leash. The
gong-beaters and I would converge on the Japanese, who were
ill at ease in a walled enclosure where they knew they
shouldn't be. Without a word they would vanish back over the
walls.

When the women discovered their enemies seemed timid
inside the compound, they grew as loud as geese in their own
defense. If a Japanese got by us and tried to enter a building
with women inside, the first one who saw him would scream,
then all five hundred, in all the buildings, would scream at the
top of their lungs, and run out to chase him. This was more
than the stoutest male could face, and the Japanese always panicked, so much so that several failed to get up over the walls in
time. Their legs were seized by dozens of hands, and some lost
their boots, their socks, even their pants before they kicked
loose and scrambled away. Then the women's screams changed
to triumphant laughter.

After a week or two, I started going downtown every few
days, to call on friends, collect news, and let the Japanese see
someone was keeping an eye on the five Lutheran elementary
schools, still closed. The Japanese ordered a curfew at dusk and
with all nerves edgy, it was wise to be home beforehand; shots
in the dark were common.

The Chinese armies had withdrawn nearly a hundred miles from Hankow, to the edge of the mountains walling off the government's western refuge at Chungking. This was open country with only a few low hills, so the armies were systematically destroying the roads, blowing up the bridges, tearing up the pavements, leveling everything back into farmland. Many refugees from Hankow and acres of refugee materials — machinery, scrap iron, office desks, hospital beds, and so forth — were reported stuck in Ichang, at the foot of the Yangtze Gorges, because the low winter water had slowed river traffic and there was no other way west except steep mountain footpaths. The Japanese continued bombing Nationalist territory but seemed to have no immediate plan for further conquests on the ground.

Oddly, the Chinese postal and telegraphic services remained neutral through the war. My fellow missionaries were still no farther away than Ichang, and often when I saw Japanese bombers take off from the nearby field, I was to hear next day that Ichang had been bombed. I wouldn't have to worry about my colleagues, though, for I would already have received a telegram from them saying "All safe. Best wishes." Such open communications naturally aided smuggling, espionage, and other kinds of corruption in the later war years.

Compared to the turmoil of the months when it was capital, occupied Hankow was a dead city. The "Safety Zone" of the International Red Cross was not violated, and enough Chinese remained to give the downtown streets a queer early-morning look — when everything was open and running but few people visible. The shouting, laughing, and zest of normal street life had been replaced by muted voices and circumspect manners, especially when Japanese soldiers were about. Even in the first weeks Japanese boats began coming up the river loaded with civilian "homesteaders." The occupation authorities seized houses and shops for them, and Hankow was swiftly assimilated into the "New Order for East Asia." Every time I went downtown there seemed to be more Japanese drugstores, cloth shops, or snack bars, more Japanese advertisements on the walls which had earlier been painted with anti-Japanese murals.

The foreign colony was reduced by half or more. The Germans and Italians had stayed because they were Axis allies of the Japanese, and the White Russians remained because they had nowhere else to go, but most of the Americans, British, and French had pulled out. Most of the few men who were left, more or less as caretakers of the big commercial or mission properties, had sent wives and children to Shanghai or Hong Kong. The Race Club and other foreign gathering places were as empty as if plague-struck.

Soon the Japanese issued identity cards. Barbed wire barricades were put up on the main streets, and to get through one was supposed to show his card and bow to the sentries. Luckily this revealed a weakness of Japanese authority; while they let their men rape, steal, and even murder in dark, out-of-the-way places, they were anxious to keep up an appearance of normality, of smiling cooperation, in the bright light of day. A little determined opposition could make them yield surprisingly. I refused to accept an identity card or bow to the sentries, and after repeated detentions, sometimes for hours while higher officers and officials were called in, they allowed me to cycle through without stopping. I had dermatitis on my hands at this time, and wore a fresh pair of white cotton gloves every day. Apparently all sentries were ordered to let "the one in the white gloves" through, for as soon as I got through once without detention, I was not stopped again.

When Japanese and puppet authorities ordered me to reopen our five schools with Japanese teachers, I was emboldened to refuse. Again they backed down, and eventually I was able to get the schools running with the same Chinese curriculum we had before the Japanese came.

Out at Three-Eye-Bridge Village, the first winter and spring of the occupation passed with periods of calm, then raids; perhaps strict and lenient officers alternated at the nearest garrison. Two or three times I had nearly all the women living in the village again, then there would be another raid and they would scurry back into the compound. By now it was obvious they weren't just seeking refuge. They liked it there, and I couldn't blame them. Never in their lives had they had so much leisure, so much freedom from services to their menfolk. Every dormitory nook seemed to contain a sewing or embroidery bee, with endless gossiping, giggling, and outbreaks of wild rowdy laughter.

When I realized that I had guests for an indefinite period, I announced they were going to have to learn to read and write their own language. As they were on Lutheran property, they were also to learn Luther's Small Catechism and sing Lutheran hymns. I brought teachers from the primary schools to help with classes.

If I had any idea this would drive them out, I couldn't have been more mistaken. Literacy in China was so restricted it was thought a great privilege. Some of the younger girls had gone to schools in Hankow, but only a handful of their mothers were literate. The older the women were, the more delighted they were at this unexpected chance to learn.

I took the class with the oldest, the "Lao Po-pos" or "old grandmothers," though many were great or great-great. I was afraid my Chinese teachers would feel they were wasting time with them. The old pupils all had bound feet, and wrinkled-apple faces with black button eyes sparkling with merriment. Their class was really a kindergarten. Just writing the ideographs for "I," "you," and "he" on the blackboard and asking them to read could set off a whole morning of laughter. Each in turn stood up and made her try, while the rest tittered and nudged one another, pointing at her and then at me with louder hoots, until everyone was overcome with mirth and they had to bury their faces in their hands. When I tried having them recognize the ideographs for their own names, the laughter was

so uproarious and the back-slappings so violent I had to give it
up. They were wonderful old ladies and it was unthinkable
that they should be left behind while their daughters and
granddaughters ventured into the new world of words. After a
couple of months most could read fifteen to twenty ideographs
from the blackboard, and their pride and satisfaction made the
trouble worthwhile.

Later I asked the wives of some of my teachers to lecture all
the women on personal and domestic hygiene, and the use of
Western-style facilities. Little instruction was necessary on
the first two counts. I was amazed at how clean the women kept
themselves and their possessions as soon as they were out of their
dark tumbledown houses. We had some misunderstandings on
the third count, though.

One day when they first moved in I found a group of women
— mainly Lao Po-pos — squatting around a toilet, busily washing rice and vegetables and exclaiming about the convenience
of this bowl. When I told them what it was, they laughed —
the Lao Po-pos were really doubled up — and all agreed it was
equally convenient for that, too. A few days later I noticed the
toilets were being used but not flushed. When I called in a
group and demonstrated, dismay showed on every face. In the
peasant tradition of returning all richness to the earth, the
women had been waiting for their men to come fetch it with
scoops and buckets.

At first I thought the men might resent having their families
live permanently in the mission, but apprehension about the
Japanese remained strong even in calm periods. The men
were pleased and proud when they heard their wives were
learning to read and write, for most were illiterate themselves;
the village had only one professional letter-writer. Every evening the men would bring food into the mission, then squat in
groups on the lawns, chatting while the women fixed supper.

In calm periods many younger women went out of the mission during the day, to work in the fields or the village.

While more and more of my guests began coming to my Sunday services, rituals of the village also crept into the mission. Sometimes I would find little clusters of punk-sticks smoldering beside a path, or red paper cutouts of the ideographs for "Good Luck" or "Prosperity" inconspicuously pasted on a door. I could see that some days were festivals, though politeness to my religion apparently prevented any explanation to me. There would be much whispering, special dishes at supper, and all evening restless, softly-talking groups would move up and down the corridors or from building to building. New Year's, which came in February, was of course the great festival, and that year it was celebrated with pagan enjoyment even in the Lutheran mission.

Days before, the men chose the biggest, fattest sow tethered in the compound. It must have weighed eight hundred pounds, a grunting, sway-backed, white monster. They led it out behind the tool-sheds and conservatory, where a huge caldron from the village was propped on rocks with a fire beneath. Most of the women and children followed to watch. The sow's throat was slit, and what seemed like a barrelful of blood drained off, into pots and kettles for sausages and blood cakes. Then metal tubes were worked under the sow's skin at all four ankles and the strongest, heaviest men — with the biggest "wind" — took turns blowing into them. The aim was to drive a layer of air between the skin and the fat inside, making it easier to pull out the salable bristles later. Everyone was in a holiday mood and the grisly performance became a gala. Small children ran round and round in excitement. With the Lao Po-pos well to the fore, the women clapped their hands rhythmically and cheered as the men huffed and puffed and their faces turned scarlet.

At last the great inflated carcass was heaved into the scalding water, and the air bubbled out. The sow was swiftly skinned, and the meat, guts, bones, and everything else carefully divided among the families. Nearly all the women returned to their kitchens in the village for the next few days, but on New Year's Day everyone crowded back in their best clothes, all freshly laundered. Each wife carried a platter with her family's sacrificial pork beautifully sliced or cubed or slivered, neatly arranged among the vegetables to cook with it. Meat scraps had been ground up and wrapped in dumpling dough. Surely every ounce of the sow was ready to eat. As if they were in a contest — and I suppose they were — the women hurried to their little charcoal stoves, fanned up fires, and in a happy din began to bake and steam and fry.

It was a peasant custom to paste up "Door Gods" at New Year's, for good luck in the next twelve months. They were big bright wood-cut prints of flag-bedecked warriors like generals in a Chinese opera. They came in pairs, to be pasted on the facing panels of a gate, and their origin was certainly pagan. While dinner cooked, I walked in the garden and noticed some Lao Po-pos making for my big front gate with a pot of paste and some giant Door Gods. I had no objection, though it could be embarrassing if an inspector of missions somehow popped through the Japanese blockade and found me protected by heathen pictures. I was a little relieved when some younger women came sprinting to catch the Lao Po-pos, and after a shouted discussion the old ladies grumblingly pasted the gods on the little gate from the village. Soon loud cries and a banging of many iron spoons on cooking pans summoned us to eat and drink.

When I saw how the Japanese occupation affected many other foreigners, I realized how lucky I was to have this big Chinese "family." I was always connected with a working, farming community, where changes of weather and season were keenly felt, where daily trivia and little religious or folk customs kept a constant drama going. In contrast, many foreigners left behind by the big exodus led utterly empty lives. They had never learned Chinese — this would have been eccentric in the pre-invasion business community — so they had to entertain themselves in the restricted group which already bored them enough. For months the Japanese blockade stifled foreign business, and few men had a full day's work. They became obsessed by food, drink, or clothes, all unsatisfactory because they relied so much on imports which were no longer available. I lived in occupied Hankow more than two years, through two long semi-tropical summers, but when I think of that foreign half-life, I remember a monotonous time without seasons, a permanent winter of the spirit.

Paradoxically, my own social life opened out. Foreigners who had ignored me in the gaiety of the full town suddenly, in the emptiness, could see a young missionary who could play tennis on his own good court, liked to ride, and in his walled compound had a pasture where horses could be safely kept. Dinner-party hostesses learned I had my own vegetable garden, and if the hints were loud enough could bring sanitary lettuce or a Bermuda onion for the salad.

"Theater parties" were our great events. The men were seldom asked to wear dinner jackets, but were expected to come in dark suits, formal enough so that the outnumbered women could dress up in their veteran evening gowns. We would have dinner in someone's grand treaty-port mansion, and no matter how unprepossessing the food, it was served in pre-invasion pomp, with soft-footed servants in mandarin silks whisking about with tureens, fingerbowls, and so forth. Then we would adjourn to a dirty little flea-bag theater near Dump Street, to watch one of the seven English-language movies existing in Hankow. Because of its scenery, the favorite was one made on the Greek island of Naxos with Brian Aherne, I think, and Joan Crawford or someone who looked like her. A hostess who telephoned the theater manager could have it shown again. Eventually I lost track, but I think I saw it sixteen times.

Several of us younger foreigners discovered we were fond of music, and about twice a month would lug our albums through the curfew lines and spend an evening before one or another's record-player, escaping farther than Naxos as we listened to Bach, Beethoven, Wagner, Debussy, Walton, and many others. Americans, Britons, and Germans were in the group. We survived the sitzkrieg, but after Germany attacked France in the summer of 1940, curiosity made us turn on the radio during the Hong Kong news broadcasts. Personal friendliness between Britons and Germans could not survive news of the fall of Paris, Dunkirk, the start of the blitz on London. The musical evenings dissolved.

The Germans in this group had been quite decent, but others, especially the Nazi party-members, were insufferable that year. They couldn't hide their arrogant pride over the victories in Europe, but the British were still top dogs in a place like Hankow while the Germans had scarcely recovered from their ostracism during the First World War. Somehow they wanted to defeat the British, yet be socially promoted by them. Few of the British would even speak to them any longer, so they would corner neutral Americans. After patronizing an American for his queer accent — they affected "Wodehouse" Briticisms — they would fawn and complain that they were so successful but nobody loved them. At length the old arrogance would come out again.

Because I spoke German I had extra helpings of this, and some Germans began badgering me to let them board at the Lutheran mission, saying they were Lutherans too. I had no experience in rude refusal, but when the Hankow Nazis hounded a Jewish doctor's German wife into killing herself by jumping down an elevator shaft, flat rejection of these would-be boarders became easier.

About twenty women from Three-Eye-Bridge Village had been pregnant the first time they took refuge in the mission, and one went into labor in the hectic first week. The Japanese were keeping me busy night and day then, so I hadn't been able to do much for her, but I soon realized we would have at least two births a month. I cleaned out a pantry in one of the dormitories, scrubbed it down with disinfectant, and had the village carpenter convert a kitchen counter into a rough operating table. I found a stock of good rags in the empty mission residences. The two village midwives performed the deliveries, but I tried to be on hand in the kitchen next door with plenty of hot water, sterilized cloths, and disinfectants.

Nearly all the babies survived, and I was flattered that the families often came to consult me about their names. Several named sons for me, translating Paul into Pao-Lo, but most asked me to pick one from their own choice of half a dozen traditional names. I remember one exception, an unfortunate girl infant, whose father was determined to name her Gin-pao ("Air raid"), no doubt because she had been conceived during one.

Nine months after the invasion a few half-Japanese children were born, or so the Lao Po-pos told me. I would never have known otherwise, for all the babies seemed to be welcomed with equal affection. Ten, eleven, twelve months after the invasion, the births were as many as ever, and I understood that Three-Eye-Bridge Village had found its own ways to survive.

By then it was late summer, harvest time, and the men were beginning to accept me as a friend, something which could have taken years if it hadn't been for the Japanese. After supper they would ask me to join them at their traditional gathering place on the threshing floor outside the village. I remember those warm evenings under the big harvest moon as a high point of my whole time in China, my closest contact with simple villagers. The threshing floor was pounded hard as marble and it gleamed in the moonlight. Hours of work in the fields, followed by a good filling meal, made for a great feeling of relaxation and friendliness in the circle of men who squatted and contentedly smoked their long bamboo pipes.

Sometimes they talked about the Japanese they could see, the soldiers from the nearest garrison, who still stole food but seldom molested women now; military brothels had opened downtown. The larger war between Japan and China was hardly ever discussed. When they weren't talking about the weather or their crops, they liked to tell old stories and legends or sing folk songs in solo or chorus. They must have heard everything thousands of times before, but chuckles and exclamations showed their lasting enjoyment. For me a door opened into a fascinating world of talking animals, beautiful maidens who turned into cruel fox-fairies, haughty princesses who fell in love with humble shepherds.

They soon asked me to tell or sing legends of my country. I explained that America was too young to have legends; I had never heard any. My religion was older than my country, I said, and preserved legends as old as the most ancient in China. Then I told some Bible stories. They were such a success I had to repeat them night after night. I had never before told these stories to adults who were hearing them for the first time, and I hadn't understood what a wonderful storybook the Bible was. The adventures of Noah, of Jonah, of David and Goliath, held them enthralled.

Jesus fascinated them too. "How could a man love others enough to sacrifice himself?" they asked. Increasing numbers of men began to join the women and children who already attended church services. Good attendance continued even after our neighborhood became quiet enough for the women to move back into the village permanently. Some families began studying for confirmation.

By the winter of 1939-40, the Japanese must have decided a quick victory over the rest of China was impossible, and it was to their interest to restore economic and social stability in the occupied areas. Military police were sent to Hankow, and though tens of thousands of Japanese soldiers were stationed in and around the city — it was a staging area for seasonal raids all through central China — the troops behaved as correctly as in peacetime. When six months had passed with no incidents at Three-Eye-Bridge Village, I decided I could risk the vacation my mission board in America was urging me to take.

Our Consulate told me the Japanese still wanted to get foreigners out, and most exit visas were one-way. Few commercial ships had permission to sail between Hankow and Shanghai. I went to the Japanese authorities, and a frank young official told me I could have the vacation and come back to Hankow as long as I spent American dollars for Japanese currency everywhere I went. Japan was the only place I could go. I would have to sail to Shanghai on a Japanese naval ship and go from Shanghai to Japan on a Japanese liner.

I went down the Yangtze on a small riverboat converted into a weapons carrier, empty except for a dozen Germans, a remarkable White Russian woman, "Ma Jenks," and her English husband. Ma looked like a retired Valkyrie, six feet four, blue-eyed, about fifty, with beautiful white skin and blond braids wrapped around her head. She ran the most respectable house of ill-repute on Dump Street, and was going to Shanghai for the wedding of one of the daughters she had put through convent schools and into respectable business jobs. "Pa" was an emaciated little sailor barely five feet tall, who had jumped ship in Hankow many years earlier and was in an alcoholic doze most of the time. Ma regally strode aboard with him casually flung over a shoulder like a fur-piece, laughing up at the surprised faces lining the rail.

As everyone on the ship soon learned, Ma thought men had been created chiefly to be bullied and humored by big women. The ship's doctor was a Japanese martinet who wanted to enjoy his authority over foreigners, and told us we could not sail until we provided him with fresh specimens for analyses. We

passengers held an outraged meeting. We had supplied specimens in Hankow and had good-health certificates not more than
twenty-four hours old. At length Pa woke up and wanted a
drink. Ma loaded his pockets with the vials and jars for all
of us, and shooed him off, promising he could have a drink when
he filled them. Four or five times on the way to Shanghai, the
doctor decided he needed new specimens, though we hadn't
even been ashore. Each time Ma chose a man to supply them
all, usually one of the younger German bachelors, who could
not resist her cajoleries though they didn't seem to know
whether they were being flattered or insulted.

Our food was prepared by two Japanese cooks in pseudo-
Western style, and it was terrible. For a few days we killed
our appetites with cheese, crackers, and canned fruits we had
brought with us, then one dinnertime when an unidentifiable
mess — beautifully garnished with radish roses, I remember —
was placed before us, Ma banged her fist on the table. Majesti-
cally she rose and heaved the food out a porthole, then went to
her cabin and returned with a big sack of potatoes under one
arm, a case of white wine under the other.

"These were supposed to be wedding presents," she said
grimly. "I grew the potatoes in my own garden." She marched
implacably into the galley and in a moment the cooks were
handed out by the scruff of their necks and dropped like span-
iels evicted by a St. Bernard.

"Come back in two hours for a real meal," Ma called to us.
Her stew was marvelous. Even the tired vegetables and stringy
meat from the ship's stores were transformed by her rich wine
sauce. Every day for the rest of the week she cooked us a stew
as bountiful as her own nature. She became our housemother,
our champion against the petty annoyances which the bored
Japanese officers liked to contrive for us. On the dock at Shanghai each of us received an embrace as mighty as a python's.
Then she clapped on a big wedding hat she had been covering

with feathers during the voyage, adjusted Pa over her shoulder, and strode off to meet her daughter.

Japan was supposed to be half-victorious in 1940, but my month there made me feel it was almost as sad as occupied China. The "liner" to Nagasaki was a little coastal steamer, so shabby and disheveled it was probably a troop transport when outward bound. Inbound it carried only a handful of nondescript middle-aged men in awkward Western clothes, traveling salesmen as I later learned, commercial pioneers of Japan's "New Order in East Asia." They did not look victorious, and the few who spoke to me in English or Chinese complained how bad business was. The pier at Nagasaki was empty except for a straggly military band playing dirges while a consignment of small white-lacquered boxes, each holding the ashes of a soldier, was unloaded from the hold.

For reasons now lost in the past, I had taken golf clubs from America to Hankow, and when I heard Japan had good courses, I brought the clubs with me. The Japan Tourist Bureau fell on me as if I were the last such traveler left in the world, and perhaps I was. For several weeks I toured the country playing golf, but the courses were depressingly deserted because of the war. Other results of the manpower shortage showed everywhere, and the departing troop trains carried off noticeably young or old soldiers. I learned I was single-handedly diverting one man from the war effort when I discovered the lugubrious little black-suited fellow who had silently shared a dining table with me on the boat was my plain-clothes detective. He followed me everywhere, waiting on the clubhouse verandas, watching through binoculars while I golfed.

Japan had a spy mania in those years, and I was surprised when I was allowed to spend the rest of my vacation on a walking tour in northern Honshu, unaccompanied as far as I could see. After the dusty plains and wide muddy rivers of central

China, the pretty coastal landscape of unexpected bays and headlands, piney slopes and green gushing streams, was a perfect change. Nothing could have been more different from sprawling, ruinous Three-Eye-Bridge Village than the neat, miniature Japanese hamlets, set among picturesque rocks and trees.

Most village innkeepers were women whose men had gone to war, and their quaint kimonos, mincing shuffle, bows, and downcast eyes, at first struck me as doll-like and false, especially when I thought of the forthright and understandable humanity of Chinese peasant women. Then I happened to be in a Honshu village when officials came to deliver one of the small white lacquer boxes to a soldier's widow. The spontaneous grief which spread from house to house made Japanese and Chinese women seem very alike.

Back in Hankow, life became so normal that I started taking Chinese lessons again, and teaching in our primary schools downtown. I had no more trouble with Japanese, except that some of the generals quartered in villas around the racecourse coveted Sandy. He was allowed to go where he liked, and was stolen about twice a month. I had three polo ponies then, left for safekeeping by British and American friends, and when I heard Sandy was gone I would gallop out of the mission whistling my special call for him, like a Marine Corps to the dog-rescue. Soon I could hear his yelps and barks behind the high walls of a villa. More whistles and barking, then a scrambling of claws on stucco, and he would sail like a bird over the six- or eight-foot wall, with a frayed rope or broken chain dragging from his collar. One day my whistles started a furious commotion of barks lasting five minutes or more, then over he came, bringing a rope and a wooden gate torn from its hinges.

The violent young Japanese soldiers who took Hankow had gone elsewhere by 1940; perhaps they were among those training for jungle warfare on Formosa and Hainan Island. They were replaced by older, quieter men, clearly bereft husbands and fathers. After my visit to Japan, I could not ignore them as human beings, and when one or two came knocking at the mission gate I would let them in. Most spoke English and just wanted to talk about the Western culture they had studied in the civilian life for which they pined. Some yearned for souvenirs of that life and as their army of occupation seemed to be turning as corrupt as any, they could procure supplies I needed. I remember swapping a record of Bach fugues for two bags of rice from army stores, a volume of Heinrich Heine's poems in German for a load of coal delivered after dark.

In early 1941, my mission board wrote that they were sending a replacement for me, a married man with a wife and eight children, all of whom were coming with him — they were later to spend four years in a Japanese internment camp, but all survived. Next, a mission inspector from St. Louis managed to reach Hankow to see how I had been getting along. His eyes fairly bugged when he saw the crowd of villagers at my Sunday services.

"Have you confirmed them?" he eagerly asked.

I did not like the way some missionaries tried to pile up records of "converts," indiscriminately enough to justify the term "rice Christians." Charity money sent from America made tempting bait for Chinese so miserable that they could not think any religion, or the lack of it, important. I had heard of missionaries using protection from the Japanese as another bait. When they had a compound full of refugees they would impose mass baptisms and confirmations, not unlike Feng Yu-hsiang, the Christian warlord, who baptized his troops with a fire hose.

I wanted to lean over backwards, so I tried to convince the mission inspector that the villagers needed a full year more of instruction. He insisted it would be great for our church to bring in so many at once. As soon as the villagers got wind of this, and of my coming departure, they began clamoring for confirmation before I left. I agreed to pick out the best half of the students and in a big ceremony they were confirmed.

In my last weeks before departure, I could not fail to see that a secret was being enjoyed. Busy conversations would stop if I came within earshot, and when I met the Lao Po-pos they nearly choked with giggles. On the day before my replacement arrived, the villagers filed into the compound in their best blue clothes, with large red or pink paper flowers — the kind worn for weddings or festivals — pinned to their jackets. They invited me into the chapel as if they were the hosts and I the guest. I sat down with them and for an hour we reminisced about our years together, making jokes out of once-terrifying incidents.

Then a din of firecrackers erupted, and we swarmed from the chapel, out to the front gate of the compound. A procession of village men was coming up the road from Hankow with a big wooden panel held broadside, flanked by boys with armfuls of firecrackers. They marched across the bridge, proud grins splitting their faces, crackers exploding around their feet, and presented the panel to me. It was professionally made, about eight feet long and four feet high. A carved and gilded border surrounded the black lacquer surface on which beautiful gold ideographs were splashed. "Yung ü Ta-wei" they proclaimed. "Brave as David." Smaller letters at the bottom said: "Presented to Paul Frillmann on his departure to America."

I nearly burst with glory, but in China afflatus never was easy. Shrill cries brought me to my senses. The crackers had set the bridge on fire. A dozen men in holiday finery jumped into the filthy canal and splashed up enough water to quench the fire, then they joyfully began splashing one another, to applause and gibes from the crowd on the canal bank. When men with ladders had hung my panel over the mission gate, we all trooped off to the village for a final feast.

Flying Tiger Chaplain

CHAPTER III

The Road to Rangoon 1941

When I returned to the United States, on April Fools' Day, 1941, I was given 14 months' leave and went to the small town outside Chicago where I had grown up. My eleven brothers and sisters were all adults, and the big house of our childhood was sold. My mother was dead and my father was living with one of my married brothers. I stayed with another.

I soon found I had nothing to do, nobody to talk to. My friends were working and most were married. Others had moved away. While relatives might show interest in China, it seldom lasted more than an hour; the war in Europe was closer. I fell into the habit of taking long walks, as I had in Hankow. I would leave after breakfast and come back late in the afternoon. "What have you been doing all day? Where have you been?" my brother and sister-in-law asked, looking almost frightened when I might answer, "I walked to the Brookfield Zoo." They thought something was wrong with me if I liked to walk miles each day.

The walks gave me time to think, and I needed it. I was certain I didn't want to go on as a missionary living in grand isolation from his parish, and I began to wonder if I hadn't been hasty in choosing a career. When I was twelve I took myself off to a Lutheran preparatory school where a friend of mine went, and was swept along through a Lutheran seminary and on out into the mission field. Now I wondered if it hadn't happened because at twelve I felt strangled by the competitive life of a big family, and took the first escape I could find.

I certainly didn't want to spend the rest of my life in Chicago. Despite the ugliness and cruelties of life in China, it had a vividness which made everything around me seem pale. Perhaps the depth of their troubles made the Chinese put so much vitality and humor into the small trouble-free part of their lives. In an American middle-class suburb, the troubles seemed to be ironed away and the pleasures equally flat. A fine atmosphere for old age, I thought then, but I wasn't ready for it yet.

One day I went to Northwestern University and learned that with my Chinese and other languages I had more than enough such credits for an M.A. I needed further work in other subjects and was making plans for financing a year at the university when I had a telephone call from John Davies in Washington.

"You remember Colonel Chennault in Hankow?" he asked. "He is here, but leaving for China on an important mission. I've spoken to him about you and he wants you to go with him."

I asked for details, but John just said: "Fly to Washington as soon as you can."

I told him this was out of the question. I hated to admit it, but I was almost broke. In some ways I had lived like a lord in China — hothouse carnations and freesias from the mission conservatory on my midwinter dinner table, for example — but my salary was only fifty U.S. dollars a month. I had no reserve for flying trips to Washington, and I knew my family would not help. "Stick-to-it-iveness" had been a great mouthful around our hearth, and I was sure they wanted me to finish as a missionary. I decided not to do anything about John's call.

Next day I had a telegram from Chennault: "If you are the

man I hear you are, you can be useful. Our work is vital to China."

That evening I spoke to some of my brothers and sisters and told them what I knew of Chennault. Any job with him would concern war in the air. I don't suppose my family was more isolationist than many Americans then, but they sat firmly on their wallets when I said I wanted to borrow enough money to fly to Washington.

Chennault's office was in the China Defense Supplies annex of the Chinese Embassy. He saw me as soon as I arrived, and fortunately didn't seem to recognize his left-fielder from Hankow. He told me the Chinese government had at last persuaded the U.S. government to allow Americans to be active in the war in China. He was recruiting a group of about three hundred American volunteers — one hundred pursuit pilots, the rest ground crewmen. He wanted fifty or sixty administrative personnel, plus doctors, nurses, dentists.

"I also need a chaplain," he said.

He said he also wanted me to be in charge of recreation and physical training. Since I was then the only member of his staff who could speak Chinese, he wanted me for liaison with the Chinese. It sounded exciting and definite after the uncertain weeks at home, so I quickly said I wanted the job.

He told me my salary, infinitely more than I had ever made in my life. I asked if a chaplain had to have any rank and he said, "This is not a military set-up. As chaplain you will be on my staff, but you won't outrank a single man in the group." He pointed to a corner of his office and said, "Now sit at that desk and make a list of the food three hundred Americans will need in China for one year — no, better make it two. Leave out the things we can buy out there."

I spent the morning trying to imagine how much catsup, mustard, mayonnaise, peanut butter, canned butter, canned bacon and ham, coffee, flour, and other staples might be needed. At one point Chennault shouted over, "Make a list of the recreation equipment too — baseball stuff, and tennis racquets and nets." Large sums of money made me nervous, and my total, with all prices quite haphazardly guessed, was only $30,000.

"This is chicken feed," said Chennault. "Are you sure you haven't forgotten something?" I knew the Nationalist government was chronically starved for foreign exchange, so I screwed up my nerve and asked who was going to pay.

"Our group is being set up by order of President Roosevelt," Chennault said proudly. "It has the full financial backing of America." He added that our salaries would be paid by China, with money loaned by America. The salaries would be paid in American dollars and, if we wished, could be deposited in any American bank we named.

I spent the afternoon with wholesalers, putting in my orders, then took copies back to Chennault's office. He would tell them when and where to ship. All these supplies were for China; nothing had been mentioned about Burma. Chennault asked me to send him some passport pictures and information for the State Department, then said I might as well go back to Chicago to await orders. I had done less than seven hours' work in Washington.

"I'll be seeing you," he said as I left. "I'll be there ahead of you."

"Where?" I asked.

"You'll find out," he said with a sardonic grin.

I telephoned John Davies to tell him I had signed up. He chuckled like a mad scientist finishing off a human guinea pig. "So it's done!" he said. "You'll never be the same again."

As I later learned, American aid to China had been slowly increasing during the past years of deadlock in China and growing threats elsewhere. Apparently we still hoped to keep out of war with Japan but wanted to give China enough to keep on entangling the Japanese. In December 1938 we had extended a credit of $25,000,000 on purely commercial terms, with China paying interest and obligated to repay in tung oil, tungsten, and tin. In keeping with America's current isolationism, the Chinese could buy only non-military supplies from us. Similar credits were extended in 1939 and early 1940. After the Germans conquered France in June of 1940, the Chinese strongly insisted on more aid, but Washington had learned that supplies purchased with the earlier credits were hardly being used, because of poor communications to and in China, therefore turned a deaf ear.

In September 1940, the Japanese occupied northern Vietnam — then French Indo-China — by agreement with the Vichy government of France. At about the same time the British, who expected to be invaded by the Germans at any moment, tried to appease the Japanese by closing the Burma Road for three months, thus completing the land blockade of China. Fearing the Chinese might surrender, we extended another credit of $25,000,000 for civilian supplies only.

In October 1940, the Generalissimo first asked for an American volunteer air force, claiming he could destroy the Japanese Navy with it; he wanted to stage what later became known as a Pearl Harbor surprise attack. In November he sent General P. T. Mao, Director of the Operations Division of the Chinese Air Force, to Washington, accompanied by Colonel Chennault. They asked for 500 combat planes to be delivered in 1941, with Americans to fly and service them. They asked also for 150 basic trainers, 15 transports, funds for 14 major airfields and 122 landing strips, plus ammunition and ordnance for one year. Representatives of the Chinese ground forces were already in Washington, asking for $30,000,000 to equip 30 divisions, the same number as there were of German-trained divisions lost or dispersed before the fall of Hankow.

In December 1940, America extended China a credit of

$100,000,000 with 25 percent of it at last earmarked for military supplies. In the race for this prize, the agents of the ground forces were hardly in the running. Although they had been clamoring for arms and other supplies for months, their plans proved vague or impractical. They wanted hundreds of four-ton trucks, for instance, so big they would destroy the flimsy bridges of rural China. Since most of China's arms came from German and other European suppliers, they needed ammunition of calibers American factories could not make without slow readjustments.

Chennault had detailed plans of what could be done if planes ever became available again, and he came to Washington with his needs and strategies carefully worked out on paper. The air force was given priority on the $25,000,000.

Even so, his full plan could not be put into effect, because the German blitz against London was at its first peak and the whole British Empire seemed to be collapsing. England had first call on any planes which could be spared from America's own build-up. After much lobbying the British purchasing mission in Washington agreed to yield to the Chinese their priority on 100 Curtiss-Wright P-40's, in exchange for future Chinese priority on 100 later-model planes. The P-40's were obsolete by American and British standards, and many of the 100 for the Chinese lacked full armament. The British promised to complete them when they arrived in Burma.

In early 1941, British gold resources in America neared exhaustion and Lend-Lease aid was set up, primarily for Britain. As plans for Chennault's air force were already formed, and were to include recruiting of personnel from the U.S. Armed Forces — strictly illegal by existing neutrality laws — it was thought better not to make it a Lend-Lease project, hence official. It would be strictly private. William Pawley, a friend of Chennault's who had imported Curtiss planes into China for years and had an assembly plant and repair shop at Loiwing, on the Burma Road just inside the Chinese border, was entrepreneur. In April 1941, he signed an officially "nonprofit" contract with T. V. Soong, the Generalissimo's brother-in-law and special envoy in Washington, agreeing to equip, supply, and operate the American Volunteer Group, or AVG as it quickly became known. In the contract, Chennault was referred to simply as the "supervisor." All expenses were to be paid to Pawley by the Chinese, out of the $25,000,000 loan.

Pawley and Chennault always seemed the closest of pals to me, and I was surprised to learn later from Chennault's autobiography, *Way of a Fighter,* that Pawley nearly sabotaged the whole AVG project at this point, by insisting on his usual agent's 10 percent cut on the $4,500,000 to be paid for the 100 planes. Secretary of the Treasury Morgenthau was outraged and tried to cancel the whole deal, but the Chinese wanted the planes so badly they persuaded him to approve a compromise whereby they would pay Pawley $250,000 instead of $450,000.

With unofficial help from American officials, agents of Chennault and Pawley visited Navy and Air Force bases, and in a few months signed up 101 pilot volunteers, roughly half from the Navy, half from the Air Force, plus four Marines. Pilots were to be paid $600 a month, flight leaders $675, squadron leaders $750. It was implied that a bonus of $500 would be paid for every Japanese plane shot down, and later this was in fact paid. About two hundred ground crewmen were recruited. Everyone signed a one-year contract, to start on the date of arrival in the Far East.

My family gathered when I came back to Chicago and told me that a young man who had spent years learning languages and missionary work was a fool to go off to die with a bunch of harum-scarum adventurers. Their objections made me more decided, for I saw that what I wanted to do would also make me independent of them.

Naturally my Mission Board was taken aback. For five years they had been investing in me, and I had just reached the point where I might pay off. They kindly gave me a leave of absence for as long as I wanted, and a year later, when the AVG broke up and I decided not to be a missionary again, I was glad I could reimburse them for some of their investment in my career.

At the end of May my passport arrived, and within a few days I had orders from Chennault to report to the Jonathan Club in Los Angeles before June 5. Following his instructions I bought a full Army officer's uniform, Sam Browne belt and all. Because I had no proof of military status, I had to go home and get my passport with its Chinese visa before the salesmen would let me have it. I also bought some civilian clothes which I hoped would make me look less like a missionary, more like a volunteer aviator. I guess I overdid this. I got the loudest suit I ever had, a regular racetrack model with stripes and padded shoulders, plus a floppy Panama hat and some screaming neckties. Then I took a plane to Los Angeles.

The Jonathan Club was a businessmen's club, but its staid lobby was full of big, tough-looking young men in slacks and fancy sport shirts. At the desk I said I was Paul Frillmann, and the clerk called over a man who introduced himself as Gene Pawley. He took one look at my rakish getup.

"Holy Smoke!" he said. "You can't be the Frillmann we're expecting."

Aware of curious eyes on my back, I suggested that I just check in quietly. Sudden introduction as the chaplain was the last thing I wanted, but several men got up and tramped after us to the elevator.

"You going out on this thing?" one asked me.

"Yes."

"Pilot?"

"Nope."

"You sure as hell ain't ground crew."

"Nope."

"What are you then?"

Luckily the elevator came. In my room Mr. Pawley said this was a top secret operation, and I wasn't to answer questions even for people who seemed part of the group. This was welcome as I hoped to get to know some of the men and let them see I was human before I was tagged as the chaplain.

All day the crowd in the lobby thickened. Everyone speculated about where they were going and what they were going to do, all on the crest of the wave with lots of new money in their pockets. I managed to scuttle through the lobby once or twice, slipping past questioners, then I was squarely blocked by a huge Irishman I later knew as Sweeney, one of our best mechanics.

"We asked you politely," he said. "Now tell us who the hell you are."

I had to admit I was the chaplain.

"Guys!" he shouted, holding up both hands for silence. "We've got a Holy Joe." I felt about the size of a peanut.

I spent the rest of the day in the lobby and found that this group were all ground crewmen except for a few office personnel and myself. All day it was a big joke to call me Sky Pilot or Holy Joe. The kidding was friendly, and that evening when I went out for drinks and dinner with some of them, a few began calling me by my own name.

Next day we heard a talk by a man named Hunter, said to be an agent in China for the Pawley brothers, who assured us that the terms of our contracts were being upheld and we would soon start our travels in first-class style. This might as well have been omitted, because a couple of mornings later, when we were told we were leaving for San Francisco, we found two broken-down old local buses parked outside; I suppose wartime shortages were closing in. Gene Pawley and a younger brother — there were five Pawleys altogether — came with us, and I didn't envy them when we stopped at roadside diners for meals. Trays of hamburgers and hot dogs were brought to the

bus, but in an explosion of curses about "first-class chow," half
the food went out the windows.

In San Francisco we found the war had really caught up with
us. Our ship was big and beautiful on the outside; we understood it was a former President liner, though the name had been
painted over. It was now a transport, full of troops sailing for
the Philippines.

Of course the AVG men had pictured themselves on a luxury
cruise with plenty of girls, and they were almost speechless with
frustration as we stumbled along decks and corridors full of
jeering soldiers and found our quarters in the former first-class
lounge. There were about fifty of us, and our cots completely
filled the room. No locker space, no bathing or toilet facilities
of our own. Apparently the ship had been waiting for us, because it sailed in a few minutes, with two relieved Pawleys waving good-bye from the dock.

Then the liquor was brought out, and the bitching really began. A soldier from the radio room came in, asked for Frillmann, and handed me a message from Chennault, naming me
the commanding officer of our group for the voyage. I quailed,
but showed it to the men, with the result I feared. From that
moment on, through forty-nine days on boats, I was chief receiver of complaints.

Soon I was also the ranking buffer between the AVG and the
military. The Troop Commander was a brusque, correct colonel, who had the public address system blaring before we were
away from the dock, announcing orders, drills, and disciplines.
This went on day after day. The presence on his ship of fifty
disorderly civilians galled him terribly. Mornings and evenings
he inspected the ship, attended by several starchy young aides.
When he came into our quarters, nobody except me would get
up from his bed. The men just stared at him, some of them
hung-over or a bit tight.

"On your feet!" an aide would bark.

"Go away, soldier," somebody would say contemptuously. "We're free men. We're civilians."

Repeatedly the Colonel called me in and ordered me to enforce military discipline. I tried to explain why I had to refuse. The AVG men were civilian volunteers for a war in which they might be killed, and had been promised a first-class trip to the Orient on a civilian boat. Of course the Colonel could say that many of his men were volunteers, they were going overseas too, and were being paid much less than the AVG. It was unfair that he had to keep them under harsher discipline, to counteract a gang of drinking, gambling, brawling civilians in their midst.

With hindsight, it was too bad that we did have a special status. Only one or two of our AVG group of fifty were later killed or wounded in the war. The troops on the transport were headed for Manila, Bataan, and the Death March.

At Honolulu, liquor supplies were replenished and some men tried to smuggle girls aboard in boys' clothes. The next few evenings were wildly confused, then the group seemed to draw together and develop a solidarity of its own. Perhaps it was just the camaraderie of having been out on a strange town together. Few of the men had been out of the United States before, and even Americanized Hawaii could give a sense of venturing into a foreign world. The fighting and bickering dropped off, so did the drinking, a little. They became more tolerant of me.

They all bragged about adventures in Honolulu, and I think I listened to more than my share because they expected me to be shocked. I pretended not only not to be shocked, but to consider their boyish depravities hardly worth mentioning. "Holy Joe" was dropped and I became "Padre."

This helped me promote daily classes in Chinese. Later, when most of these men learned how safely, though dully, they could live in China without speaking Chinese, I wouldn't have been able to teach them a single word, but on the ship they feared they might starve or be assassinated if they couldn't talk to the "natives." Some days I was able to get most of them out on deck, studiously grouped around a blackboard, when the Troop Commander made his evening inspections.

On the long haul from Honolulu to Manila, with the ship creeping westward in beautiful tropical weather, we all got to know one another better. I liked nearly everybody, but a pattern was clear. Most men were escaping from frustrations or disappointments, as perhaps I was. They hoped an unknown future in unknown places would somehow give them a second chance. One of the oldest was a tough former sergeant major about forty-three, irreconcilably divorced. One of the youngest was a boy of nineteen who had enlisted in the army, then got right out again for this junket; he was longing for adventures with lots of shooting, perhaps because he was small for his age. A majority came from the South and West, and Texans were the largest group from any one state.

Shore leave in Manila repeated the Honolulu celebration, except that everyone had white tropical suits tailored in six hours. Several men discovered that if they sat in the big hotel bars looking like mysterious soldiers of fortune, awed tourists would crowd around to ply them with the best in drinks and meals. Others found that they could play golf or ride horses within a few hours of arriving in this completely strange port. It amazed me how men who had no foreign languages and didn't seem resourceful outside a familiar setting could disappear into an Asian city, then weave back after dark, having found every novelty they fancied in the way of sports, drinks, or girls. As often as not, they were laden with other novelties to mail back to their dear old grandmothers — stuffed rats in hula skirts, for instance.

In Manila the troops from our transport marched off to their fate, and we had the freedom of an empty boat on the short run to Hong Kong. There Mr. Hunter met us and handed out some overdue pay, but before the men could start work on Hong Kong, he told us we were going to Rangoon in Burma, and clapped us aboard a small Dutch freighter. The new ship was comfortable, despite the heavy Dutch food, but its speed was better suited to the easy colonial years than a final prewar summer. I don't remember how many days it took to Singapore, and there the captain casually told us he would have to wait two weeks for a shipment of heavy machinery for Rangoon.

Chaperoning fifty AVG men for two weeks in a British colony is not a job I would recommend. They thought British accents were affected and sissy. Although they wore Hawaiian shirts in floral prints, they thought the British civilian uniform of khaki bush-jackets and shorts was sissy; this was before the age of the barbecue pit and pink Bermuda shorts for American suburbanites. In bars, when they expansively asked Britishers to drink with them, they were insulted if their guests declined to hang around drinking double whiskeys until closing time. On the contrary, many were tough young British or Scots planters from the Malay Peninsula, unwilling to take any nonsense from "damn Yanks," and I was often telephoned by frantic cafe-owners who needed help in breaking up fights and collecting damages.

Among the special cases were two young mechanics who played golf for the first time in Manila and were crazy about it. They had a big room together at Raffles Hotel, where we all stayed in Singapore, and liked to practice in their room, whacking a ball around until it hit a window or mirror and the management called for me. Two older men bought an advertisement in the paper, and printed their own photographs with the news that they were Hollywood talent scouts sponsoring a beauty contest. Applicants were to meet them any evening at a certain bar. The prize — a trip to Hollywood and a screen test — would be awarded on such-and-such a night, which happened to be the one after we were to sail. I was appalled, but didn't see anything I could do; also, I couldn't help being struck by their ingenuity.

When the machinery arrived we sailed slowly up the western side of the Malay Peninsula. The little radio in the dining room began mumbling about a Japanese invasion in southern Indo-China but said it was bloodless, so it didn't seem like a war. On July 28 we crept into a jungle river. Great lumber mills with mountains of teak and a huge oil refinery spread along the western shore. A mile or more of modern cement docks within a tangle of loading cranes and warehouses covered the eastern bank. Dozens of ships were unloading. The warehouses were full to bursting and thousands of tarpaulin-covered crates were piled around them. Beyond the docks the pale low-lying city of Rangoon was dimly visible under black monsoon thunderheads, the golden spire of the Shwe Dagon Pagoda its only tall structure.

Chennault was waiting for us with two Pawleys, Mr. Hunter, and several men I later knew as staff officers of the AVG.

"Hello, Frillmann," he called as soon as we were within earshot. "I told you I'd be here first. I'm glad to see you." Then he turned back to talk to his staff officers.

I don't suppose anyone could have called Chennault "glamorous" to his face without being punched. But he was a vain man, and obviously relished making an impression. Like MacArthur, he had immense natural magnetism on which to base his public figure. That day on the docks he was wearing some slapdash adventurous costume as usual — mosquito boots, officer's shirt with Chinese insignia, beat-up Air Force cap — which emphasized his gamecock look. Watching him for only a few minutes, anyone would get the impression of informality and lack of military pomp, plus a quick, sure air of decisive authority. I don't think any of the men on our ship had ever seen him before, and as I looked down the rail where they were lined up, staring silently at him, I could see that for the time being anyway, Chennault had them all in his pocket.

Long after the war, when secret papers began to be published, and public events fell into better perspective, I got an inkling of what was happening in those last quiet months. In April a Russo-Japanese Neutrality Pact had been signed, dismaying the Chinese who until then were still getting a trickle of supplies from Russia. America's first Lend-Lease aid to China was allocated immediately, mainly for the air force and ground communications. It would total more than $25,000,000 by the end of the year. Unlike the earlier credits, no stipulations were made for the repayment of Lend-Lease. Massive shipments of Lend-Lease supplies to China via Burma started, and steadily increased through the year. In all the later months of 1941, more freight for China was unloaded on the docks of Rangoon than could possibly be moved inland. It became one of the most expensive bonfires in history.

Soon after the Germans invaded Russia in June, American cryptographers broke the Japanese codes and learned that instead of collaborating with the Germans in attacking Russia, as some had hoped, the Japanese intended to advance south against American, British, French, and Dutch holdings. On July 21 they began moving into South Vietnam — then French Indo-China — the perfect base for attacks on Burma, Malaya, and Indonesia. Allied intelligence learned that the government of Thailand, while declaring neutral intentions, had given the Japanese secret permission to build up Thai air bases.

On July 26 all Japanese assets in America were frozen. No further licenses for oil exports to Japan were to be issued. Within a year at the most, Japan would have to abandon its aggressive plans and reach an understanding with America, or it must attack the rich oil fields of Dutch Indonesia.

Rather grotesquely, it is also on record that on July 23 President Roosevelt approved a Joint Board paper which recommended that America equip, man, and maintain a 500-plane Chinese air force with American pilots in China "to embark on a vigorous program culminating in the bombing of Japan in November 1941." This was us, the AVG, of course, and the grandiose notion would have provoked savage laughter if it had become known in the under-manned, under-equipped, and primitive AVG camps that November, one month before Pearl Harbor.

On our arrival in Rangoon in midsummer, Chennault told our group on the dock that we were not going to China right away. The pilots were to train at an airfield in Burma, near the small town of Toungoo, about one hundred and seventy miles inland from Rangoon. I later learned we had been slated to go directly to Kunming in southwestern China — after all, we were working for Chiang Kai-shek — but a Pawley flew there in early summer and found the Chinese had hardly begun enlarging the airfields and building ground installations as promised. Chennault and the Pawleys negotiated with the RAF — Royal Air Force — to lease the field at Toungoo, a secondary one which the RAF did not use during the monsoon rains. It was strictly stipulated that the AVG should use the field only for training, not combat, as the British still hoped to avoid war with Japan.

Chennault told us ninety-nine of the AVG planes had arrived in June, the hundredth having dropped into Rangoon harbor while unloading. A few American and Chinese mechanics from the Pawleys' plant at Loiwing were assembling them, very slowly because they were so short-handed. The mechanics in our group were to go immediately to help them at Mingaladon, the Rangoon airfield. We others would wait in Rangoon hotels until the rest of the AVG arrived on a Dutch passenger liner, expected in a few days, then all would go up to Toungoo by train.

Chennault called me over and handed me a scribbled and smudged paper. I saw it was a long list starting with plane and auto parts and tires, electrical and telephone supplies, then tapering off in a miscellany of musical instruments, screen doors, typewriters, coffins, hunting rifles, American-style cooks, and the like.

"A few other things I thought we might need," he explained offhandedly. "Get the money from the Pawleys and bring the stuff up to Toungoo when you come."

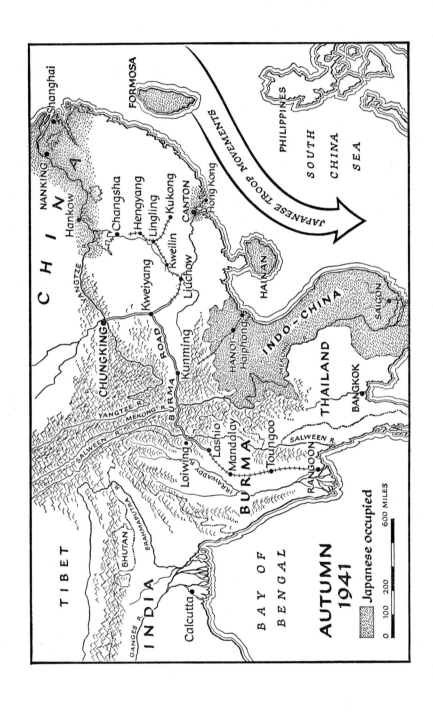

CHAPTER IV

Training at Toungoo 1941

NEXT DAY Chennault flew to Singapore to ask the RAF Command to permit the AVG to practice bombing and strafing over the empty jungles near Toungoo. This was granted, though not without delay. The rest of the AVG soon arrived in Rangoon, bragging about the pleasures of first-class passage on a Dutch luxury liner which also carried female travelers. They had passports as students, salesmen, musicians, and other dummy identities, but Radio Tokyo had announced who they really were and threatened their ship with destruction. West of Hawaii, two U.S. Navy escort cruisers lurked discreetly on their horizon, very much in defiance of our current neutrality laws.

A week after everyone else disappeared up the railway to Toungoo, I had only a fraction of the things on Chennault's list, but decided I should deliver what I did have. I was afraid it would take months to locate everything, bargain for it, then untangle the red tape which hampered buying anything of war value. British Burma was technically at war with Germany, but there was none of the emergency atmosphere which could help the purchase of supplies against Japan. Instead, the calculated lethargy of many British officials and wholesalers seemed blandly intended as insult: "You Yanks! Always in a rush." The mock-obsequiousness and profiteers' prices of the Indian and Chinese merchants were just as aggravating. This was my first experience of a colony, and when I looked for Burmese merchants, thinking they might be more helpful, I was startled to find there were practically none.

On the train north I was so tangled in my notes and inventories that I scarcely noticed exotic Burma flowing past the windows. Toungoo, reached in a monsoon downpour at the end of the day, was a shabby little bazaar of tin-roofed Indian and Chinese shops, sprawling around the Victorian railway station and a few other brick hulks of Empire. I had wired for an AVG truck to come for my cargo, but instead a Burmese telegraph clerk handed me my own telegram and asked me to deliver it to the airfield, six miles away. I found an Indian trucker who would take me at a pirate's price. We drove out through patches of jungle and teak plantations where the fading light made tethered elephants look big as dinosaurs.

In another downpour and total darkness we came to the airfield. Everyone was sensibly indoors and the buildings, lit only by dim kerosene lamps, were hardly visible. At the closest, I was greeted by a hail of empty beer cans and blurry voices shouting: "We don't want none of you wogs around here!" After much more slogging through mud and underbrush, bulldozed down and rotting in the wet heat, I found a hut for the cargo and a bed for myself.

Disintegration always seemed close to the surface in the AVG, and those early days at Toungoo were one of the worst times. Chiang Kai-shek had summoned Chennault from Singapore directly to Chungking for conferences, while the capital was going through the heaviest air raids of the summer. Traffic through the city could be halted for many hours by each attack, and Chennault was long overdue in Burma. None of his staff at Toungoo could assert enough authority, and the idle pilots and ground crew were close to mutiny. They hated the weather, the mud, the food, and the bugs. All were in fact terrible.

Hot rain poured down for hours every afternoon and evening. Two landing strips crisscrossing in the jungle were the airfield. Only one was paved, for only 4,000 feet — everything else was sticky mud. Our food was made by Burmese cooks on loan from the RAF, who could botch the simplest materials and served claimedly British dishes like tepid fish for breakfast and a repulsive dessert they called "Cold Shape." The dormitories were new and well-carpentered, of teak, but with no screening — I had learned in Rangoon that not a square foot could be bought in all Burma — and bugs the size of sparrows flopped in at night. Sometimes we had electricity, more often not.

The men who had joined the AVG to escape were now anxious to escape from the AVG. They also had to convince themselves they were injured parties. Many pilots lied when they claimed experience with P-40's, and they were whining against Chennault: "Who the hell does he think he is anyway, a broken down ex-captain hiding out in China for years? What can he teach me?" A few assembled P-40's had been delivered from Rangoon, and the ground crewmen were discouraged by the work still to be done — armament, radios, bomb racks, auxiliary fuel tanks. They had little of the equipment or material they needed, so they settled for doing the minimum.

On August 22 Chennault flew in, and was immediately handed the resignations of five pilots and several ground crewmen, some of whom had cabled home to have messages sent back saying they had sick wives or dying children. We later heard a couple of the pilots soon got good jobs with commercial airlines; they had apparently joined the AVG just to get out of the service. A few ground crewmen moved into Rangoon and picked up with Burmese girls who became their partners in the extremely lucrative business of black-marketing and smuggling up the Burma Road.

With his face like a chunk of lava ready to explode, Chennault accepted the resignations and ordered everyone else into a meeting. Full preparation for combat would start next day, he said grimly. Only about a dozen P-40's had arrived from Rangoon, so the pilots would have to take their sixty hours of flight training in two batches, but all would attend all lectures, getting two courses of seventy-two hours each. The first lecture would start next morning at six. He reminded the ground crewmen their contracts with the AVG allowed fines or dismissal for failure in their duties.

Within twenty-four hours, it seemed, the air of the camp freshened. The pilots found Chennault a good teacher, and his information about Japanese planes and tactics was new and fascinating. After his morning lectures, in the few hours before the monsoon thunderheads built up, he would send his pupils aloft in P-40's, one at a time, following them with binoculars, directing and suggesting by radio from his lookout tower, a crude bamboo scaffold beside the operations shack. In the first days he concentrated on the pilots who had no earlier experience in P-40's, especially the Navy fliers accustomed to flying boats — great slow airships big enough for bunkrooms and kitchenettes. The little P-40's with hair-trigger maneuverability and a landing speed of 100 mph baffled and no doubt terrified the Navy men; their flights could be comic and horrifying. When we had electricity we sometimes had old movies, mostly Laurel and Hardy comedies, and on the ground we used to speculate which was at the controls overhead.

Still, having planes overhead was a great morale-booster for the ground crewmen. They began to treat the shortage of parts and tools as a challenge, and to enjoy improvising. They rigged up contraptions of bamboo, rope, and pulleys, and used gangs of Burmese workmen instead of mechanical hoists. They taught themselves how to rip up one plane for the parts to put several others back into the air. Filing and hammering at odd bits of metal, they began to manufacture some of the simpler spare parts themselves.

By early September life was much easier. The monsoon was passing and the mud began to dry up. Chinese cooks hired away from a Rangoon nightclub took over the kitchen. Chennault ordered everyone to do daily calisthenics — and me to lead them — so we all felt healthier. On every dry afternoon we had a baseball game, sometimes with Chennault pitching. For more fitness, he told his staff to make our vehicles hard to get, when the men wanted them for jaunts around the field or into town.

After a few days of sweaty walking and bitter complaint, someone discovered a stock of cheap Japanese bicycles in the Toungoo bazaar and nearly all of us bought one. In somewhat slow motion we had afternoon bike races into Toungoo, where we liked to gawk and shop, our one real amusement. Cashew nuts were local, delicious, and cheap, so we bought them by the bushel. Leather shops could make fancy wallets, belts, and mosquito boots. Pilots with spare cash began to collect rubies and star sapphires from northern Burma. Some men liked to cycle into the teak plantations and watch the elephants hauling timber; their circus memories made this seem a big deal, a bargain, a free treat.

After dark there was not much to do except stay home, drink, play cards, and talk. I was quartered in a dormitory with some staff members and pilots, and Chennault lived in a semi-partitioned cubicle at one end. He usually spent his evenings with us, and I found he was not at all the taciturn forbidding character I had thought. He was affable and talkative. He didn't drink with us, but was a cribbage fan and liked to joke and reminisce as he played. This fascinated us. We were naturally curious about the career which had brought him — and all the rest of us — to a little airfield in the Burmese jungle. By the end of the training months we felt we knew the outline.

He was born in 1890, son of a small cotton planter in rural Louisiana, and spent a hunting, fishing boyhood in the forests and bayous. After high school he put himself through two years at the state university and two years of normal school by farming his own cotton patch in vacations. For a few restless years he taught grade schools in small Louisiana towns, meanwhile marrying and starting a family of eight. He moved to New Orleans and taught in a business school while he studied physical culture at night, then he took a job teaching it at YMCA's in Kentucky, Tennessee, and Ohio.

At the start of the First World War he found work as inspector of military balloons in one of the booming rubber factories in Akron, Ohio. He volunteered as soon as America entered the war, and was assigned to Officers Training School. Because he knew balloons, then widely believed the most promising aircraft, he was commissioned a Lieutenant in the Aviation Section of the Signal Corps—there was no separate Air Force yet. He applied for flight training but was rejected with the barb, "Does not have the qualifications of an aviator."

A few days before the Armistice he applied again and was accepted for training as a pursuit pilot. Afterward he studied aeronautical engineering for six months and was honorably discharged in April 1920. He tried cotton farming in Louisiana again, but one hot, dry summer was enough. That September he was one of the first thousand officers to volunteer for the brand-new U.S. Army Air Force.

An early assignment was flying the Mexican border patrol, where one of his colleagues was Jimmy Doolittle, later the leader of our first air raid on Tokyo. Together they made what were probably the first experimental parachute drops of supplies to ground units. Then Chennault had routine ground-officer jobs until 1922, when he was assigned to active pursuit flying, his chief interest. In various units and several places — Texas, Hawaii, Texas again — he continued with this until 1929. In his last eight years in the Air Force, he was an instructor in pursuit flying, at bases in Virginia, Georgia, and elsewhere.

One of Chennault's noticeable foibles was a tendency to feel slighted or persecuted even when he wasn't, but some of the things he told us about the early U.S. Air Force helped explain this. The 1920's and early 30's were paradoxical years for military aviation. Private interests and civilian inventors were hurrying the airplane through more technological development than wheeled vehicles had creaked past in many centuries, but the U.S. Army seemed unconvinced that the plane was here to stay, especially the pursuit plane. Funds for the Air Force were so small that flying officers often had trouble finding the planes and enough gas to fly the four hours per month needed to qualify for flight pay.

In 1921, American planes with thousand-pound bombs had destroyed two obsolete German battleships — war prizes — anchored off the Virginia Capes. Later, obsolete American ships were successfully sunk, and Army brass and the public alike were persuaded that bombers were the weapon of the future. The development of the Martin B-10 bomber, which had more than double the armament and almost the speed of the Boeing-26, then the most advanced pursuit plane, was taken to confirm this. A popular book of the period was *The War of 194?* by the Italian General Douhet who theorized that wars could be won by air bombardment alone. The dogfights of the First World War were dismissed as archaic, even funny; this notion survived in the U.S. Army and Air Force until blasted by the RAF and Luftwaffe in the Battle of Britain, then the AVG in Burma. As late as 1931 the real possibilities of pursuit planes were so neglected that the U.S. Air Force still had a plan to use them to drop ball-and-chain obstacles into the propellers of attacking bombers.

The flexibility of all air power was slighted because of the dream of massive squadrons of bombers. When Chennault was at Brooks Field about 1928, he and some younger officers staged a maneuver in which a big V of two-seater pursuit planes escorted a tri-motored bomber. A paratrooper rode each wing of every pursuit plane and a third sat in the extra cockpit. When they jumped, trench mortars and a piece of light field artillery, plus ammunition, were tumbled from the bomber. On the ground the men quickly collected into one fighting unit.

The routine was kept a secret until the U.S. Army Chief of Staff came to inspect the field. As soon as this general saw the parachutes blossoming, he turned his back and stamped away muttering, "More of this damned aviation nonsense!"

Later the demonstration was staged for a group of Russian officers, in America on a purchasing mission. They were impressed enough to offer Chennault a job in their department of experimental aviation, at a salary more than four times his U.S. Air Force pay. He declined, fearing he would have to give up U.S. citizenship.

Closer to the threat of another war, Russia and the European powers were constantly experimenting. Many innovations must have appeared in several countries almost simultaneously. Still, it may not be coincidence that within a few years of Chennault's demonstration for the Russians, the newspapers of the world were printing pictures of Russian skies as thick with parachutes as a June pasture with daisies. The Germans evidently took notice, for in 1940 German paratroops captured Rotterdam and held it until ground troops could fight their way to them. In 1941 the stunning German paratroop invasion of Crete at last startled America into training parachutists in quantity, more than a decade after Chennault's demonstration for our Chief of Staff.

During part of his Air Force career, Chennault's real abilities were obscured by the fun he had as a stunt performer. In a bid for public interest, the infant Air Force encouraged its fliers to put on shows at gatherings ranging from country fairs to the big air races popular in that period of slower and more visible planes.

This suited Chennault perfectly. One of his early shows began with the megaphoned announcement that Grandma So-and-so, who had arrived as a pioneer in a covered wagon and had tried every new wheeled contraption since, was to have her first airplane ride. A shaky old lady in a big black bonnet and voluminous dress was ushered onto the field and helped into the second cockpit of a pursuit plane. The pilot went to whirl the propeller, but to his great surprise the plane took off before he could climb aboard.

For half an hour the crowd in the grandstand shrieked and gasped at what a daffy old lady could do. The plane spinned and rolled and looped-the-loop. It dove to treetop level, then headed for a barn or the grandstand itself, swooping up at the last moment. Then it made a perfect three-point landing and the old lady bounded out. Laughter and applause followed as Chennault whipped off his bonnet and dress before bowing.

Later he organized a show of acrobatic flying, "Three Men on a Flying Trapeze," famous for several years as an attraction at the big air races in Miami, Cleveland, and Birmingham. With two other airmen who were willing to spend hundreds of hours in practice, he perfected an act in which eighteen spectacular maneuvers — wingovers, spins, rolls, Immelmanns — were flown in formation. Sometimes the planes were tied wingtip to wingtip with twenty-foot ropes, but often they flew as little as eight feet apart. After the Miami Races in 1934, Chennault received his first offer of a job in China, from General P. T. Mao, then Chief of the Chinese Air Force, who had been an astounded spectator.

Under the bravura, Chennault was a deadly serious airman with an obsession for pursuit flying. In his years as an instructor, he did research on its beginnings in the First World War. With his flying students he experimented in new techniques. He was a frequent contributor to service journals, and wrote a primary manual of pursuit flying which continued in use as a textbook for years after his retirement. He was one of the few Americans to keep posted on the new ideas about airpower in general and pursuit flying in particular, then appearing in foreign countries.

His experience with "Three Men on a Trapeze" had shown him it was hard for three pilots to coordinate perfectly. One was always a little out of pattern, a little extra. Two pilots could keep better track of one another, so he began building combat plans around pairs of pursuit planes. He found precedent in the pioneer ideas of a German pilot, Oswald von Boelcke, who had been killed in 1916 after teaching his tactics to the young Manfred von Richthofen. Von Boelcke discovered many surprises and traps two could use against one, and von Richthofen adapted them for his "Flying Circus" which entered combat with sensational success in 1917. The "Circus" was never defeated until von Richthofen was killed, and Hermann Goering — later Hitler's air chief — took command. He may have felt that the teamwork was demeaning or democratic, for he went back to the earlier tactics in which each pilot entered the fray alone, like a medieval hero on a horse. The "Circus" was soon cut to pieces.

As Chennault experimented with pairs of pursuit planes, he became convinced they could fight as well against bombers as against other pursuits. Their combined firepower would almost equal a bomber's. It was a revolutionary idea then, and when he asked Air Force technicians to equip pursuits with four wing-cannons synchronized to fire through the propellers, instead of the existing two, he was told it was impossible. Not until 1938, when Russian pursuits with four wing-cannons appeared in China and Spain, did America begin developing such a plane. Chennault also asked for timed fragmentation bombs for his pursuits to drop among squadrons of bombers, but nothing was done about this until after Pearl Harbor, when the Japanese began using such a weapon against our bombers.

The ground air-warning net, as later established in China, was perhaps the most important non-combat innovation pushed by Chennault while he was in the Air Force. His ideas were based partly on British and German prototypes, partly on his own diagnosis of what a defense by pursuits needed; this got little attention from the bomber-oriented Air Force. Chennault was also among those who first proposed, quite as fruitlessly, that the Air Force back a training program for civilian pilots to provide a reserve in case of war.

By the mid-30's he was very much the prophet without honor in his own country. He was also growing deaf in one ear and had chronic bronchitis. The Air Force restricted him to flying two-seater planes with an emergency pilot in the other cockpit, then grounded him completely. But he was reluctant to leave aviation without proving his ideas about pursuits, and had been corresponding with friends in China, including his former sidemen in "Three Men on a Trapeze," who were teachers in a Chinese flying school. Through one of them he received an offer from Madame Chiang Kai-shek to make a three-month confidential survey of the Chinese Air Force. He resigned from the U.S. Air Force on the last day of April, 1937, and on the following day left for China. He was then forty-seven years old.

*

In my Hankow years I had heard a bit about the start of aviation in what now seems prehistoric China. Since the 1920's, many a warlord had prided himself on his private "air force," usually one or more old crates flown by White Russian or other mercenary pilots. The planes might be used as much for smuggling or for flying concubines to the Shanghai dressmakers or dropping rocks on rebels, as for orthodox purposes. No national Air Force existed until the early 30's, after Chiang Kai-shek took control of the coast and was then threatened by Japanese encroachment.

Under the aegis of T. V. Soong, an unofficial American mission of about twenty U.S. Air Force officers led by Colonel John Jouett went to China in 1932 and opened a flying school. Large Chinese orders for American planes, aviation gas, and equipment were made, but disappointment followed when no official American government sponsorship was offered. American reluctance to give air support to Chiang's drive to crush a rebellion in Fukien province, on the southeast coast, led to the withdrawal of the Jouett mission in 1934.

Soon afterward, H. H. Kung, Chiang's conservative banker brother-in-law, visited Italy and received an imperial welcome. No doubt irked by the Far Eastern prestige Hitler was gaining with the Nazi mission to train Chinese ground forces, Mussolini offered Kung an official Italian Air Force mission of about forty pilot-teachers and one hundred ground personnel. Though a few Americans from the Jouett mission stayed on to teach as private citizens, and a corps of American-trained pilots remained an elite in the Chinese Air Force, Italian influence was dominant until the Japanese invasion.

The Italians opened a flying school in Loyang, and at Nanchang built an assembly plant for Fiat pursuits and Marchetti bombers. In the capital at Nanking, their chief of mission, General Scaroni, and his high-ranking Fascist officers vied in size of limousines and flags with General von Falkenhausen and his Nazi staff.

Axis influence was indeed so strong in Nanking when Chennault arrived in 1937 that Madame Chiang and her Australian adviser, W. H. Donald, had to pull hard on many strings to arrange for an Air Force survey by an American. Chennault soon learned why. Corrupt Italian and Chinese practices had combined as smoothly as olive and sesame oil. Wrecked or disabled planes were not removed from the rolls, lest that cut off the money for their maintenance. Funds for new planes were raised in the big cities by pretending to name a plane for each city. All the planes were added to the rolls, while in fact only one demonstration plane was flown around the country, a new city-name painted on it for each new fund-raising campaign. The funds disappeared. On paper the Air Force had nearly five hundred planes but only ninety-one were really in existence and ready for combat.

At the Italian flying school all entrants were graduated and given commissions, regardless of merit. The Air Force was chic, and most students came from rich or highly-placed official families who could make trouble if they flunked out. Later it was nearly impossible to get them to practice or take refresher courses, because this would be a loss of face, an admission that they had not already learned everything.

Chennault was at the Loyang school when the Japanese invasion began near Peking, on July 7. He wired to Chiang volunteering to help in any way. He was ordered to Nanchang to complete the training of a class of pursuit pilots, but it was too late to do much for these novices soon to be in combat. In midsummer he was summoned to Nanking. He remained a civilian adviser, technically in the employ of Madame Chiang, but within a few days was in partial command of the air defense of the capital. Though he only made "suggestions," they had the force of orders because Chiang Kai-shek was known to back them.

While the Japanese were still busy with the battle for Shanghai, a few Chinese successes were scored over Nanking. In their first bombing raids the overconfident enemy sent bombers in daylight without fighter cover. Chennault's hastily-taught pursuit tactics knocked down enough to cause the Japanese to switch to night raids. Chennault devised a night defense using searchlights to dazzle the attackers while pursuits flew in at a lower level, then swooped up to strafe the brightly-lit bombers. After that Nanking was left alone until October, when Shanghai fell and Japanese ground forces began converging on the capital.

A hundred to a hundred and fifty attacking planes would appear on every clear day, with each V of twenty-seven bombers escorted by a swarm of pursuits. The Italian-trained Chinese Air Force simply disintegrated. A few dandies from the Loyang school died in combat after surprising feats of courage; others cracked up their planes and themselves in panicky takeoffs or landings. Before the fall of Nanking, Mussolini suggested to Chiang that he accept Japanese surrender terms. Instead, Chiang demanded the recall of the Italian Air Force mission.

It is generally forgotten now, but the next year and a half were the Russian period of Chinese aviation. Chiang Kai-shek had asked military aid from all the great powers as soon as Japan attacked, but America and Britain declined. Russia responded with an air force and other aid. The Chinese always tried to keep the Russians out of sight, so the size and nature of their intervention were a mystery at the time. Chennault said in his autobiography that the Russians maintained four fighter squadrons and two bomber squadrons — complete with ground personnel — a force about twice the size of the later AVG. The squadrons were changed every six months, for the Russians were training pilots against the Japanese, just as they were then using Spain to train men against Germany and Italy.

According to Arthur N. Young, an American financial adviser

to the Chinese government, between 1937 and 1939 the Russians extended to Chiang Kai-shek credits equaling U.S. $250,000,000. By 1939 they had supplied him with 1,000 planes and sent 200 "volunteer" pilots in rotation. Many of them were flying for China at a time when America was so isolationist that American civilian flying instructors, hired by the Chinese Air Force before the war, could not get passports from the State Department.

The Russian credits were also used to purchase anti-aircraft guns, artillery, and the materiel for artillery and flying schools. It was brought in on a truck road the Russians built along the remains of the old Silk Route across Central Asia. All aid was supposed to have gone to Chiang's government, none to the Chinese Communists.

By the time the capital moved to Hankow, the Russian aid was arriving and Chennault found himself somewhat on the sidelines. He still advised Madame Chiang, and sometimes collaborated with the Chinese and Russians in planning air strikes — the victory on Hirohito's birthday, for example — but the Russians had the airpower and did most of their own planning.

Before Hankow fell, Madame Chiang sent him to Kunming to train a new air force. He collected a teaching staff of about a dozen Americans and opened a primary flying school to prepare cadets for further training in the United States. A new kind of young Chinese had become available, not just the sons of the rich, but earnest volunteers who had lost homes and families in the invasion. Some trekked west to Kunming with great hardship, walking for weeks over the rough mountain roads.

The following two years were mainly routine for Chennault, full of the small problems of running a school, but it was a terrible time for China. When clear weather came in the spring of 1939, the Japanese launched a massive bombing offensive.

No doubt they were training pilots for the Pacific War, but the raids were so extensive, and so costly to them, that they must have hoped also to defeat China by bombardment alone. Their attacks were smaller than the American raids on neighboring Vietnam more than a quarter of a century later but were comparable, though they were purposefully aimed at civilian as well as military targets.

Chungking and other larger cities were bombed repeatedly, with tens of thousands of casualties. Bridges and roads, railways and riverboats, were bombed or strafed. Half a dozen provinces would be under air alert for hours, all business stopped and traffic halted.

Before the end of the summer, however, it was obvious bombing would not win the war. The damage and deaths increased hatred of the Japanese, and renewed the Chinese will to resist. Ways of living and working despite the raids were found. City people would disperse into the country during alarms, then come back to do their day's work in the evening. Main lines of communication were so well equipped with warning signals — usually red cloth globes hoisted on poles by men alerted by the main air-warning net — that traffic could move except when enemy planes were within a few miles. Because the communications were so primitive they could usually be repaired and re-opened in a few hours, by manpower alone.

When war in Europe threatened in the late summer of 1939, Russian air aid was withdrawn, and after a winter's lull the unopposed Japanese bombers ravaged western China through the clear months of 1940. That autumn Chiang Kai-shek called Chennault to Chungking and told him he was worried about the eventual effect on Chinese morale if the raids should continue many more years. America was already giving him civilian aid, and he wondered if he could buy enough American planes and hire American pilots to stop the bombers. Chennault was not hopeful, because he had heard of the intense rivalry between the U.S. Army and Navy — and our allies — for new planes, but in October he left on the mission which would result in the AVG.

After our life at Toungoo settled down, I was sometimes able to sit in on Chennault's lectures, and I marveled at the care he had put into them. While at the training school in Kunming he had collected Japanese flying and staff manuals, taken from downed planes and translated into English by the Chinese Air Force. He had records of long interviews with captured pilots. He had copious notes on late-model Japanese planes, crashed in China then repaired and tested by the Chinese. He had information on the new Zero pursuits, then unknown outside Japan — when he first described the Zeros, two or three more of our pilots discovered urgent reasons for going home. On his studies Chennault based combat plans which exploited the differences between Japanese and American planes and temperaments.

Lightly armored and of flimsy construction, the Zeros were more maneuverable than the P-40's, with faster and steeper climb, and higher ceiling. This advantage was partly offset by the inflexibility of the pilots, who were sergeants drilled in precise formation flying and tactics learned by rote. Each group was directed by an officer who flew above and behind, but ordinarily did not go into combat himself.

The P-40's with heavy armor and more guns were faster in dives. If the American planes could start above the Japanese, pairs of reasonably quick-witted and independent pilots could dive on the rigid enemy formation, breaking it into confusion and singling out their victims. Much of the classroom time was spent studying the Japanese textbook attacks one by one, and inventing surprises which might jolt the Japanese out of their prepared pattern. Chennault always emphasized that our men should exploit the P-40's great advantage and dive away immediately after an attack, then climb and dive on the enemy again. A tumbling turning dogfight with the more maneuverable Zeros should be avoided if possible.

When news of these novel tactics spread, a sarcastic note on the RAF bulletin board in Rangoon announced that any pilot diving out of combat would be court-martialed. In the Chinese Air Force, of course, a pilot who did so would be summarily executed.

When Chennault started flight practice with pairs of planes, then larger formations, we had our first casualties. Armstrong was killed in a mid-air collision with another P-40 during a simulated dogfight; the other pilot lost a wing but was able to parachute safely. Atkinson's propeller governor gave way in another practice battle and he power-dived into the earth beside a Burmese village. Hammer crashed in a monsoon storm. At the airfield we had a chapel of thatch and bamboo matting where I read modified Lutheran services before we buried them in the little Church of England cemetery in Toungoo.

From a military point of view, our losses of planes were more serious than the casualties. With 99 planes, the AVG should have been a consequential force in the Far East that year, but training accidents at Toungoo destroyed or damaged the P-40's almost as fast as they could be assembled and flown up from Rangoon. We seldom had more than twenty flyable planes on the field at once. One day six P-40's — most of them flown by ex-Navy flying boat pilots — overshot the field and cracked up. Chennault ordered all further flights canceled for the day, then a ground crewman bicycling along the edge of the field, looking over his shoulder at the wreckage, crashed into the aileron of a seventh plane and disabled it. This was a heavier toll than any one day's losses in later combat. Chennault had a line whitewashed across the runway a third of the way along it, and put a fifty-dollar fine on any pilot whose wheels touched down beyond the line.

The ground crews had become expert at reclaiming planes which seemed hopelessly wrecked, but maintenance was a terrible problem because of the chronic shortage of spare parts, for either planes or engines, and the lack of new tires. Some planes had to be grounded because their tires were worn out in training. At one time Chennault had twelve of his staff flying all over the Far East looking for spare parts and tires. One was Joseph Alsop, the columnist, who was captured by the Japanese when they took Hong Kong, and repatriated after months of internment.

With hindsight, this spare parts problem suggests that the AVG had become obsolete even before it was organized. Americans were apparently beginning to treat planes like cars, not repairing them and making them last, but discarding them when something went wrong. The Chinese had been unable to buy spare parts from the Curtiss-Wright Company when they purchased the 100 P-40's, and a vice president told Chennault his firm was under U.S. Air Force orders to make only complete planes, disposable like Kleenex. It was a waste of time producing the spare parts which could keep an ailing plane flying. This was all very well for an air force with a ready supply of complete planes, but it was disastrous for an outfit like the AVG which could not obtain new planes.

Except for this problem, the end of November saw the AVG as ready for combat as it ever would be. Everybody had lost weight and the pilots were fit, tanned, and alert. All day pairs of closely aligned P-40's twisted and sideslipped overhead as Chennault's maneuvers were practiced with growing skill. The men were so fascinated by them that at the bar in the mess hall they spent most of their evenings talking tactics, weaving their bodies as they swooped their aligned hands around. I used to think how odd it would look through a soundproof window, seeing these extremely tough young men behaving like a gaggle of ballet dancers.

Most of the problems which had bedeviled us since summer were solved. After some conflict with British and Chinese officials, a supply of Lend-Lease gas and ammunition was assured, and enough Lend-Lease trucks and jeeps were obtained. The RAF originally refused to let us make any changes in their field, even to build revetment areas, but the ban was somewhat relaxed and a gunnery butt for sighting machine guns had been built. When the first P-40's arrived, the British forbade us to post American guards or to hire Burmese — we supposed because this would infringe on colonial sovereignty — but they had since rented us some Gurkha soldiers. None of our planes had proper Air Force radios, just light civilian models on which the pilots could not talk to one another, only to the ground, but an earlier tendency for them to go dead entirely seemed to be licked. Modern gun sights had never arrived, but the ground crewmen hammered out old-fashioned ring-and-post sights; the pilots were at least accustomed to them since they were like rifle sights.

Not long before the AVG flew into the attention of the world, someone noticed a photograph in the *Illustrated News of India* showing P-40's Lend-Leased to the RAF in North Africa. They had grinning shark faces painted on their snouts, perfectly fitting the shape of the plane. One pilot painted a shark on his P-40, then everybody had to have one. In a week or two, all AVG planes had the decorations which would become part of the legend.

CHAPTER V

First Combat 1941–42

FROM FRIENDS who were in the United States on Pearl Harbor day, I later heard how thunderstruck they were, eating their Sunday chicken or watching a football game when the news hit. At Toungoo we were less surprised. During the autumn British and Chinese intelligence had brought many warnings.

In October and November Japanese transports began moving crack troops southward from China; their garrison duty was taken over by reserves and Chinese puppets. Japanese naval vessels were concentrating at Camranh Bay in Indo-China, and included shallow-draught landing craft. Zeros were seen on the Saigon airfield for the first time in November, and Japanese air strength in Indo-China was reported to have increased from about 75 to 250 planes. Unidentified aircraft were heard over Malaya at night.

For months, Japanese engineers with gangs of Thai coolies had been working on airfields in the jungles of Thailand, including one hardly a hundred miles from Toungoo. Starting about the first of November, Chennault secretly sent scouting patrols over, and found the scale of work steadily increasing. A single Japanese reconnaissance ship began appearing over Toungoo about twice a week, just before dark and too high and fast to intercept.

Because we were on the far side of the International Date Line, it was December 8 by the calendar when we heard about Pearl Harbor and the raids on the Philippines and Wake Island. Around noon, as I recall, one of the radiomen ran out to the control tower waving a paper. Chennault glanced through it, shouted the news to the nearest men, and a great clamor of voices spread over the field. After months of boredom and discomfort, elation was the first response.

We had only eighteen P-40's fully equipped for combat at Toungoo on the 8th. Our only warning of air attack could come from one British civil servant stationed near the Thai border — sixty miles away — with field glasses and a telephone. Chennault had tried to get the British to set up a complete warning net like the Chinese, but was told that British spotters could not survive in the jungle, and the Burmese were not to be trusted. That afternoon, while our ground crews worked feverishly to finish more P-40's — luckily, about twenty-five were almost ready — the rest of us spent hours peering into the skies over Thailand. We knew the Japanese could avoid the lone British watcher and come bursting over the nearest mountains without warning. We became uneasily conscious of how many strange Burmese were wandering about our field despite the Gurkha guards. Several were intrusive and specially curious Buddhist monks in saffron robes; monks or men disguised as monks later proved to be among the most active enemy agents.

Next day several reconnaissance ships came over, and we had half a dozen false alerts, each setting off a mad scramble. The usable planes were outnumbered by fully trained and terribly excited pilots. Although every ship was supposed to be assigned to one man, the pilots would race down the field pell-mell when the alarm — an old ship's bell loaned by the RAF — sounded. The fastest runners leaped into the planes and sat there grinning, with the rightful pilots furiously yelling and shaking fists at them until the alert was called off.

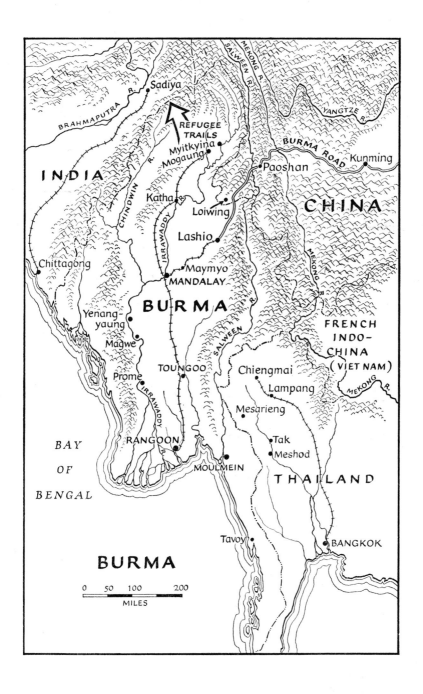

INDIA

BRAHMAPUTRA R.

Sadiya

REFUGEE TRAILS

Myitkyina
Mogaung

SALWEEN RIVER

MEKONG RIVER

YANGTZE R.

BURMA ROAD

Paoshan

Kunming

CHINA

CHINDWIN R.

IRRAWADDY R.

Katha

Loiwing

Lashio

Chittagong

Maymyo
MANDALAY

BURMA

Yenang-
yaung

Magwe

SALWEEN R.

MEKONG R.

FRENCH
INDO-
CHINA
(VIET NAM)

Prome

IRRAWADDY R.

TOUNGOO

Chiengmai

Lampang

MEKONG R.

Mesarieng

BAY

OF

BENGAL

RANGOON

MOULMEIN

Tak

Meshod

THAILAND

BURMA

Tavoy

BANGKOK

0   50   100   200
          MILES

On December 10 we heard Thailand had formally surrendered, and Chennault sent a stripped-down P-40 on a reconnaissance mission over Bangkok. With a borrowed RAF camera, it photographed twenty-six Japanese transports in the river, docks jammed with troops and equipment, one airfield packed with about fifty bombers, another with as many pursuits. A few formations of American bombers could have crippled the looming invasions of Malaya and Burma, but the only ones within range were burnt-out wrecks on Clark Field in the Philippines.

I think it was on this day that Chennault got a radio message from China Defense Supplies in Washington, saying that a cargo plane full of spare parts for the AVG had been flying the Pacific at the time of Pearl Harbor. It was stopped at Wake Island, the AVG cargo dumped, and the plane used to evacuate civilian personnel to Hawaii. The next load for the AVG was flown around the world the other way, but did not arrive in Kunming until three months later.

Despite America's entry into the war, we were still under Chinese command, and our first orders were to defend the Burma Road, a large job for so small a force. The port at Rangoon was more than a thousand road miles from the terminus at Kunming, and the cities were about six hundred and fifty miles apart as the P-40 flew. Chennault originally wanted to base the whole AVG around Kunming, but he had already divided it into three squadrons, and on December 12 he sent the Third Squadron, under Arvid Olson, to Rangoon, where its fifteen planes were to bolster the RAF's ridiculously inadequate force of about thirty Brewster Buffalo pursuits, a few Hurricanes, and a dozen old Blenheim bombers.

On the morning of the 18th we heard that the Japanese were bombing Kunming, and Chennault ordered the First and Second Squadrons, under Bob Sandell and Jack Newkirk, to fly there in the afternoon; he had always planned the AVG as a guerrilla force which could move suddenly from one base to another, using surprise against the enemy's greater numbers. At dusk, when the danger of Japanese attack was less, three battered old China National Aviation Company cargo planes landed at Toungoo and loaded the other men and equipment needed for combat. A dozen unfinished P-40's were left at Toungoo, along with twenty-five partly trained pilots, and some ground crew. Other men were sent off to Kunming by truck.

I was somehow classified as combat personnel and flew over the black mountains in a CNAC plane, landing at Kunming around midnight on a field dimly marked by a few auto headlights and many crude little peasant lamps. After hours of confusion and rush in the dark, thirty-four P-40's were loaded with gas and bullets and lined up on the field at dawn. Our headquarters was linked with the Chinese warning net, and coderooms which could intercept and translate Japanese messages.

A day of giddy anticlimax followed. P-40's patrolled the Indo-China border about two hundred miles to the south, but met not a single Japanese plane. Sleepiness and excitement and the stimulus of being in a new country, a new climate, made everyone in the alert shacks light-headed. We couldn't see anything that looked specially Chinese — just open farmland and bare reddish mountains beyond the adobe airfield buildings — but the thinner cooler air of a high plateau was like a shot of iced gin after the Burma jungles. Lots of horseplay, Indian wrestling, acrobatics, even tag, helped the long hours pass.

At quarter to ten next morning, we were warned of ten Japanese bombers crossing the border, heading toward Kunming. We could hear sirens howling from the city and in the distance saw red warning globes hoisted on hilltops. Long lines of people trudged out into the country.

Chennault sent the Second Squadron south in two groups to intercept. He ordered the First Squadron to climb to top altitude near Kunming and circle there in reserve. The warning net kept reporting the bombers' approach, then snatches of confused talk among pilots of the Second Squadron came in on the radio. The war was so new, the men could not convince themselves the bombers they saw were the enemy. They were still arguing when static drowned them out. The warning net reported the bombers were turning around, and we heard a rumble of heavy explosions from the southern mountains. Chennault ordered the First Squadron to follow in pursuit, with the great speed which diving would give them.

The Second Squadron came in soon afterward, sheepishly reporting that their few moments of incredulity had given the Japanese time to jettison their bombs. Emptied of their loads, the bombers gained enough speed to escape P-40's flying at the same altitude.

When the First Squadron returned much later, the pilots were grinning triumphantly. They had dived on the Japanese about thirty miles south of Kunming and harassed them in a running battle. The tactics and teamwork taught at Toungoo were forgotten in this first helter-skelter, and some P-40's narrowly escaped colliding or shooting one another down, but three bombers were sent crashing in flames, and most of the others were trailing smoke before they got away. The warning net reported three more went down before reaching Indo-China. Ground intelligence from Hanoi later said only one returned to its base. Radio Tokyo announced the arrival of the AVG at Kunming and Rangoon, and boasted the "unprincipled American bandits" would be totally destroyed, but this was the single time the enemy tried to attack Kunming while the AVG was there.

The Japanese had plenty to do elsewhere, of course. The invasions of Malaya, Indonesia, Hong Kong, and the Philippines were under way by mid-December. After the abortive attack on Kunming, Chinese intelligence reported many planes on fields near China were flown off to the new fronts. Air patrols over the Thai-Burma border increased, and about 150 bombers and pursuits were discovered massing on the Thai fields closest to Rangoon. On December 21 twenty-seven unescorted bombers approached the city. They were intercepted by fourteen AVG P-40's and twenty-three RAF Buffaloes, and fled without a fight, dropping their bombs on the small coastal town of Tavoy.

I had already realized that my work as a chaplain was not likely to include much care of the wounded; our casualties tended to be fully alive one minute, dead the next. Still, I knew the Third Squadron in Rangoon was shorter of general help than the larger group in Kunming, and as the action seemed to be moving there, I got Chennault's permission to return to Burma on a CNAC plane flying down to evacuate civilian refugees.

In the dry heat of the Burmese winter the AVG men at Mingaladon, the Rangoon airport, were camping in a dirty bivouac of frayed tents, across the dusty runway from the rather trim RAF quarters. Their food was removed from its cans by the hands of Burmese boys they had hired. Vague agreements about housing and food had been made with the RAF, but they broke down in the first distraught days of war. It hardly mattered, since everybody was so busy and keyed-up.

The partly-assembled P-40's had been dragged away from the runway, and the ground crews were hastily finishing them under towering jungle trees. Four trucks to service planes during combat were almost ready. One was for ammunition, one for gas, one for engine and body repairs, one for oxygen. They would be kept in revetments, ready to speed out and cluster around a plane so fast — it was hoped — that they could service it and get back to shelter before a Japanese spotted them. Farther out from Mingaladon, teams of other ground crewmen

were flattening emergency landing strips in the dry rice pad-
dies. Two of these became known as "Johnny Walker" and
"Haig & Haig," because of the bottles hidden in the nearby
jungle.

December 23 started as a blazingly hot cloudless day. At ten-
thirty in the morning, the RAF alarm system — a primitive
radar plus some spotters — picked up about fifty planes heading for Rangoon. The AVG had twenty-one pilots but only
fifteen flyable P-40's at Mingaladon, and in the rush for them,
several men took off for freezing altitudes wearing nothing but
shorts, holsters, and mosquito boots, comfortable in the hun-
dred-degree heat of the alert shack.

The P-40's and an RAF formation of sixteen Brewsters
climbed and were quickly lost in the glare. With growing thunder the Japanese formations came from the east, silvery dots
suddenly visible on blue. A big V of twenty-seven bombers
flew first, at about 15,000 feet. Above and behind came twenty
fighters on two levels, Zeros and Nakajimas — an older, lighter
version of the Zero. Higher still, the noncombatant battle commander rode a speedy two-engined ship. All the planes flew
straight ahead as levelly and evenly spaced as a toy armada on
horizontal wires.

Explosions peppered the smooth thunder and we could see
the P-40's and Brewsters flickering down through the rigid formation, the sun glinting on their wings as they dove and
turned. The Japanese pursuits gave chase and for a moment
the little planes tumbled around the sky like mayflies. Puffs
of black smoke, splotches of scarlet flame, and the pink needles
of tracer bullets marred the calm blue, and at intervals a long
trail of smoke and flame spiraled to earth. Because of Chennault's instructions to attack and dive away immediately, each
engagement was over in a minute or two.

Watching from the ground, I was never able to follow and
understand what happened in combat, but when the pilots

came down, every battle was naturally refought many times in talk, until the next one started. On that first day the AVG planes had split, with one group of nine to attack first, the other six to stay in reserve. The nine climbed as high as they could, then went into single file and dove out of the sun, sideslipping past the bombers with all guns open. Five bombers including the lead plane were shot down. Some P-40's turned immediately and attacked the bombers head on, shooting down two more. The bombers fled, jettisoning their loads over the dried-out jungles east of Rangoon and starting huge fires.

The twenty Japanese pursuits now dived on the P-40's, and over many square miles and through thousands of feet of height the battle tangled and snapped out, so fast and intricate that even the pilots never could agree on some details. When a second wave of twenty-seven bombers came in, three of the reserve P-40's attacked them head on, while the other three came in at right angles. The leader of the second trio, Martin, became the AVG's first battle casualty when fire from the bombers' turret guns converged on his plane and blew it to bits. Although one bomber exploded in mid-air and two more went down in flames, the Japanese had too great an advantage of numbers. They bombed Mingaladon and the docks, while Zeros strafed ships in the harbor and crowds in the streets of Rangoon. In the running fight which followed the bombers back toward Thailand, the AVG suffered its second battle casualty over Mingaladon, when six Nakajimas dove on two P-40's diving on some straggling bombers. As one bomber started to smoke and spin down, a P-40 piloted by Gilbert was set afire and crashed.

The other P-40 was put out of control, but its pilot, Greene, parachuted. As ground crewmen at Mingaladon watched, a Nakajima came back repeatedly to machine-gun him, but each time he escaped by pulling at his parachute harness and swinging aside. Then he seemed to be hit, and hung like a sack. The Nakajima left. When he came down, the ground crewmen ran to the parachute expecting to find a corpse. He was lying on the ground laughing, and said he played dead because he got tired of pulling the ropes.

AVG pilots claimed only fifteen Japanese planes downed on the 23rd, but RAF searchers found the wrecks of thirty-two. Several planes had crashed into the sea and could not be verified. The RAF claimed only seven victories, leaving twenty-five for the AVG. Since many downed ships were bombers with crews of five, enemy casualties were probably around ninety. The AVG lost only two pilots and three planes, the RAF five pilots and eleven planes.

In keeping up this extraordinary record, the AVG and its successor — Chennault's 14th Air Force — later got a bad name for wishful battle reports, but I think the figures for the early fighting over Rangoon were quite accurate. After all, they were largely supplied by the RAF, which had no wish to blow trumpets for any "Yanks." I suspect the Japanese Air Force was simply flabbergasted, not having had any real opposition in years, and like many military outfits took some time to adjust to a new fact.

On the evening of the 23rd Radio Tokyo announced that Rangoon's air defenses had been destroyed, and gifts of poison gas and parachutists would be brought to the city on Christmas Day. Our Burmese servants at the airfield fled in panic, and we began living on old bread and warm beer. Most of the P-40's had battle damage, and until dawn ground crewmen with pressure lamps worked on them in the jungle hideaways.

At eleven on Christmas morning, the RAF warned that three waves of twenty-seven bombers each, escorted by forty-two pursuits, were flying toward Rangoon. One hundred and twenty-three planes altogether. The AVG could put only twelve hastily-repaired P-40's into the air, the RAF sixteen Brewsters.

After they had taken off, we had a rather horrifying example of how our own high command could operate. As the first V of Japanese wheeled overhead, a single Blenheim landed and the ranking British and American generals in Asia, Wavell and Brett, debarked in full regalia, blithely ignorant of the attack. Olson and some ground crewmen ran out and herded them into a slit trench as the first bombs fell. One man who looked hastily into the Blenheim reported that its bomb bay was fitted with a rug and wicker lounge furniture for the brass.

The Christmas battle went on for an hour and a half of many separate and quick engagements. The AVG planes divided into two groups of six. The pilots had learned that the light Nakajimas could not catch up with the bombers they were protecting if they were diverted into a dogfight. With a diving speed up to 400 mph, the heavy P-40's could, so they began attacking the pursuits first. They had also observed that the Japanese tended to be more careless leaving a battle, so they made a point of following them to shoot down stragglers. With practice in battle the AVG pilots began to make more use of Chennault's tactics for pairs of pursuits.

For the first time Japanese pilots speaking plausible English gave confusing orders on the AVG radio frequencies. One pair of pilots was told to "pancake" — AVG slang for "land" — and almost reached the field when Nakajimas dived on them. By putting on all power and gunning as straight up as they could, they managed to escape with only a few bullet holes.

The AVG had no casualties that day, though it lost two P-40's in forced landings. The RAF lost six pilots and nine planes, and again claimed seven downed Japanese, leaving the rest to the AVG. The wreckage of twenty-eight was found, and eight more had been seen crashing into the water. Japanese casualties were estimated at more than a hundred.

On the ground the day was no doubt a Japanese victory, because many bombers got through to Rangoon and did much destruction. At the airfield we were out of reach of the panic

and distress and had our own victory banquet. William Pawley
unexpectedly arrived in a truck with hams, roast chickens, cold
beer and liquor. We rigged up trestle tables in the open, and
feasted with Wavell and Brett. This was one of the high points
of the AVG, and it seemed a pity that Chennault was not only
absent in Kunming, but in bed with bronchitis.

It later became known that Wavell, Brett, and Chennault
had been in Chungking a few days earlier, for their first conference with Chiang Kai-shek on Burma. It had been less than a
love feast.

Wavell wanted to assimilate the AVG into the RAF but was
adamantly refused by Chiang and Chennault. He wanted as
much as he could get of the Lend-Lease supplies for China, then
piling up in Burma. It was doubtful whether all this material
could be trucked into China, but Chiang was cagily noncom-
mittal. He did offer Wavell two of his best armies if they could
be supplied by the British in Burma, but Wavell instead suggested borrowing one division to be supplied from China; and
one regiment to be kept in reserve on the Chinese side of the
border.

The British thought there was still time to get Indian and
East African reinforcements, and that it was better to have
Burma defended by "imperial" rather than foreign troops. The
Chinese, ever since their own years of empire, had made claims
on northern Burma and the border was still in dispute, so the
British feared they might have a Chinese as well as a Japanese
invasion.

Chiang felt Wavell was snubbing him, and furiously declined
to send the division or regiment. For about six weeks his two
armies stayed inactive near the border, until the defense of
southern Burma became hopeless and the British asked for
their help.

At this conference Chiang again made his demand for a

huge air force to be based in his coastal provinces. The Hump airlift was nonexistent then, and if every ton on the Burma Road went to the air force it could still support only about eight squadrons on the eastern fields — a force less than three times the size of the little AVG.

In Rangoon at about this time we had our own crisis among allies, when an American ship, the *Tulsa*, came in loaded with Lend-Lease munitions for China. With the Japanese threat so much closer, the British need for support was better recognized than in Chungking and a Chinese-American-British committee to divide supplies had been set up. Yu Fei-peng, a cousin of Chiang Kai-shek's and supervisor of traffic on the Burma Road, was the Chinese representative.

The British were frantic to get the munitions off the *Tulsa*, and out to their armies. Because of the air threat to shipping, many stevedores were deserting and quick unloading was essential. When Yu seemed to be stalling, someone launched rumors to reach him, suggesting the British Governor of Burma might confiscate the *Tulsa* cargo. Soon afterward, in an entirely unconnected incident, British troops without authority seized 150 trucks from a Chinese agency which had them in dead storage.

Yu got in touch with relatives, and on Christmas Day Ho Ying-chin, the Chinese Minister of War, told the Allied Military Council in Chungking that Chiang Kai-shek had decided twenty Lend-Lease machine guns were all he could spare for the defense of Burma. Ho read a telegram from Yu, accusing the British of stealing Lend-Lease supplies with American help. He said Chiang Kai-shek had decided this was a hostile act, and future Lend-Lease should be given to the British or returned to America. Chinese military personnel in Burma — presumably including the AVG — would return to China, and Sino-British military cooperation would end.

Yu, meanwhile, was amicably continuing his work on the al-

lied committee in Rangoon, and when General Magruder, our
ranking officer in Chungking, called on Chiang Kai-shek, he
was received with friendliness, and Chiang suggested he send
an officer to Rangoon to smooth the transfer of Lend-Lease to
the British. Much was later transferred. This could have
been an oriental comedy of "face," but Lend-Lease and its passage over the Burma Road had extremely lucrative angles. Yu
may simply have wanted to show the claws in his velvet paw,
and warn that he was not a man to interfere with.

After hours of squinting up at swirling air battles, then lis-
tening to the pilots' confusing tales, illustrated with enough
arm-swooping and spiral-staircase sign language to make anyone groggy, I couldn't retain a very clear idea of the stories of
individual men. One exception was a quiet young flyer, Hed-
man, who at Toungoo had much kidding from the self-styled
"hot pilots." He was slow and conservative, climbing, turning,
and diving his P-40 as moderately as if it were a full school bus.

At the first alert on the 23rd, he suddenly exploded into a
different man. His own ship was under repair, so he tore across
the field and stole another, while its rightful pilot threatened
him with a pistol. He nearly crashed into two Brewsters in his
haste to get to the runway. He was the first man into combat
and the last to leave, after shooting down five planes and becoming an ace in a single battle. To get his fifth he flew nearly
to Thailand, more or less inside a formation of enemy bombers, explaining later it was safer because the Japanese gunners
were afraid they would hit one another if they fired at him. He
landed at an emergency field with five gallons left in his tank
and not a bullet still in his guns.

Christmas Day he made off with the same plane, though the
ground crew tried to prevent him because it was still full of
holes and the gunsight was shot away. In that battle he was
credited with several probables, but when he came down —

again at an emergency field with empty guns — he said it was bad luck to try to count them. He never put in for confirmation or bonus money, and refused to do so after later battles when the other pilots were sure he had shot down more planes.

Another story from those days has stuck in my mind though it took place far from the shambles of Rangoon. On the 23rd three pilots were sent to ferry newly-arrived Interceptors from Mingaladon to Kunming. One of them, Shilling, who usually flew our reconnaissance plane and was beginning to know the country, drew sketches from memory which were their only maps. They followed the Irrawaddy River north to Lashio, the railhead, where they refueled, then in the late afternoon they headed east over the mountains to Kunming.

Shilling's engine failed and he managed to crash-land on a mountainside with only minor injuries. The other pilots continued eastward in growing darkness, over jagged country utterly unknown to them. One belly-landed on a dry riverbed, but the other, Mangleburg, crashed and was killed.

When Shilling painfully crawled out of his wreckage, he was seized by a band of swarthy little men in shaggy clothes, with ancient rifles and daggers. Many primitive non-Chinese tribes lived in these border mountains. The tribesmen roughly stuffed Shilling back into his plane, built a bamboo fence around it, and stood guard all night. They must have had, or heard of, air raids and decided to take no chances with any unidentified man from the sky.

In the morning they allowed him to sit in the sun by the fence, brought him a bowl of gritty rice, then covered the plane with a camouflage of branches. After hours of uneasiness, Shilling remembered he had a crank-up phonograph and a few jazz records, so he got them out to distract himself. As soon as the music tootled out, his guards shouted in delight and called everyone from their village. Men, women, and children squatted around the fence all day, setting up a menacing outcry if he let the music stop. When he asked for more food and some bedding by sign language, roast pork and greasy quilts were brought.

Next morning it all started up again, and he feared he had a bleak future as a captive jukebox, then Chinese soldiers arrived, called by a spotter of the warning net who had seen him go down. They told the tribes-people he was an American and explained what that was, so his captors released him with grins and much back-patting. They built a rough sedan chair and carried him jubilantly down to the town in the valley. After that, all AVG pilots wore identifications in Chinese sewn on the backs of their flight jackets.

On New Year's Day, Newkirk's Second Squadron came to Rangoon to relieve Olson and the Third. The pilots of the Second had been idle except for patrol duty and still seemed embarrassed by their fiasco in the first battle of Kunming. They were anxious to prove themselves, and when no Japanese came over on January 1 or 2, Newkirk and two pilots, Hill and Howard, who had been raised in China and Korea and were anti-Japanese from personal experience, made a foray into Thailand on the 3rd.

At a field called Tak they discovered a line of bombers being serviced, and dove to strafe them from a height of about thirty feet. They were up and away so fast they couldn't guess how many they hit, though they saw flame and clouds of black smoke billowing up from the jungle. On the way back they found a brand-new field at Meshod, also with planes being serviced. They made repeated strafing runs, so intently they did not notice a patrol of six Zeros diving on them, straight down out of the sun.

Newkirk and Hill were attacked head on, and peeled off into a brief combat in which each shot down one Japanese.

Howard, going the other way, went on obliviously strafing the field although the plane Hill destroyed was diving on him and apparently filling him with bullets. It wasn't until they landed at Mingaladon and he discovered the holes in his plane that he realized he had been under fire for the first time.

Next morning the sky was full of big puffy tropical clouds, and the RAF alarm system could report only that the noise of many planes was coming toward Rangoon. A first group of six P-40's climbed to 21,000 feet and circled about, looking for the enemy among the clouds. Observers on the airfield soon spotted a formation of twenty-seven Japanese pursuits coming in at about 18,000 feet and tried to warn the P-40's, but through a mechanical failure all their radios were dead. They continued their search in wide downward circles and reached 11,000 feet before the Japanese dived on them. Another group of eight P-40's had climbed above the clouds, but their radios were dead, too, and they never joined combat. The ensuing melee was the closest thing to a victory the Japanese had over Rangoon. They lost three planes and pilots, while three AVG planes were destroyed or damaged in crash landings, and their pilots had to be hospitalized.

Gil Bright was one of the few pilots with whom I kept in touch after the AVG dissolved, and years afterward he told me that while this battle had dimmed for him, he vividly remembered his landing. The plane was in flames when he slid it to a stop in a dry rice paddy, and he was burned when he ripped off his mask and goggles to make sure of the fastest way out. Without thinking, he ran straight ahead and was nearly killed when the fire touched off his wing guns, sending fusillades of bullets on either side of him. He was blown flat when the plane exploded.

He tottered to the only building he could see, and found it was a tiny railway station. The Burmese stationmaster showed him the phone, and although he still felt shaken and rattle-headed, he telephoned RAF Headquarters in Rangoon to ask how to get back.

"Take the train!" a pip-pip British voice told him impatiently.

"But I don't have a ticket," he complained feebly, and instantly realized what a fool he must sound.

"Bugger the ticket, old boy!" the voice replied with a ducal swagger. "Just get on the train."

The attacks of January 5 and 6 were a little lighter than the Christmas raids, but in some ways worse, because the Japanese had recovered from their first surprise and were replacing their rigid approach with varied tactics. They would come in from two or three directions, on many levels. Small groups of low-flying bombers decoyed the P-40's up to be attacked by scores of following pursuits, or the bombers would lure the P-40's up high while pursuits swept in near roof level to bomb or strafe the airfield and the city. The AVG lost no planes or pilots in the two days, but Japanese casualties were probably smaller, too. Only thirty wrecks were found for both attacks.

The moon was full then, and we began having nuisance raids at night, two or three planes attacking the field at irregular intervals, aiming to keep us awake and exhausted for next day. After a couple of nights we loaded into trucks after supper and drove into the jungle to sleep on the ground, away from the explosions though not the mosquitoes. On the bright night of the eighth, three pilots took off, believing they could intercept the enemy by following radio directions. They failed. Coming into the field badly lit by auto headlights, one crashed into a truck where a pilot, Merritt, had fallen asleep, and killed him.

Earlier that same day we lost another pilot, Mott, who was strafing Meshod with three others when his engine was hit and he had to crash-land. We thought he was dead, but a week later heard his voice on the Bangkok radio, saying he was comfortable in a Thai jail.

Though the night raids continued, we had no day attacks for more than two weeks. Eight planes of the Second Squadron, led by Bob Neale, arrived from Kunming, and the combined force made many sorties over the airfields of Thailand. At one, the Japanese seemed ready to give some kind of air show for Thai puppets; half a dozen planes were parked by the runway, near a little grandstand packed with people. As the P-40's dived and strafed the planes, the crowd had a show it didn't expect and scattered in screaming panic.

As far as I can remember, even when I first signed up with Chennault, I never expected to be a chaplain in the Hollywood style, a Crosby or Hope type in a backward collar, chucklesome yet reverent, always lifting the mens' spirits with brave jokes. I really didn't know what my life would be. By doing what was most needed and within my ability, I had discovered I was mainly a Service of Supply man. During this quieter period at Rangoon, I scrounged a jeep and spent most of my time in the city, looking for canned food, Fruito, and things like insect-repellent and sunburn lotion.

These trips brought a shock, for at Mingaladon we seemed to be holding our own even when there weren't victories. Inside Rangoon, it was appallingly clear that this capital and single metropolis of Burma was crumbling in defeat before a single Japanese foot soldier had crossed the border.

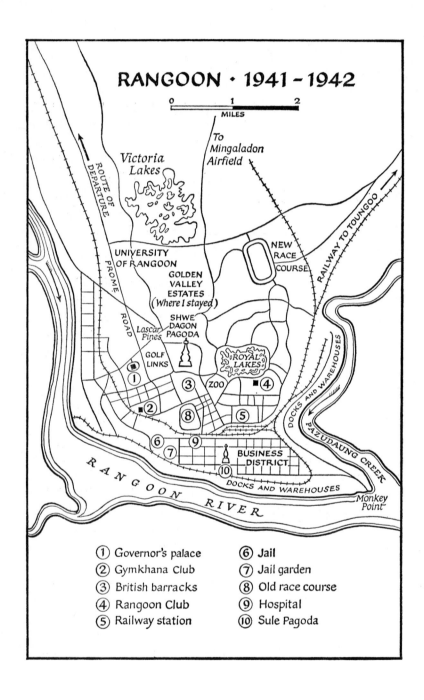

RANGOON · 1941–1942

0   1   2
MILES

ROUTE OF DEPARTURE

Victoria Lakes

To Mingaladon Airfield

RAILWAY TO TOUNGOO

NEW RACE COURSE

UNIVERSITY OF RANGOON

GOLDEN VALLEY ESTATES (Where I stayed)

PROME ROAD

Lascar Pines

SHWE DAGON PAGODA

GOLF LINKS

ROYAL LAKES

① ③ ZOO ④

② ⑧ ⑤

⑥ ⑨

⑦ ⑩ BUSINESS DISTRICT

DOCKS AND WAREHOUSES

DOCKS AND WAREHOUSES

PAZUDAUNG CREEK

Monkey Point

RANGOON RIVER

① Governor's palace
② Gymkhana Club
③ British barracks
④ Rangoon Club
⑤ Railway station
⑥ Jail
⑦ Jail garden
⑧ Old race course
⑨ Hospital
⑩ Sule Pagoda

CHAPTER VI

Up the Burma Road 1942

RANGOON had been a city for centuries, a port for Chinese and Indian merchant-sailors, and a shrine for Burmese Buddhists. Its great turnip-shaped Shwe Dagon Pagoda holding relics of Buddha's body stood three hundred feet high and was plated with gold brought by generations of worshipers. The British first seized the city in 1824, in revenge for a Burmese general's attack on British India, and they occupied it permanently — as it then seemed — in 1852, when all southern Burma was taken as prize in a small war provoked by racial friction. A grid of wide streets was victoriously surveyed and a modern port city spread beside the ramshackle old Asian town. For eight decades, trade with the rich hinterland boomed, and Rangoon grew into one of those enclaves of Victorian prosperity, solidity, and comfort which the British Empire scattered across Asia from Suez to Manchuria. Parts of it reminded me of the British Concession in Hankow, with the same big square brick and masonry buildings, arcaded with heavy columns.

When I arrived in the summer before the war, British Rangoon still held the settled, colonial life for which it had been built. The quick-growing tropical trees along the avenues were as large as the elms or oaks around a New England common, and in their shade little British children in starched playclothes promenaded with their Burmese nannies. The taipans — the big businessmen — were driven to their offices in dark limousines like submarines, piloted by liveried Burmese chauffeurs with matching footmen to open the doors. Stylish young British matrons whizzed by in bright roadsters, on their way to lunch or tea at the club.

After one of the Christmas raids, a squadron of Japanese fighters strafed Rangoon. Most of the outnumbered RAF and AVG planes had already landed, out of gas, and could do nothing. The people of Rangoon had been warned to take cover during raids, but heard the noise of aerial combat and gradually edged into the streets to see what was happening. When the Japanese fighters flew low along the main avenues with their machine guns blazing, they slaughtered hundreds, perhaps thousands. The total was never announced.

These scenes of carnage and screaming panic in the staid familiar setting shook the city to its roots. Everyone expected Rangoon to be invaded from the sea, as Hong Kong had been, and the news of Hong Kong's surrender on Christmas Day increased the dread. Within a few hours of the strafings, Rangoon's evacuation and collapse were under way.

The British announced a schedule of departures, with all military and civil ranks of Britons and their dependents bureaucratically graded. The Indian and Chinese merchants began moving their families and goods out of town, off to India by boat or plane if they were rich and lucky, up the roads and railways into the interior if they weren't. British shipping lobbies had never allowed overland links between the Burmese railways and those of India, Malaya or Thailand, so the chances of exit in those directions were poor.

For a few days the streets were lined with merchant trucks loading, then they drove off and Rangoon was noticeably more deserted. Later I was sorry I was too busy to keep a journal of the steps in the city's death, but as I remember it was the buses and taxis that disappeared next, driven off full of refugees. Then the newspapers died, the restaurants closed, the street-sweepers and garbage-collectors disappeared, and the street lights and electric signs went dark. Then the electricity itself was turned off, so was the water. The telephones went dead and the police deserted. In Hankow we had always known many of us were neutral; so was part of the city, but in Rangoon nothing was safe. Each day the emptying streets slipped back a little farther toward jungle.

Before Pearl Harbor the AVG had been ignored by the Rangoon British. We were obviously a bunch of yahoos, superfluous at that, since any loyal subject knew the RAF had full command of the air. After our Christmas victories, however, we had many British invitations, and most were accepted. One of our doctors, several pilots, and I went to stay with a Mr. Johnson who was in charge of oil refineries up country. His family had been evacuated and there was plenty of room in his magnificent house. With its gardens and stable of riding and racing horses, its well-stocked wine cellar and library, its vast living room with splendid oriental rugs and a concert grand piano, it seemed the epitome of this comfortable Western city built in a Far Eastern swamp.

We never did know how many Burmese servants staffed the house, but when we came in from the airfield at dusk, one in immaculate native dress was always waiting in the hall, offering a silver tray with stiff Scotch-and-sodas to enjoy while we bathed and changed. When we came downstairs to have our second and third — and sometimes fourth, fifth, and sixth — drinks with our host, he liked to interrupt the conversation to play Bach ferociously on his great piano. We always listened to the evening radio news, and every night it was worse; this was the period of rapid Japanese advances in the neighboring British colony of Malaya.

Mr. Johnson had spent many years building up the oil refineries, and was now planning their destruction. He drank much faster than we, and by dinnertime, which seldom came before ten, he was worn out. He would sit at the head of the richly laid table and, plunk, down his silvery head would go into his soup.

"Eat your soup, sahib," the Burmese butler would say, gently sitting him up again, but that would be the end of Mr. Johnson for another evening. We had to leave for the airfield at 4 A.M., hoping for naps during the day, but Mr. Johnson would always have left before us, tirelessly destroying his life's work.

Through him, we began to know others in the rapidly diminishing British community. They had first priority for evacuation, but many seemed to be disintegrating in a hectic "tomorrow-we-die" attitude. There was much drinking, and the pilots told me many frosty-seeming married women were pushovers. There was fierce backbiting about who preceded whom in the evacuation, and — as in Hankow — some high officials were said to be sending out property like porch furniture in space which could have been used for lesser evacuees. In the end I believe most British civilians got out of Burma safely but, through misadventure or foolishness, some did meet horrible deaths in the jungle.

Many of the AVG men had found Anglo-Indian girls, and they and their families were more pitiable than the British. In the colonial world they were half-people, treated contemptuously by whites and pure Asians alike. Some of the girls were daughters of British fathers and Indian or Burmese mothers, others came from families which had had mixed blood for generations. A few were bar-girls, others were well-educated clerks or typists, desperate to leave ahead of the Japanese. All were attractive, a few were beautiful, some had fair complexions and light curly hair. They were too westernized to be inconspicuous in a Japanese-occupied city. There must have been as many Anglo-Indians in Rangoon as there were pure British, but as far as I ever heard the only thing British officialdom did to help them evacuate was to assign one train to them, on one day only. Some who left in it may later have reached India by air, but I am sure many died struggling through the jungle.

It still makes me uncomfortable to remember the phone calls I used to get nearly every evening from a distraught girl of mixed blood, very much in love with one of our pilots who had been killed. "But what can I do? Where can I go?" she would implore, and it was agonizing not to be able to imagine any word of useful advice. She was a tiny voice weeping in the night, and after about a week her calls stopped. I never heard what became of her.

In contrast, I recall one of the few pure Burmese I met, a calm stunning girl called Ma Tah-ne. She taught Basic English at the University of Rangoon, and was a friend of several American war correspondents, all of whom were trying to persuade her to flee. She would just smile mysteriously and say she could take care of herself. This led some of us foolishly to conclude she must be a Japanese agent, though a Burmese girl in Burma could easily hide herself in complete anonymity.

Fifteen years later in New York I went to a lunch in the delegates' lounge in the United Nations, and across the room saw a familiar-looking girl in Burmese dress. Surely it was she. I kept staring and she stared back. After lunch I went over and said, "This may be very rude, but I am sure I know you."

"I know you, too," she said. "I am Ma Tah-ne."

She told me that when we met in Burma, she already belonged to an underground group and worked with it through the Japanese occupation. In New York she was the operating head of the Burmese delegation to the UN.

*

In early January, daytime air raids on Rangoon slackened off, but the Japanese bombers began making successful visits at night, guided by fires lit by spies or fifth columnists. The AVG had no night fighters and the RAF too few to be effective. These were incendiary raids, but most Rangoon fire engines had already been evacuated to the north. From about the middle of the month on, some part of the city was constantly burning.

The land invasion of Burma started January 20, with about eighteen thousand Japanese troops moving across the Thailand frontier. They were experienced jungle fighters, cleverly camouflaged, and seemed to have full knowledge of back roads and paths. Many had collapsible bicycles or inflatable rafts in their packs — along with enough rice rations for days — and their guerrilla advance confused and outflanked the British Empire forces of British, Burmese, and Indian troops. The defenders were heavily dependent on motor transport and paved roads, and they were badly prepared for a land invasion because they had expected one by sea.

Even in those early days of fighting, Burmese nationalists began helping the Japanese as spies and saboteurs. Following the British line, we Americans called them fifth columnists and traitors, although in Rangoon most of us had noticed passive Burmese attitudes toward the British Empire's war and could see reasons for it. I understand many former "fifth columnists" are now respected members of the Burmese government.

Daytime air raids on Rangoon began again, with six big attacks between January 23 and 28. Some brought as many as a hundred planes each, but now three fighters escorted every bomber, in tribute to the AVG and RAF damage of December. The enemy came over in waves timed to catch our planes on the ground, refueling and rearming, but the speed of the ground crews threw their schedule off. The official score for the five days of battle was 50 enemy planes downed, at a cost of

2 AVG planes downed and 10 RAF pilots lost with their planes.

A few days later, at dawn on February 4, the Japanese retaliated with a surprise attack on the airfield at Toungoo. In one of its few failures, the air-warning net did not pick them up, and all the men at Toungoo were asleep when the first bombs fell. The operations building and a hangar were destroyed, but luckily the field was almost empty and only three of our P-40's, grounded for repairs, and half a dozen RAF bombers, were lost.

Singapore fell on February 15, releasing fifteen thousand more ground troops and scores of planes for the attack on Burma. By February 22 the front came within seventy-five miles of Rangoon. Here the Japanese ambushed and routed Indian troops defending the bridge across the Sittang River, the city's last natural defense. They could now shell the main road and rail links north from Rangoon to Mandalay. At last the Chinese troops who had been waiting and ready on the north Burma border since December were given British permission to cross and come to the aid of Empire.

In the final days before its fall, the only organized activity in Rangoon were the efforts of a few hundred British, Chinese, and Americans to remove or destroy the still-mountainous heaps of Lend-Lease and other military supplies on the docks. About a thousand tons a day were sent north but this was not enough. Huge fires were lit to consume the rest. AMISCA, the U.S. Army Mission in Chungking, for example, with only a few men in Rangoon, had nearly a thousand half-assembled trucks to wreck, plus five thousand tires and some thousands of tons of ammunition, blankets, and other gear. The harbor had been mined and closed but was still full of loaded freighters to be scuttled.

The Chinese had a tremendous glut of Lend-Lease supplies, assigned directly to them by Washington. Now, when it was clear this couldn't be moved out, they released a thousand submachine guns and several hundred trucks and jeeps to the British Empire forces deployed between us and the Japanese. Even the AVG was invited to come to the docks and take anything we needed or wanted.

Until I left, I spent every day there with whatever ground crewmen could be spared from the airfield, smashing open crates and barrels, loading our trucks with spare parts for planes and vehicles, tires, tools, radio equipment, guns and ammunition. We tried to round up a three-month supply of canned goods and liquor for the whole AVG. When time ran short we just snatched whatever crates were handy and portable, with no idea of contents.

The trips to and from the docks were weird. We traveled in convoys because Japanese agents or Burmese nationalists were reported sniping at stray Westerners. Nearly everyone had fled or was hiding, and we roared through empty sun-baked streets under a burning blue sky. Over the roofs we could see the pale gold spire of the Shwe Dagon and the great black and red pillar of smoke and flame from the docks. Smaller plumes of smoke rose from every part of town; twenty-five blocks were said to be burning. The air-raid clean-up squads had evidently fled, for masonry lay tumbled out onto the pavements and the sweetish smell of decay hung over many fields of ruins. For blocks we would see nothing alive except the scavenger dogs, crows, and buzzards.

In the richer business streets many locked shops had been looted, and the pavement was littered with broken glass and spilled cameras, clocks, typewriters, broken liquor bottles, silks, even jewels. Sometimes we approached as a shop was being rifled, and could see dark-clad figures scuttle into doors or alleys with their arms full. Down the vistas of the side streets we saw mysterious tight-packed groups of running figures, some chased by soldiers or police who were shooting at them.

The last civil authorities to flee had opened the prisons, insane asylums, and leprosariums, driving their inmates into the city, and it was rumored the Burmese keepers at the zoo had maliciously liberated their great snakes and jungle cats. I'm glad to say I don't know about the zoo creatures, but one day we came upon a leper at a downtown gas station. It was an American station, exactly like all those selling this brand in the United States. The leper with his filthy rags, his great lion head and thickened features, looked as if he had escaped from a medieval dungeon. He was laughing insanely as he pumped the gas into the street, shaking the hose above his head to make the fluid scatter and sparkle in the sunlight.

On one of our last trips back from the docks we took a new route to avoid spreading fires and passed the Buick agency, where we saw three beautiful new Buicks gleaming in the show window. Inside the open door, the debris-littered office was utterly deserted. We knew the Japanese were within thirty miles, and the fires were just down the street. The keys were in the cars, so we filled them with gas and two ground crewmen and I drove them away. Steve — I think that was his name — got so excited at again driving a powerful smooth-riding car down empty roads that he wrapped his around a tree in a few minutes. He limped away from the wreckage but did not seem seriously hurt.

As I recall, it was next day, February 26, that the Japanese began their last big air attacks on Rangoon. More than a hundred planes came over, still more on the following day. On the 26th only nine AVG planes and six RAF were fit to take to the air, next day six AVG. None was lost. It was no longer possible to hunt for wrecks and make an accurate count, but it was hoped that at least forty Japanese planes had been shot down. We nevertheless knew we had reached the end. Our planes were simply worn out, and we had no replacements for engine parts.

On the night of the 27th, some of the remaining RAF officers invited the few AVG last-ditchers to the dedication of their new officers' club. We knew they had been fixing it up for weeks, but it seemed crazy to dedicate it with the Japanese arriving in a day or two. I said as much to the officer who invited me.

"You Americans," he replied with lofty amusement, "always getting the wind up."

We went to the party and had a rip-roaring time, with the British proposing erudite toasts and singing quaint dirty songs. We turned in at about two, but at four were wakened by planes taking off and trucks grinding away. We found the British had pulled out entirely, taking their air-warning equipment which was all-important to us. It was only a primitive radar set-up, and gave less than five minutes' warning, but without it our own staying would be suicide.

We had already experimented with the evacuation of extra people in P-40's and found it wouldn't work. If the radio were pulled out, a small man could squeeze into the cramped airless space it left, but those who tried it couldn't stand it even to the end of the runway. It wasn't feasible to fly slow transports into a field with no warning system, so all of us except the lucky half-dozen pilots who still had P-40's would have to get out on the ground. We began hastily loading the trucks.

In the middle of the morning Bob Neale who commanded the squadron at Rangoon — the Third — called me over and said, "You're it. You are taking the first convoy up the road."

"You're out of your mind," I said. "I'm the chaplain. I'm not taking any convoy anywhere."

"The Old Man says so," he replied, showing me a radio message from Chennault: "Convoys start this morning. Frillmann takes the first."

"Where is this convoy?" I asked wildly. "What's on it? Is

there an inventory or a bill of lading?" As soon as I said that I realized how silly it was.

"Forget it," he said. "Just get out. The Japs are closer than twenty miles and may cut the road anytime."

The convoy was waiting at the end of the field: twelve jeeps and eighteen trucks, loaded to the hilt with goodness knew what. Beside most drivers sat pretty Anglo-Indian girls dressed as for a picnic, with frilly blouses and harlequin sunglasses. I had a twinge of morality, then thought what might happen to them if they didn't come with us. I got my Buick, which I luckily had already loaded to the roof, and led the parade through the deserted smoke-hazed streets.

About a week earlier, Mr. Johnson's efforts had . been crowned by giant explosions in his oil refineries. I talked with him at the airfield before he was evacuated by the RAF, and he told me he never expected to see Rangoon again. We were to keep on living in his house, he said, and take anything we wanted, then set the rest afire when we left.

We moved out of his house almost immediately because the servants disappeared when he left, and water and electricity were shut off. Bands of looters and nationalist assassins were said to be active in the nearly-empty British residential section after dark.

On that last morning my convoy passed Mr. Johnson's house and I couldn't resist stopping. A house at the other end of the block was in full flame, crackling loudly in the empty sunlight, so there was no need for conscience-racking on whether or not to set Mr. Johnson's afire. I had greedy ideas of taking the wonderful piano and some of the books, but all our vehicles were overloaded and we had to keep going. I ran to the stable and drove the horses into the street, where they might escape burning, but reserved a beautiful big black stallion which I tied to

the last truck with a long rope. Then I drove behind to keep
an eye on it.

Since most refugees had left long before, the first miles of
road were empty except for a few British-Chinese military
convoys also heading north, and we were able to make good
time. So good, it immediately became clear the horse couldn't
last. It was terrified, beginning to skitter and stumble, so I had
them stop the truck, then sent the convoy on ahead while I took
the animal into a ricefield where I calmed it, then shot it. In
the confusion of the day I had no idea whether I was doing
right or wrong, but this saved the marvelous thoroughbred
from becoming a Japanese trophy or a country pack-animal.

Ten or fifteen miles farther on I caught up with our last
truck, stalled with an Anglo-Indian girl frantically signaling
me to stop. The driver, slumped unconscious over his wheel,
was Steve who had cracked up the Buick. Nothing I could
do would rouse him. Feeling stupid and desperate, I walked off
into the Burmese countryside to look for a doctor.

All along the road, the fields and villages had seemed eerily
empty as Rangoon, but I couldn't help feeling every house and
grove must be packed with people hiding. I could see a sizable
village behind some trees and went to it hoping to find at least
a semi-modern doctor, perhaps a Rangoon refugee. I did find
a few refugee families squatting uneasily under the village
trees, their city luggage piled incongruously in the dust, but
nobody was a doctor. It was early afternoon and the villagers
were having their naps, comfortably snoring on mats on the
raised bamboo floors of their open-faced huts. I later learned
Japanese patrols may have been as little as five miles away from
this village and probably arrived by evening.

After what seemed hours I found a young country Burmese
with scanty English, and he aroused the village doctor, a pic-
turesquely unmodern old gentleman in white turban and blue
skirt who readily came with me. Steve was still unconscious, so

we eased him out on the roadside. One of his legs looked an inch longer than the other. He must have dislocated his hip in the crash of the Buick and had been going through agonies to keep the injury hidden.

The old doctor gently pulled and poked at the leg, then he sat back on his heels, lit a white Burmese cheroot, and thought. Suddenly he seized the leg with surprising strength and after a few deft movements popped the joint back in. Steve soon recovered consciousness and after limping up and down a few times said he felt well enough to drive. He drove for the next seventeen days, all the way to Kunming.

My memory of that trip has blurred, each day being equally strenuous, uncomfortable, and exciting. We were bothered by Japanese planes only on the first day, and they seemed to be on reconnaissance. We parked the trucks and ran into the fields when we saw them, but they did not attack. They were not even trying to destroy the bridges, no doubt because their command looked forward to using them in a few days.

We spent the first night somewhere south of Mandalay, camping by the road as we did through the trip, partly because inns were too primitive when they weren't too crowded, partly because the vehicles had to be guarded. British drivers warned us that Japanese agents or Burmese nationalists were beginning to sabotage military trucks, slashing the tires or stealing engine parts.

We rummaged in our cargo for supper and had the first of many surprises, in the crates snatched at random. We had a five-year supply of shoelaces, perhaps a year's store of facial tissues, plenty of kitchen cleanser. We had more liquor than could be accidental, especially case after case of Harvey's Bristol Cream sherry.

I remember that evening as a peaceful interlude between two kinds of frenzy. We had a meal of canned asparagus washed down with plenty of sherry. We were far enough away from Rangoon's deathly emptiness so we could see peasants peacefully working in the fields, and far enough south so we were not yet tangled in the refugee hordes which had gone ahead. Long red and purple clouds streaked the golden sunset, and the landscape was pure *National Geographic*: thatched villages and crumbling Buddhist shrines, clusters of bamboos and palms, busy farmers in the rice fields, elephants bathing in the river. I was sorry that after months in this country I was leaving it still so ignorant that it meant little more to me than an exotic picture in a magazine. I could not hope to understand the stresses and hates the war was beginning to uncover beneath the picturesque surface.

Next day we caught up with the backwash of the motley refugee traffic and our pace often fell to a crawl as we moved through the stragglers, mainly poor Indian and Chinese shopkeepers from the lesser towns above Rangoon. They seemed to have resurrected their escape cars from the junkyards. Some were dilapidated old wrecks twenty or more years old. Many had reached their last mile, and their abandoned hulks lay in the ditches while their former passengers were strung out along the road ahead — men, women, and children plodding through the dust with what little they could carry on their backs.

In spots the motor traffic was congealed by high-wheeled bullock carts moving at less than a walking pace, full of rural families in soiled white drapery, so humble and obscure-looking, so completely removed from the modern world, it was hard to imagine why they fled. I later learned they were the tiniest "running dogs of imperialism," country versions of the great Indian landlords of Rangoon. Their forebears had followed the British from India a century earlier, and settled in small villages where their slightly greater commercial sophistication helped them become little landlords and money-lenders, poor but hated as rich by their poorer Burmese neighbors whom they did in fact victimize. When order broke down ahead of the invasion, the Burmese in some villages began lynching whole Indian families, and now many of these wretches from all over Burma were fleeing, without any real idea of where or how.

Closer to Mandalay the road was a mad jam of cars including new ones of the well-to-do, all in a cloud of heat, dust, and flies. On the flats outside the city a swarm of vehicles was parked, among them taxis, buses, delivery wagons, ice trucks, fire engines, and hearses from Rangoon. Tents and cooking fires dotted the parking lots. Many refugees hoped the Japanese would stop at Rangoon and were delaying here to see what happened next.

From the brief glimpse I had of it before we went on and camped by the road, Mandalay was an exotic Asian river city such as I had expected when I arrived in Hankow years earlier. On the broad Irrawaddy, flat-bottomed paddle wheel steamers, strange native craft, and huge rafts of teak logs were moored. The ornate royal compound built by the next-to-the-last King of Burma, Mindon Min, survived at one end of town, an ants' nest of palaces and temples surrounded by crenelated red walls and lotus-filled moats. More than half of the milling crowds in the streets and bazaars might be refugees, but here they were having a breathing spell and they bargained, bickered, joked, and amused themselves much as usual, dressed in all the rainbow hues a mixed crowd of Burmese, Indians, and Chinese can flaunt. The city had never been bombed. All shops were open. There was electricity, water, everything.

One month later, at noon April 4, Japanese bombers were to make their first and only visit to Mandalay, without warning because the air-alarm system had been mysteriously sabotaged the day before. Their explosives killed an unknown number, and their incendiaries lit fires which burned half the city before next morning. The fire was to continue for twenty-seven days and nights, constantly relit by looters and fifth columnists.

Even with the extra engines from Rangoon, the fire department was hopelessly inadequate, then the water supply was sabotaged. By the end of April, picturesque Mandalay had vanished into ashes.

Beyond the city the refugee tide divided, with the Chinese heading northeast up the one paved road through the mountains to Kunming, and the Indians going northwest or north into their giant mountain-and-jungle death trap. Across the Irrawaddy the slightly emptier road to China sloped upward through wooded valleys to our next stop, Maymyo, high and cool enough to have become a favorite hill resort for the British.

The lower town of Maymyo was packed with Chinese refugees but after we camped by the road I drove higher and found luxurious British villas and gardens as peaceful as prewar Rangoon. Many British refugees had come here to wait for evacuation to India by air, and I saw pale-skinned children, matrons, elderly gentlemen, all in freshly laundered clothes. I even saw two proper blondes in long-skirted evening dresses, one blue, one pink, walking sedately with two young British officers. Off to a dance, I supposed. They looked strange as Martians to me.

Maymyo was the rear-echelon headquarters of the British Empire forces in Burma and the whole hill crawled with high brass and staff cars. Though it was a struggle, I had managed to keep myself shaved and roughly presentable on the road, and I felt I could venture a drink in a hotel bar. It was full of British officers, none of whom wanted to talk to a questionable Yank, but I did overhear a covey of colonels telling one another that the Japanese could never come north of Rangoon because they were already over-extended.

Lashio, the end of the Burma railway line and the real beginning of the Burma Road into China, was about a hundred air miles beyond Maymyo, but much farther by winding road. As I recall, it took us two or three days. The highway narrowed as it climbed through higher hills, and now we had traffic in the opposite direction: hundreds of trucks full of Chinese troops. One evening we camped near a Chinese convoy and I learned they were heading south to make their first stand at Toungoo, our old training base. They said an American general named Shih Ti-wei was coming from Washington to command them.

The other AVG convoys never caught up with us in Burma. They left Rangoon a day later than we, and because the road we used was then cut by the Japanese they had to take a roundabout way farther west. Between Maymyo and Lashio, however, we began to learn that we had other American company. In the crowds at garages and restaurants we noticed some of the ex-AVG men who had gone into smuggling or the black market. We never caught their station wagons and light trucks following directly behind us, but when the road zigzagged down one side of a valley and up the other, we could see them discreetly tagging along a mile or two back, no doubt planning to catch up at the Chinese border and cross as part of our convoy.

Lashio, much smaller than Mandalay, was more swamped by refugees. Those who had fled this far by train had to wait while they struggled for places on the trucks and buses into China. Mobs had set up housekeeping in the streets, amid squalor and many flies. The warehouses around the railhead were bursting with supplies for China, military and civilian, all waiting to be hauled away. The roads outside town were lined with Lend-Lease trucks for China, waiting for gas or drivers, or just the orders to go. Much of this materiel was not moved before the Japanese took Lashio a few weeks later. An estimated 44,000 tons of arsenal supplies alone were lost. The Japanese, too, failed to empty the Lashio bonanza, and some supplies were still there three years later when Sino-American forces recaptured it in 1944.

When we reached Lashio, Chinese soldiers in great number were camping on its outskirts, and in town I was astonished to run into two U.S. Army Signal Corps sergeants. They told me Shih Ti-wei was General Joseph W. Stilwell, and he had just arrived in Lashio. I had known Stilwell slightly, as a serious and somewhat austere military attaché who sometimes ate at Bishop Root's table in Hankow. If his headquarters was here, I naïvely thought, this was our chance to get baths, clean beds, and some American food. I asked for directions and we set off with great expectation.

Since the war, new background to Stilwell's appointment in China has been revealed in U.S. Army histories. Because of President Roosevelt's great admiration for China and Chiang Kai-shek — and, no doubt, because of the Chiangs' hints that they would make a separate peace if they didn't get massive American aid — Pearl Harbor was followed by American plans to give China much face. Britain was persuaded to join us in suggesting an Allied China Theater under Chiang as Supreme Commander, responsible only to himself, a unique position. He was to have an American Chief of Staff, however.

When Chiang agreed to this, the first officer selected was General Hugh Drum, the senior line officer in the U.S. Army, who could bring plenty of face to the job. This was an unpleasant surprise for Drum, who had been expecting an important mission to Europe, and he managed to decline. Stilwell had been slated to command the North African landings and occupation, but Secretary of War Stimson now suggested him for China, since he spoke the language and had many years' experience in the country. The suggestion was rejected at first because others in Washington feared that high Chinese would remember Stilwell as a lowly military attaché, lacking enough face to deal with them.

In accepting the idea of an American Chief of Staff, the Chinese had said they did not necessarily want an officer with previous knowledge of China. Chiang Kai-shek, it was explained, feared that anyone who knew the old warlord armies might fail to understand the difference in the new Nationalist armies. The obvious implication that the Chinese wanted a figurehead or puppet who would believe what he was told eventually helped carry the day for Stilwell. He left Washington in mid-February, arriving in Karachi on the 24th. After conferences in New Delhi he flew on to Lashio about March 1 for his crucial first conference with Generalissimo and Madame Chiang.

We found his headquarters in a British Army compound, a group of comfortable bungalows in park-like grounds. The British soldiers guarding the gate grinned and waved us past, so we went blundering on with a great grinding of gears and honking of horns. As luck would have it we stopped right in front of Stilwell's own bungalow, just as he was coming out to see who was making the noise.

His days in the dust and mud of Burma were still ahead, and he looked as if he had stepped out of a military tailor's shop in Washington, with dress uniform crisply pressed and decorations all in place. We could not have looked worse or less military. Most of the men had several days' growth of beard and we were all filthy, dressed in patchings of civilian and army clothes. The Anglo-Indian girls, quite a bit the worse for wear, could hardly be passed off as WAC's or WAVE's. They were vigorously shaking the dust out of their hair and beating it off their finery before settling down with their lipsticks and compacts.

I got out of my Buick, shoving the cats back into it behind me. Perhaps I have forgotten to mention that I was taking two Siamese cats to Kunming for one of the RAF officers who always cooperated with us at Rangoon. The female cat was in heat, as they immediately began proving.

In the next few minutes I learned how Stilwell earned his

nickname, "Vinegar Joe." I was glad he didn't recognize a former young Hankow missionary as chief of what he saw as a gang of bums, but he didn't need the extra ammunition. Before I finished trying to tell him who and how many we were, and what billets we hoped to find, he was launched. I'm afraid he most resented our being a disgrace to the U.S. Army, which we weren't in. None of us realized he might be dressed up because he was expecting the straitlaced Generalissimo and Madame for tea. Without us he still had plenty of problems with them.

The drivers gathered behind me, muttering about desk pilots who didn't understand a real war. I kept mumbling excuses, then a station wagon came swerving up the drive and skidded to a halt beside us. It was driven by an ex-AVG black-marketeer called Dutch, and in his load were his fat and rather old Anglo-Indian girl, her dark and spidery mother, a varicolored batch of her children, and a full cargo of contraband gin. Dutch and the women must have been drinking all day, for he could hardly keep his eyes open and they were waving empty bottles at us weeping all the while. This skirmish was lost by the AVG.

"See what I mean?" said Stilwell sarcastically, going back into his bungalow and slamming the screen door with a crack like a pistol shot. We drove on up the road to China and camped for the night on a barren mountain ridge.

CHAPTER VII

Fortress Kunming 1942

THE SOUTHWESTERN MOUNTAINS crossed by the Burma Road held China's most colorful minorities, related to the Thais, Burmese, Tibetans, and other neighboring peoples. Cut off from one another and the outside world by high ranges reaching down from the Himalayas, their groups varied from primitive tribes to sophisticated little sultanates similar to the Shan States of Burma. Their customs and costumes were as distinctive as any in the world. The Padaung giraffe women, for example, once featured by the Ringling Brothers Circus because their necks were lengthened by stacks of brass rings, came from here.

On our first afternoon over the border we reached what must — for China — have been the most exotic of the tribal kingdoms, the vest-pocket empire of the Pawley brothers at Loiwing. An aircraft assembly and repair shop lay beside a sizable airstrip, and beyond it were bungalows for the married American staff, a clubhouse with dormitories for the bachelors. All machinery, furnishings, plumbing, had been imported from America when Rangoon was still open, and it was eerie to drive from the primitive countryside into this patch of modern efficiency and comfort.

A matronly American housekeeper ran the clubhouse, and

after showers we had the good meal we vainly sought in Lashio. Our hostess firmly chaperoned the Anglo-Indian girls, indeed causing them to vanish until time to leave next morning. Before going to our comfortable beds, we spent the evening in a big chintz-upholstered lounge, playing jazz records on a bubbly jukebox and staring at the darkening province of Yunnan through a wide picture window draped in chintz.

Next day we passed many little tribespeople walking by the road in embroidered blouses and kilts, but I became very aware that I was back in China. Most big villages, and the men connected with the motor traffic, were purely Chinese, and though this was more than a thousand air miles from Hankow, everything looked familiar, especially the swarming blue-coated people with their endless energy and humor. I could speak their language, only a little filtered by a strange provincial dialect. It was a relief after the Burmese who were unreachable and might be hostile. These Chinese were wildly pro-American, for news of the AVG victories had spread along the road. Crowds would wave and applaud as we drove by, and children ran out shrilling *"Ting hao"* (Very good) as they held their thumbs up in approval.

When we climbed the ridge of the Salween gorge we left the last of the jungle and came up into austere windswept country of red clay and rock slopes, sparsely fuzzed by vegetation, with only a few green fields around the villages. The view from the top was stupendous. The gorge ahead stretched straight from north to south, and it seemed we could look down it for a hundred miles in each direction, far into blue distance. Some six thousand feet below, the bright green Salween tumbled among giant white boulders. We could see our road zigzagging down, crossing a toy-like suspension bridge, and winding up the facing slope through countless steep hairpin turns.

Later we found the Mekong gorge, a hundred miles farther on, was only a little smaller, and tributary gorges flanked it.

Much of western Yunnan was a gigantic washboard of ridges and river trenches. The road snaking across it was the stretch of the Burma Road so publicized in the American press a few years earlier, when praise of China was helping us not to see our aid to Japan. The road was indeed a great achievement, brought off mainly by a few American-trained Chinese engineers, working with hardly any equipment except dynamite and the strength of tens of thousands of peasant laborers, who dug, broke up stones with crude hammers, carried the gravel in handbaskets.

As early as the 1860's, British Empire surveyors had come into Yunnan from Burma, hoping to get a railway to Kunming before the French could build theirs from Indo-China. The gorges defeated them, and when the Japanese invaded coastal China in 1937, the Chinese back entrance into Burma was only an ancient pathway passable to animals or men on foot. Within two years of rushed work, cars could use it, and before Rangoon was closed it became China's most vital supply route.

When I talked to peasants along the road, I was sorry to learn this triumph for their country meant tragedy for many of them. Labor on the road was commonly forced, with the peasants rounded up by soldiers who kept an armed guard over them while they worked. The mountains were so thinly inhabited that workers were brought from as many as a hundred miles away and did not see their homes again until the road was finished. They were paid little or nothing, fed badly, and lived in filthy camps. Thousands died of exhaustion, malnutrition, or malaria, without ever being told they were doing patriotic work.

The gorges gave us the toughest, slowest driving of the trip, and I can't remember how many days it took to get through. Our overloaded vehicles needed constant repair. Sometimes we had to dispose of one that had cracked under the strain, then we had to reshuffle all cargo and abandon a carful. It could take more than a day to get up or down one side of one gorge.

I think we discarded at least two trucks and three jeeps. Whenever we could, we pushed or coasted the dead car to a place where no road ran below, then stripped off the tires and other usables and gave it the old heave-ho. This was wonderful. I think everyone must be fascinated by utter destruction, and we would crane our heads over the side, laughing and cheering like boys as the car bounded down the cliffs in a cascade of rubble, perhaps sliding out of sight for a moment then hitting a rock and arching into the clear again, turning over and over before it hit the river with a great splash.

The road was crowded with trucks and buses heading for Kunming, crammed with Chinese refugees, but for miles the mountainsides were empty except for a few shacks of pauper farmers, wedged high in crevices beside steeply tilted fields which, if they were lucky, might be the size of a tennis court. The inns were so dirty and bulging with refugees, many of them ill, that we stopped getting anything from them, even water. We found Bristol Cream sherry could be used as eau de cologne and tooth water. Even today I sometimes imagine a toothpaste flavor in sherry.

All this was exhilarating, at least for me. I began to realize how deeply the last weeks in Burma had made me dread situations beyond control. Here I was on home grounds and felt I could handle anything. The peculiar mixture of the awful, the funny, and the incongruous which always seemed to color life in China was engulfing me again. I remember one morning when I stood on a crag above the river, squinting into the brassy dawn and brushing my teeth with sherry as I watched a dismantled jeep spin down thousands of feet to its big splash. I couldn't help laughing at the thought of the life in China I had expected when I signed up as a missionary with the Missouri Lutheran church.

I must have been so cheerful at breakfast that I seemed to infringe on an iron rule of the convoy — except when we were destroying cars we were to act as if we were having a perfectly terrible time. A few hours later, after a lunch break oiled with lots of sherry, since it was a hot dusty day, the drivers were most reluctant to get back on the road. Apparently I overdid my "Come on, fellows" pep talk. Suddenly I had a mutiny on my hands.

"Okay, Padre," the spokesman said. "You've just been breezing along in that Buick with those damned cats. You don't know what a tough job it is in the trucks. This afternoon one of us is going to drive the Buick and you'll take a truck."

I didn't see how I could refuse, and the next couple of hours were torture. I didn't have the build or conditioning for truck driving, and my arms and legs were soon trembling with the effort of steering and braking. The hairpin turns were so tight that our big trucks could not get around without stopping in the middle, then backing out on the shoulder — sometimes soft as cake, always unfenced, often with a thousand-foot drop below — before easing on around. Luckily at the next stop all seemed agreed that I had passed my test, or taken my punishment, so I went back to the Buick, glad even to see the squalling cats again.

The final hazard of the gorges were the hundreds of Chinese army trucks we passed speeding to Burma, empty except for a few civilian "Goldfish," as illegal passengers who had bribed the drivers were called. In Lashio I had heard rumors that Yu Fei-peng, cousin of Chiang Kai-shek and manager of traffic on the road, was slowing the Chinese advance into Burma because he was more anxious to move supplies out of Burma — including civilian and black market cargo — than he was to move Chinese troops in. These empty convoys rushing toward the front certainly suggested hanky-panky.

They were most troublesome to us when we were going uphill. To save precious gas the Chinese drivers would shut off

their motors and careen downhill, trusting their lives and ours
to overworn brakes. They were careless about keeping to their
own lane, and after a few of our vehicles were nearly forced
over the edge, we made our own traffic laws. We always drove
on the inside, whether it was our right or left lane.

This caused a hair-raising series of close calls, funny and awful like a primitive movie, a Chinese production at that. The
other trucks were light enough to fly around the hairpin turns
without backing or even reducing speed. They would suddenly
pop into view and if we happened to be in the wrong lane they
would come straight for a head-on collision. Everyone in both
convoys would scream and wave, urging the others toward the
brink. After indecision whether to pile into our larger trucks
or go off into thin air, the downhill group always straightened
out enough to plunge by with a few inches to spare, leaving us
breathing easily until the next ones sped down without warning. One group of Chinese fired rifles and submachine guns
over our heads, so at our next stop the AVG drivers dug arms
out of our cargo and began firing over the heads of everyone
who offended us.

Some jeeps of our second convoy from Rangoon caught up
with us in the gorges and when we got to Paoshan, the first real
Chinese city, halfway between the Salween and the Mekong,
we must have been a party of fifty or more vehicles, quite conspicuous from the air since we were now on bare slopes instead
of driving under jungle cover. A Japanese reconnaissance plane
had been checking on us and I wanted to keep going but everyone else was crazy to sightsee in Paoshan. I was the only one
who had ever been in a Chinese city, and despite all I told them
about remote provincial places, and all they could see of the
crumbling medieval walls in front of their faces, they were mes-
merized by the word "city." After days on the road they seemed
to expect cocktail bars, steak restaurants, perhaps something
like a Paoshan Hilton.

We parked near the Chinese military airstrip outside the walls, along with hundreds of dusty cars and thousands of refugees who were cooking supper at campfires. Nearly all other Americans went into town. They had hardly disappeared when I heard the soft thunder of approaching bombers, eighteen of them as I recall. I ran to shelter in a ditch, but the Japanese ignored or couldn't find the American target. Most bombs were dropped inside the walled town, crowded with refugees, and one stick was laid across a corner of the refugee camp by the airstrip, causing dreadful casualties.

All our men returned in a few minutes, shaken and pale, and it was decided that we must go on immediately; no use trying to do rescue work in a lousy little town so backward it probably didn't even have a hospital. We had almost certainly led the bombers to Paoshan, but as we drove away, while flames were still spreading over the city, flocks of children pattered beside us in dusk, fluting, *"Ting hao! Ting hao! Mei-kuo-ren ting hao!"* (Very good! Very good! Americans very good!).

After the days in the gorges we came out on fertile plateaus with wide green fields bordered by lines of poplars and willows. As this was March, the red earth of the uncultivated hills bloomed with many shrubs familiar in American gardens, but here growing wild, especially azaleas and rhododendron. We passed more modern cities, some with a few miles of paved road on either side. The roadside food-stalls improved and I began having lunch in them. Two or three of the more venturesome drivers would join me, and as we ate delicious hot dishes like chicken with peppers, or beef with mushrooms, we could see the other drivers down the road superstitiously scooping cold beans or spaghetti out of cans.

We still had several days before Kunming, and I became conscious of goings-on in the convoy. Some of the ex-AVG black-marketeers were openly following us, and in the evenings would come to talk with the convoy drivers. Without taking a one-man count every day I couldn't be sure, but the cargo seemed to be shrinking. On the last morning before Kunming, I noticed that the tarpaulin on a truck I had searched for cigarettes the night before had a noticeable sag in one corner. I looked under, and found some radios and tires missing. Several other trucks had sagging tarpaulins.

We reached Kunming about ten at night and found comfortable quarters in the hostel the Chinese had finally arranged for the AVG in a former university building northwest of the walled provincial capital. Chennault lived here, but he was asleep. An early mission was slated for next day, and it was his habit to get up at three or four to see the dawn flights off. I reported to him at breakfast, after he returned from the airfield, south of the city and about ten miles away.

He greeted me cordially as ever, but was quite matter-of-fact about our trip. He never thought anything was impossible for himself, so he evidently considered it routine that the convoy had come through. Indeed, his sharp questions about the lack of an inventory, the destruction of vehicles in the gorges, and the black market intrigues — I was astonished that he already knew about these — made me creep away from breakfast fully deflated. The third Buick from Rangoon had started out with the second convoy but had to be given the heave-ho in the gorges, and at lunch I somehow found myself suggesting that the Old Man should have my Buick, the only one left. The offer was accepted matter-of-factly.

Before we left Rangoon, we knew the few AVG planes left there were retreating to Magwe, a British airstrip beside the Irrawaddy about a hundred and fifty miles north. This hastily-built new field in the jungle was hoped to be secret from the Japanese. More AVG planes and some ground crewmen were later flown to it from China, but soon after we reached Kunming, news came of disaster at Magwe.

The field had no dispersal or revetment facilities. Its only radar could be set in only one direction, and was usually tuned toward Rangoon, which had fallen on March 6. Emergency field telephone lines were also strung south down the Irrawaddy and Sittang valleys, but in the east, toward the busy Japanese fields in northern Thailand, there was no warning except for one antiquated RAF bomber which would go up scouting every day until its gas ran out.

With all Burma so infiltrated by agents, it was inconceivable that the Japanese did not soon learn of Magwe, but they seemed to be giving themselves a rest after capturing Rangoon and they ignored it until March 21. At dawn that day a British reconnaissance plane reported fifty Japanese bombers on the ground at Rangoon, and before noon RAF bombers from Magwe successfully attacked them. The Japanese retaliated in the afternoon with two waves of twenty-seven bombers coming from the east. They evaded the warning net and caught the RAF bombers on the ground at Magwe, leisurely being rearmed and refueled. All were destroyed, and the ones that were full of gas exploded, setting fire to other planes and the ground installations. Only two AVG P-40's and two RAF pursuit planes could get into the air. They shot down four Japanese.

In the next twenty-four hours more than two hundred enemy planes attacked Magwe. On the second day no allied pursuit planes could be put in the air. One AVG crew chief, Fauth, was killed and a pilot, Swartz, so badly wounded that he later died in an Indian hospital. All ground installations were pulverized. On the third day the RAF retreated to India. Three AVG P-40's had been put back into operation and they were flown to Loiwing in China. Other AVG personnel were evacuated to China by truck.

This ended allied air operations from Burmese bases, and the Japanese quickly exploited their victory with fire raids on all larger towns, Mandalay among them. The raids clogged the roads with refugees and encouraged fifth columnists to further sabotage. The enemy's ground push for the rest of Burma was launched March 19, when they attacked the Chinese troops fortifying Toungoo, and in all stages of this later campaign the Japanese had decisively better air cover and reconnaissance.

On March 23, everyone in the Kunming AVG hostel got up at dawn and went out to watch the takeoff of what by then seemed a big mission to us. Reconnaissance had proved that most of the Magwe raiders came from Chiengmai and Lampang in northern Thailand, and our First Squadron — reduced to six P-40's — and Third Squadron — only four — were going to punish them. That day they flew to Loiwing and refueled, then at dusk went on into Burma and spent the night at two little RAF emergency strips in the jungle near the Thai border. Before dawn the First Squadron appeared over Chiengmai, and the Third over Lampang, both without warning.

When the Third Squadron came back to Kunming late that afternoon, the pilots said they found no planes at Lampang, and while strafing an armored car their leader, Jack Newkirk, an ace with ten Japanese to his credit, and one of the outstanding men in the AVG, crashed in flames. Our sadness was not dispelled when the First Squadron returned with a report of forty bombers and fighters surprised on the ground at Chiengmai. Not one had time to get into the air. After repeated strafings, at least twenty planes were set afire and ten more riddled with bullets. Many fleeing Japanese were killed. One P-40 was damaged by ground fire, and its pilot, McGarry, also an ace with ten kills, had to bail out on the way back. He parachuted safely into the jungle, but we feared we would never see him again.*

---

* He turned up in Kunming three years later. After days of wandering in the jungle he had been picked up by jolly Thai constabulary who kept him in a comfortable village jail and had no thought of turning him over to the Japanese. American OSS agents with good Thai connections made contact with him in early 1945, and he was whisked out of the country months before the Japanese surrender.

Chennault was again confined to bed by bronchitis, but in early April he went forward to Loiwing to see what could be done with what was left. Postwar U.S. Army publications show that some 450 American planes were allocated to the Chinese Air Force and the AVG at this time, but some were still being finished in American factories while others were awaiting delivery on fields in the United States. We later learned that the first medium bombers for the AVG had already been brought to India by the U.S. Air Force, and at least fifty replacement pilots had left America for China, but neither arrived until the Burma campaign was over.

Meanwhile the AVG had only thirty-five usable planes. Thirteen were new P-40's which AVG pilots had gone to Africa to claim and ferry back over the newly-established Hump air route from India to China. The other twenty-two were over-age P-40's, veterans of countless repairs and rebuildings in Burma and China. Twenty more old P-40's might be used again after much work. The British had temporarily loaned Chennault a few RAF pursuit planes and pilots, flown over from India.

Loiwing was within the protection of the Chinese air-warning net, and this more than evened the odds when the Japanese first attacked it, on April 8. Word came that twenty Zeros were approaching, in plenty of time for eleven P-40's and four RAF pursuits to climb high enough to dive on them as they came in. Ten Japanese were destroyed, at a loss of two RAF planes shot down, and two P-40's ruined on the ground. On April 10, five Zeros strafed Loiwing at dawn, then twenty-seven bombers approached in the late morning. They stayed above a heavy overcast, and when our pursuits appeared they flew off without dropping their bombs. Another twenty Zeros attacked in midafternoon and eight were shot down with no AVG losses.

These two days evidently convinced the Japanese they should stay away from Loiwing, and they attacked it only once again, just before it fell. April was nevertheless a busy month for the tiny air force, for General Stilwell, the British, and the Chinese all had tasks for it. Many were not what the pilots had agreed to do when they signed up in America.

In Burma friction and poor liaison between the allies was helping the Japanese continue their mobile guerrilla advance. Air reconnaissance was the only remedy and General Stilwell constantly asked for it. The AVG pilots found this extremely dangerous, because they often had to fly within range of ground fire to get clear vision. By this time nearly all Burma was hazed with smoke from the burning towns. Many fields had been fired by fifth columnists, and even patches of jungle were aflame, for this was the driest time, before the monsoon rains.

The British wanted AVG fighter cover for their bombers flying over from India to hit targets in Burma and Thailand. The AVG pilots hated these missions because they so often ended in futility; the rendezvous were too hard to keep for planes coming from so far in opposite directions. The bombers — mostly Blenheims — were also so slow that it was hard to protect them from the high-speed Zeros, and the AVG pilots began to feel they couldn't help them but were simply sharing their vulnerability.

"Morale missions" requested by the Chinese were just as dangerous, and most pilots found them pointless. They were supposed to fly over the battlefields, not to fight but to show themselves to the Chinese troops as proof of air power which didn't really exist. They thought that the altitude ordered was too high for the troops to recognize their insignia, and so low they would be easy victims for Japanese fighters higher in the haze.

Real air support for the ground troops was not practical without direct air-ground communications and trained liaison officers, neither of which existed. A few attempts to communicate through roundabout army channels, and to use cloth direction panels laid out on the ground, had poor results. Some Chinese troops were strafed by our planes, and AVG pilots flying over what they thought were Chinese positions suddenly found themselves the target of Japanese flak. Most of the Far East was conquered by now, allowing the Japanese to bring more anti-aircraft guns into Burma. All this was a far cry from the perilous but simpler early days of the AVG, when it was just plane against plane and a $500 bonus for every Japanese knocked down.

In mid-April I flew to Loiwing for two or three days. It was gratifying to spend a few hours soaring over the steep miles which had taken more than a week of struggle on the ground, but the atmosphere at Loiwing was most depressing. The Second and Third Squadrons were there, and pilots and ground crewmen alike had dropped into a pit of disgust and exhaustion. It wasn't just the different work the AVG was now expected to do. They had been through months of tension and combat without any break. Few new planes or supplies, and no personnel replacements, had ever arrived, so they felt they were stranded and forgotten, expected to go on until they dropped.

As early as January, the U.S. Air Force had tried to assimilate the AVG, but the proposal was rejected by unanimous vote; most of the men had joined the AVG to get away from formal discipline and they all wanted home leave before joining the regular forces. Chennault himself agreed to go back into the Air Force in March, and on April 18 his new rank of brigadier general was announced. He had made no secret that he thought all his men should follow him in, and this raised a barrier between them.

I was back in Kunming by April 20, but the news of that day in Loiwing spread quickly. An escort mission for Blenheim bombers from India, coming to attack Chiengmai, was announced, but the pilots refused to go. Only a day or two earlier, the AVG escorts spent dangerous time circling over the jungles, waiting for Blenheims which failed to appear. Northern

Thailand was thought hexed anyway, since the loss of Newkirk and McGarry.

Hours of angry talk ended with all but four of the twenty-eight pilots at Loiwing signing a mass resignation. The four took off on the mission to Chiengmai, but soon returned when word came that the Blenheims had turned back because of bad weather. Chennault called a meeting and reminded the rebels that America was now at war and they could be held as deserters for resigning. They would certainly get dishonorable discharges, perhaps other punishment. All but three or four resignations were withdrawn, and the holdouts were so obviously at rope's end that they were given honorable discharges and later returned to America.

Chennault could look grim at the best of times, and for days after the mutiny his face was like a sprung trap. I never heard him mention it, but we later learned that just at this time he was handed another bitter pill.

General Doolittle's token air raid on Tokyo occurred on April 18. The bombers were launched from aircraft carriers in the Pacific, and after attacking Japan, sixteen of them landed in eastern China, at night and in a storm. Only a few pilots were lost in the crash-landings, but all planes were damaged beyond repair. They were to have been assigned to Chennault, and if the AVG had known, our liaison with the Chinese air-warning net might have helped guide them safely into fields the Chinese had already built in that area. But neither Washington nor Chungking told Chennault about the raid until it was over.

By the end of April it was clear that all Burma would soon be lost. Like western Yunnan, the country was striped with parallel north-south valleys — of the Irrawaddy and Sittang and the southern stretches of the Salween. The British Empire front was on the Irrawaddy in the west, and the Chinese under

The Koehler family with missionary houses. The author lived in the second from the left. *From the author's collection*

A gathering after church. The author is at the right in a white robe. *From the author's collection*

Farmer women weeding the mission lawn. *From the author's collection*

Hankow after Japanese bombing, September 1938. Eight hundred were killed and several thousand wounded in this raid. *United Press International Photo*

Pete Atkinson "dives in," Toungoo, Burma. *Courtesy Gil Bright*

Atkinson's burial. *From the author's collection*

Wright lands on top of Newkirk's car. Merritt killed. January 1942.
Courtesy Gil Bright

Tom Jones (later killed) and his pet leopard. *From the author's collection*

Rangoon, December 1941. *From the author's collection*

An alert — pilots run for their planes. *United Press International Photo*

Pilot J. Gilpin Bright from Reading, Pennsylvania, grabs lunch between raids over Rangoon, January 1942. *George Rodgers, LIFE Magazine* © *Time Inc*

Left: General Chennault. The hawklike face that invoked Churchill's remark, "I'm glad he's on our side!" *Wide World Photos*

General Chennault speaking at Madame Chiang's dinner in honor of the Tigers. The Generalissimo is at the right. *Wide World Photos*

Flying Tigers study their next "strike" with General Chennault. *Wide World Photos*

Left to right, above: Neil Martin, first Flying Tiger casualty; shot down December 23, 1941, over Rangoon. Hank Gilbert, second casualty, December 23, 1941. Below: Al Christman, shot down January 23, 1942. Louis Hoffman, one of the oldest Flying Tigers, shot down over Rangoon, January 26, 1942. *Photographs by Peter A. Juley & Son from portraits by R. P. Neilson*

Left to right, above: Tom Cole, killed on strafing mission over Moulmein January 30, 1942. Jack "Scarsdale" Newkirk, shot down March 24, 1942, over Thailand. Below: John Donovan, shot down May 12, 1942, over Hanoi. Bob Little, downed on strafing mission, May 22, 1942, over Salween River. *Photographs by Peter A. Juley & Son from portraits by R. P. Neilson*

Left to right, above: Pete Petach, brought down over Nanchang, China, July 10, 1942 — six days after the Tigers were officially disbanded. He volunteered for extra duty. Frank Schwartz, wounded during bombing of Magwe, Burma, March 22, 1942. He later died in Poona, India. Below: Johnny Fauth, killed in bombing of airfield at Magwe, March 22, 1942. Ben Foshee, killed in bombing of Paoshan, China, May 4, 1942. *Photographs by Peter A. Juley & Son from portraits by R. P. Neilson*

General Yu Ch'ien-wan, Commander of the 57th Division, court-martialed, exonerated and later murdered in Hong Kong. *Courtesy Stephen Wong*

Changteh, China. Chinese re-enter the ravaged town captured by the Japanese December 2, 1943, and abandoned by them December 9. Only three hundred of General Yu's 57th Division survived this battle. *United Press International Photo*

Corporal Charles Annell and a Chinese sentry. *From the author's collection*

Chinese junk bought by Shoemaker. It was returned to its former owner in gratitude for helping the downed American pilots. *Courtesy Commander Shoemaker*

Kweilin, China. Flying Tigers in their P-40's take off after a Japanese raid. *United Press International Photo*

Hengyang, China. American airfield abandoned to Japanese. *United Press International Photo*

Chinese railroad blown up to delay the Japanese advance. *Wide World Photos*

Walking to the coast. Corporal Bichan and Commander Shoemaker.
From the author's collection

Right: General Stilwell and General Chennault confer. *Wide World
Photos*

The author (center) attends a one-man art show of paintings by David Kwok (at left). Hong Kong, 1952. *From the author's collection*

Louise Frillmann (center) at a diplomatic party; left, Lula Ballerand; right, Mrs. Bagley, Greek wife of British Colonial Officer. *From the author's collection*

Governor Dewey, Consul General Walter McConaughey and the author on the launch of the Governor of Hong Kong. *From the author's collection*

Foreground: U.S. Consulate residence in Hong Kong occupied by the author. *From the author's collection*

Stilwell in the center, on the Sittang. The Chinese were also supposed to guard the Salween, but the terrain was so rough and the roads so poor that their defenses were light. East-west communications between the three valleys were few and poor.

The Chinese made a good start in their defense of Toungoo. The enemy surrounded one division inside the town, and a pitched battle raged for three days. Japanese records seized after the war classed this as the stiffest resistance anywhere in Burma. Another Chinese division was camped near Toungoo, and Stilwell, who had reached the front by now, ordered it to attack. The division stayed put, and Stilwell, who must have seen similar incidents when he was military attaché, concluded Chiang Kai-shek was treating him like one of his own Chinese commanders, bypassing him and sending orders directly to the generals at the front.

Unaided, the defenders of Toungoo fought their way out and retreated. The British on the Irrawaddy had been attacked too, and their exhausted forces soon retreated fifty miles, so the whole Chinese front fell back to keep step. Stilwell sent word to Chiang Kai-shek that he would resign unless he was given full command, without interference. This was readily promised.

The British made their next stand a few miles up the Irrawaddy beyond Magwe, around the big oilfields at Yenangyaung. The Japanese threw in roadblocks behind them, and the British blew up the oil installations. Stilwell wanted to take Chinese troops to aid the British, but Chiang Kai-shek was already interfering again, sending contradictory orders to the American's Chinese subordinates, apparently uncertain whether he wanted to risk any of his men to aid the British whom he mistrusted. At last he agreed, and in a big confused battle following the belated arrival of Chinese troops at Yenangyaung, most of the trapped British troops were released. Then the whole defense of Burma was thrown into confusion by the biggest Japanese encircling movement of them all, up the lightly guarded Salween valley.

There the Chinese front just melted away, and in about two weeks columns of Japanese tractor trucks spearheaded by light tanks thrust north for three hundred miles, threatening Lashio and the land link with China. There was marching and countermarching of British and Chinese forces all over central Burma, but no effective defense could be put into the Salween valley. In a last minute effort to speed reinforcements, Stilwell asked the Chinese authorities at Lashio for 150 of the 850 trucks still parked there. They granted him twenty-two. Lashio fell on April 29, with many of the trucks still there.

In a series of diminishing battles the defenders fell back to the north, then began threading their way out of the country through the mountains and jungles. Stilwell retreated to India on foot and so did many Chinese troops. He already had plans to retrain them, equip them with American arms, and lead them in the reconquest of Burma.

As invasion approached Loiwing, Chennault expected the Japanese to make a final air attack. Recalling the great Emperor's Birthday raid over Hankow on April 28, 1938, he expected something similar, but perhaps a day earlier. The overload on Japan's wartime communications, he suspected, might call for an extra day to saturate the home press with the holiday news of the destruction of the AVG. On April 28 he sent all operable P-40's into the air with orders to patrol the approaches to Loiwing until their gas ran low, then land at Mongshih, an emergency strip farther up the Burma Road.

Twenty-seven enemy bombers were discovered heading in along the railway near Lashio, escorted by an uncounted number of Zeros, enough to engage all the P-40's while the bombers went on unmolested to Loiwing. The smoke haze made accuracy impossible, but it was believed at least twenty

Zeros were shot down. The bombers reached Loiwing and blasted great craters in the dirt runway, but these were quickly filled in by hundreds of peasant laborers and the P-40's were able to return from Mongshih next morning.

An ignored portent of troubles Chennault had to face on a much greater scale two years later was the fact that this airfield which had been a hornets' nest to the Japanese had to be evacuated the very next day, because of threats on the ground. The Japanese had hardly paused at Lashio, and their tanks and trucks were racing up the Burma Road toward Loiwing. Organized Chinese resistance collapsed in a pell-mell rush back into China. Small units and gangs of stragglers fought with Burmese who tried to waylay them. Others fought with civilian Chinese refugees, trying to hijack their trucks.

The air-warning net vanished, its watchers murdered, bribed, or in flight. The remaining Americans burned the Loiwing installations, jukebox and all, and took off in planes and trucks. Left behind in flames were twenty-two partly wrecked or dismantled P-40's, a gold mine of spare parts. The Japanese reached the field on May 2.

AVG headquarters moved back to Kunming, leaving five P-40's of the Third Squadron under Bob Neale at Paoshan, to cover the escape of the trucks from Loiwing and to escort Chinese Air Force bombers from Kunming, which had begun attacking the Japanese as soon as they crossed the Chinese border. On May 4 fifty Japanese bombers raided Paoshan without warning, again hitting the refugee-crowded town with terrible results. One AVG pilot, Foshee, was killed by bomb fragments. Only one pilot, Bond, was able to get into the air, and he was credited with two bombers shot down. On his way back he was caught by three Zeros who set his plane afire. He bailed out, but his clothes were in flames and he was badly burned before he landed.

Next day the Chinese Air Force code room in Kunming intercepted a Japanese message indicating bombers were taking off from Rangoon and Chiengmai, apparently heading for Paoshan. Nine P-40's were sent to reinforce the three planes which still had pilots at Paoshan. All twelve climbed so high they did not see the first wave of bombers coming in below, so the attackers made craters in that dirt runway. Our pilots estimated they shot down eight of a large group of fighter escorts. The second wave of bombers, with fewer escorts, fled at sight of the P-40's.

On that same day, May 5, Japanese motorized columns reached the western rim of the Salween gorge, pushing their way without resistance up the road packed with refugees and demoralized Chinese troops. At the top they set up artillery and began shelling the bridge and the road opposite, covered with thousands of vehicles and refugees fleeing on foot. All Americans had gotten through by now, but Chinese I later met in Kunming told me the panic that followed was unimaginable. Terrified drivers rammed one another off the road, or took too many chances trying to get ahead and went over the brink with carloads of people. Many vehicles that had stalled or broken down were mobbed by passengers rushing up from cars trapped behind. They were pushed off into space, complete with any people who had been too slow to get off.

On May 6 the Japanese descended to the bridge, blown up by retreating Chinese forces just before they reached it. Some of the multitude of Chinese soldiers and refugees now trapped in enemy territory on the western side of the river tried to get off the road, but most stayed because there really was no other place to go. This was the only road, and there was no way for crowds to live in the surrounding wilderness.

In postwar interviews, Japanese officers who were in the push to the Salween have said that their orders were not for deep penetration into China. Their lines were at last overextended, and Japan could not assimilate large new chunks of China at this time. They were to make a destructive and disruptive nuisance raid, pushing as far as they could without much reinforcement, then digging in.

In Kunming Chennault and his intelligence officers had no way of knowing this. They feared that if the Japanese crossed the Salween they would push on to Kunming and Chungking, knocking China out of the war. Chennault radioed Generalissimo and Madame Chiang for permission to attack Japanese targets on the road west of the Salween, even where Chinese soldiers or refugees must be slaughtered too. This was granted, and for the next two weeks AVG planes from Kunming attacked whenever the cloudy, turbulent, pre-monsoon weather allowed.

For the first time they bombed as well as strafed. The ground crews had spent many hours trying to modify the old P-40's to carry bombs, but they were so heavy that nothing seemed to work. Whiskey bottles full of gasoline and home-made lead-pipe bombs had been dropped, but these were hardly worth the bother. The new P-40's ferried in from India had wing racks for fragmentation bombs, and each carried one big demolition bomb on its belly. These could start landslides in the gorges, wiping away whole stretches of road with everyone on them.

The Japanese made one attempt to rig a bridge across the Salween, but their engineers and pontoons were quickly blasted by the AVG. Before the clouds pressed down and the monsoon rains began in mid-May, the front was stabilized. The Japanese were entrenched on the western rim of the Salween gorge and the Chinese were building forts on the eastern banks of the river. As later years showed, the Japanese Empire here reached its high tide mark.

CHAPTER VIII

End of the Flying Tigers 1942

I REMEMBER LATE MAY and early June as weeks of relative quiet for the AVG. Most of us were living in the one big hostel in Kunming, and for the first time since Pearl Harbor the Japanese left us alone. On all sides we were protected by hundreds of miles of the Chinese air-warning net, and the monsoon rains made the unsurfaced Japanese airfields in Burma and Thailand almost unusable for attack.

Missions were still flown, and a few of our men were killed. The Hanoi airfield was raided May 12, and more than twenty planes were believed destroyed on the ground, at the cost of one young pilot, Donovan, who wasn't fully trained but volunteered to go anyway. On May 16, another pilot, Jones, crashed while practicing dive-bombing near Kunming. He had four Japanese to his credit, though he had picked up malaria while trying to hunt tigers near Rangoon at Christmas-time, and had been in bed during the most active months of combat. On May 22, another ace, Little, with a record of ten downed Japanese, was killed while bombing Japanese artillery west of the Salween. Ground fire touched off the bombs in his rack.

Outside our mountain hideaway, terrible things were still happening in the Far East. In southern Burma the first of the

British prisoners-of-war from Singapore had started their three years as slave laborers in jungle heat, condemned to build a Japanese railway from Thailand to Burma. In northern Burma, the last of the refugees were on the steep jungle footpaths to India when the monsoon struck. Rain fell steadily for days, and it took only ten to complete the life cycle of the malarial Anopheles mosquito. Soon many refugees were too sick to climb further. It was believed that some thirty thousand tried to flee this way, and only about twenty thousand made it. When Sino-American forces re-entered Burma two years later, they found jungle glades literally white with skeletons sprawled among bits of rotted luggage.

In eastern China, near Shanghai, the Japanese launched a campaign against the airfields which could have been used by the Doolittle raiders but hadn't been. Neither the Chinese Air Force nor the AVG could spare planes to help their defense. The enemy advanced against little ground opposition, blew up the fields, then moved out, and the Chinese forces flowed back. The big losers were the peasants whose spring crops were destroyed and farm animals and grain reserves stolen. Many villages were burned and thousands of farmers killed in casual massacres.

In Kunming, such grim news seemed unreal. Even the hard fact that the AVG was still fighting and suffering losses was assimilated into the oddly prosaic atmosphere which began to result from our more settled and comfortable life. Everyone was still hectically busy: the ground crews trying to get more over-age planes ready to go back into the air, the pilots practicing new tactics to combat the new Japanese planes we expected. But there were no more panic scurryings or last-minute improvisations. The war was a job on which everyone spent a scheduled number of hours, reporting back to the hostel for meals and relaxation.

The hostel had been a college administration building, but with several pilots, or ground crewmen, bunking in each spacious whitewashed room, it looked as if it had always been a dormitory. There were clean showers and toilets on each floor. It was like being back in school, or living in a fraternity house, since two busy bars were the centers of social life. Despite Chennault's wish that rank be ignored, the lines had been drawn — quite spontaneously on both sides, as far as I could see. One bar was for the pilots of officer rank, the other for ground crewmen.

By strange luck, all the canned goods and games equipment I had ordered in Chennault's Washington office more than a year earlier had come through the shambles of Rangoon and Lashio. Afternoon games of baseball, volleyball, and tennis filled the park-like grounds with shouts and cheers. Occasionally Chennault came out to pitch baseball, but for all the leather-spitting, tough-talking formalities, these games were more like ritual than sport. He was obviously ill with bronchitis. While everyone loyally tried to keep on calling him "The Old Man," we couldn't forget he was a General now.

It was peaceful enough to worry about food. I got our Chinese cooks to use American canned bacon and ham, pancake and biscuit mixes, dried and preserved fruits, but these were breakfast or dessert trimmings, and I was never able to do much about our basic diet. Our meats and vegetables were locally produced, but unfortunately our Chinese hosts thought that as Westerners we should eat in Western style. The cooks claimed to have worked in Shanghai or Hong Kong hotels, but they just didn't understand Western cooking. I never caught any of them eating it themselves, and their over-boiled or over-fried foods showed why.

The hostel was run by the War Area Service Corps, WASC, a Chinese government outfit headed by a former YMCA secretary called "Fatty" Huang — he insisted on the nickname —

who seemed to be something of a court jester on the fringe of the Chiangs' inner circle. When I suggested to one of his aides that we might try switching to Chinese food for some of the meals, I was clearly told — though with much embarrassed laughter and lengthy indirection — that I was implying a flaw in Chinese hospitality, suggesting that our hosts were too uncultured to understand Western cooking. I saw I'd better forget it, since any complaint would go right to the top.

I wasn't even sure the men would welcome a change to Chinese food. Like most Americans, they seemed to have enjoyed meals in Chinese restaurants at home, but they distrusted Chinese food in China. It was much better than Chinese food in America, of course, but most restaurants did look dirty even when their fresh-cooked, scalding food was perfectly safe. Except for two or three expensive semi-Western restaurants in downtown Kunming, none had English-speaking waiters. Most of the men formed a grouchy routine of avoiding both Chinese food and the pseudo-Western fare at the hostel. At every meal they ordered familiar and safe-seeming scrambled eggs or fried rice. I gave up, and began eating in Chinese restaurants as much as possible. Before long, enough eggs were consumed in the AVG hostel to inflate their market price in Kunming.

If the Communists hadn't taken China, a Kunming Hilton might well tower over the little city by now. Climate and location made it potentially one of the world's great resorts. Within easy flying distance of the great sweltering metropolises of the Asiatic coast, it sat on a six-thousand-foot plateau at the edge of the tropics. The beautiful blue lake beside it offered year-round swimming, out in the middle where the water was clean. Nearly perfect weather lasted all year, frostless, with warm days and cool nights. Even in the monsoon, we had sunny mornings in Kunming, followed by brief afternoon showers and clear evenings.

In its isolation it was the most picturesque Chinese provincial capital I ever visited. Its main streets were still cobbled with glistening irregular stones and many shop fronts were carved and painted in peacock colors like those of old imperial Peking. Medieval gateways arched over the streets, and on the north side a crenelated city wall separated the crowded streets from empty grave-lands where little grass-covered knolls marked the dead of centuries.

After the Anglo-American quarters of Hankow, a novelty for me was the French flavor in what little modernization had reached Kunming. The one-track railway from Haiphong and Hanoi had been the single link with the outside world for decades; the Japanese closed it only the year before. Most of the French had left, but a big compound full of French offices and residences surrounded the railhead south of the city. Elaborate houses in Mediterranean colors, the summer villas of merchants and officials from Indo-China, stood in lush gardens on the reedy shores of the big lake. Good loaves of crusty French bread were still sold in some Chinese bakeries, and as the AVG lost no time in discovering, excellent French brandy and champagne could be found in a few groceries or at the small French Hotel de Commerce.

In about one week, incidentally, it became an old tradition of the AVG that a pilot who shot down a Japanese would invite his friends into town for French champagne. At a semi-Westernized restaurant they would drink it with hundreds of fried chicken livers, one of the few Chinese banquet dishes they recognized and ate.

For me, a great surprise after the earnest, patriotic Hankow of 1938 was the frivolous, cynical air of supposedly beleaguered Kunming in 1942. Buildings in Hankow had been camouflaged black or gray, streaked with anti-Japanese murals or war slogans. Kunming seemed sure the AVG had ended the threat from the air. Fancy new banks, offices, and apartments were painted white or gay pastel colors. Movie posters and cigarette ads took the place of war slogans.

In Hankow, showy dress and open luxury had been frowned upon. Many people who could afford better wore simple cotton uniforms — blue, gray, or black. Kunming was a much poorer and more backward city, and half its people seemed almost paupers in their threadbare robes, their faces pale from the opium which was only technically illegal here. A step above them were the usual solid bourgeois of a provincial town, old-fashioned merchants, absentee rural landlords and their peers, perhaps more comfortable here than elsewhere because slavery, too, was illegal only on the books. At the top of the heap was a new class of black-marketeers, speculators, hoarders, corrupt officials, and successful gangsters. Most made no effort to hide their wealth. With their new American cars, their smartly tailored Western clothes, their women in brilliant silks and jewels, their new glass-and-concrete suburban villas, they reminded me of wicked old prewar Shanghai. The downtown shops were bursting with technically illegal luxury goods smuggled up the Burma Road: American cigarettes and liquor, coffee, fancy clocks and pistols, trick razors and fountain pens, radios, everything that had inflated value in a blockaded country.

American aid, promised or arrived, was one reason for this flowering. Out on the end of the longest supply line, the AVG might be starving for specialized material, but millions of dollars worth of Lend-Lease, both civilian and military, had come in before the closing of Rangoon. The few transport planes already flying the Hump from India showed that Kunming would be the entry port for future American aid, and propaganda from Washington promised it would be huge. New airfields were abuilding, and Stilwell planned Kunming training camps for Chinese troops. Idle capital and the wheeler-dealers who controlled it, from Japanese-occupied China as well as the free part, had been attracted to profiteer on the American ef-

fort. Already, the problem of how to give war aid to a backward, exploited people without letting it be corrupted by their
traditional exploiters, was emerging. Nearly a quarter of a
century later, and not many hundred miles from Kunming, we
are still struggling with the same difficulty.

Then as now, some Americans thrived on the rackets and
deals. Several dishonorably discharged AVG men had set up
in Kunming hotels, and were apparently up to their ears in
everything from black-market money-changing to gunrunning.
They kept up friendships with AVG men and made new ones
among the pilots flying the Hump. The temptations were enormous. Just by turning his back at the right moment, a ground
crewman could deliver a jeep or a pile of tires to a customer,
pocketing a black-market price of thousands. A pilot flying
from India to Kunming or on to the more remote cities of free
China could make a similar profit by taking a small satchel of
medicine or watches.

I couldn't begin to guess the volume of this secret trade, but
the possibility of the social involvement of the AVG with the
Chinese in it was always there. Many of our men had been stationed in Kunming nearly a year. Naturally the pilots were
glad to know rich English-speaking Chinese who could invite
them to parties where they might meet pretty girls. Their hosts
were often the biggest black-marketeers, usually with the respectable front given by official or bank jobs. For the ground
crew there was a rough-and-ready world of refugee pimps and
prostitutes, newly arrived from Hong Kong or Shanghai, and
the gangsterish petty black-marketeers who were their friends.
Simple boredom drove our men who had no under-the-counter
dealings to associate with English-speaking Chinese who did.
I'm afraid a majority of non-English-speaking Chinese, who
knew no Americans, assumed all the AVG was corrupt.

One day Chennault called me in for a lecture. I think he

must have had some outside needling, perhaps by Madame Chiang or some moralistic senator on a flying junket. He said he hoped I was seeing to it that the men learned to like and respect the Chinese. He assumed I was giving them Chinese lessons. He wanted me to help them see the countryside and meet the real Chinese. College students, for example.

I had to bite my lip. He had been in China five years, and I had never heard him speak more than a few common Chinese phrases of the *"Ting hao"* variety. I never heard rumors of corruption against him, but his choice of Chinese friends was as limited as that of any of his men, and many rich and dubious characters wanted the prestige of knowing him. A few worldly, attractive, but quite questionable foreigners also managed to get themselves identified with him. I always felt that China to him was mainly the Chiangs, especially beautiful Madame with her fluent southern-accented English.

I did try what he suggested, but it was like teaching Sunday School in the basement of a nightclub. My language lessons were a washout, since even the rickshaw pullers had learned how to ask the important questions in English. "Hey Joe! You wanchee . . . ? Joe, Joe, wanchee . . . ?" they would shout, filling in the blanks with vigorous sign language. Naturally, none of the men wanted to hang around the hostel with the chaplain, learning the Chinese for "America and China are good friends," or "Please bring me a glass of cold boiled water."

Several colleges from the coast were in refuge in Kunming and I did arrange basketball matches between student teams and the AVG. Wartime diet in the colleges prevented overweight, while beer had made many of the Americans thick and slow, so the Chinese won every time. After some AVG grumbling about student draft dodgers, the games were abandoned.

I arranged for co-eds to come to AVG dances, but these weren't much of a success either. The girls had heard of wild AVG behavior and were extremely reserved. A few romances began, soon ended by the girls when they learned what happened to their reputations if they were seen in public with Americans. This only increased anti-Chinese feeling among the AVG, who took the snubs as proof of anti-American feelings among Chinese.

Chennault was an enthusiastic hunter and the swamps around the big lake teemed with ducks. He used to take off-duty pilots out to shoot, and they liked it so much I began doing it too. Often I found the men simply wanted to explore the strange countryside. These were the most natural and satisfactory Sino-American contacts in which I had any hand.

Many of the men were from small towns or farms and were fascinated by the Chinese farmers' different ways of doing things. The handicrafts in the villages, entirely new to them, were still understandable ways of making useful things. Sometimes we happened on a village market fair where peasants from miles around had gathered to sell or barter their goods, exchange news, and just have fun. Far from the corruption and wolfishness of the capital, the simple curiosity and friendliness of these holiday crowds easily came through the language barrier. The market-goers were always loudly amused at the "I am your American friend. Return me." inscriptions WASC had sewn on their pilots' clothes.

On clear mornings we climbed into the hills and sunbathed on the empty upper slopes. No place in crowded China was really empty, though, and sooner or later a ring of farmers would be squatting around us, volubly discussing the unusual spectacle. They ridiculed our hairiness, and the bolder ones would poke at our discarded clothes with sticks, trying to see how they were made. This in turn amused the Americans.

"Hey, Padre, what's that old joker with one eye saying?" somebody would ask. Or, "Why is that gimpy little one laughing? What did he just say to the ones behind?"

It never occurred to the farmers that I understood them, and I would let them rattle on to hear their notions. I remember one who exclaimed, "Look at their eyes! How pale they are! All the blood has drained out!" We were the first non-black-eyed people he had seen.

When I began speaking Chinese, the farmers would ignore me for minutes. They were utterly confident foreigners spoke a foreign language they didn't understand.

At last the big double-take would come, and someone would cry, "Ai-yah! He's speaking our language!" Then the eager questions would bubble out. Who were we? Where did we come from? Where was that? What was it like there?

It was fondly believed by some of Chennault's non-Chinese-speaking staff officers that the arrival of the AVG had galvanized all the millions in free China into new hope and determination. Our shark-nosed planes were supposed to be a token that a great power far across the seas would soon send much aid to China. I found that these peasants within a few miles of Kunming were dimly aware of new planes flying about, but when I told them we were Americans, they had only the foggiest notion of where or what America was. Many didn't know that water lay between American and China. Some thought America was just another part of China, perhaps over there beyond the farthest mountains we could see.

We received so few American magazines and papers after the war started that we had only a sketchy idea of the great publicity given the AVG; for a long time we didn't even know the pilots were "Flying Tigers." But we could tell we were on the world map by the dignitaries and journalists who began dropping in: people like Alfred Duff Cooper, and Mountbatten, and Jinx Falkenburg, as well as high-powered war correspondents, rank-conscious enough to make a general flinch.

Stilwell came, soon after he walked out of Burma to India,

and Chennault called a formal meeting of his staff to present us. As I recall, this was one of the times I wore my dress uniform, and I spent a long time trying to get everything right, hoping Stilwell would not recognize me from Lashio. In vain.

When Chennault introduced me, Stilwell frostily stared me up and down. "We've met," he snapped, moving on to the next man.

At about this time I pulled another Frillmann coup when I was wakened one night by noise and laughter from the pilots' bar. I blearily struggled into my old robe and made my way there. The commotion centered around an attractive blonde in a well-tailored version of Churchill's air-raid suit, as I recall, with war correspondent's insignia attached. She was charming everyone, and it was a great party, but I saw some pilots who were slated for a dawn mission, only a few hours away.

"It's late and I'm afraid the lady should go," I said. This wasn't as priggish as it sounds now, because we all were supposed to help get the dawn pilots to bed at a reasonable hour.

"But don't you see who she is?" several asked.

"I don't care if she's the Queen of England," I said. "It's time to go." That ended the party.

At breakfast I found her sitting next to Chennault, who called me over and introduced me.

"This is Clare Booth Luce," he said.

"We've met," she snapped, with as heavy a frost as Stilwell's.

Among other silly things I remember from Kunming was an evening with a French family, one of the few left in the railway compound. They wrote me saying that they appreciated the end of the air raids and asked me to bring half a dozen pilots for dinner. We had a marvelous meal, with rare treats like homemade eclairs, then our host asked if we would like to smoke or play cards.

"Well, I'm the world's worst bridge-player," I said heartily. "I'll just smoke."

The others began playing cards, and he led me down into a curtained room in the cellar, with soft chairs and sofas, rather like an American rumpus room. Instead of a bar, a long table was laid with silver pipes and jars. This was the family opium den.

My host was so polite and matter-of-fact that I tried a couple of pipes before I had to excuse myself hastily. I threw up in the nearest gutter and walked back to the hostel before my head cleared.

As a staff officer I had a room to myself, but for several weeks I had to share it with the Siamese cats I had brought from Rangoon. The RAF officer who owned them never showed up — I'm afraid he was killed — and nobody else wanted them. They soon got badly on my nerves. I would come home late in the afternoon, tired out after hours of odd jobs and errands all over the airfield and the town, and there they would be, sitting on the mantel like a pair of candlesticks, staring contemptuously at me as if to say, "Well, where the hell have you been all day?"

One evening the staff and pilots were invited to a reception by the Governor of Yunnan, Lung Yun, the white-haired and reverend-looking little warlord who had stayed in power for decades, it was said, through as much bloody intrigue as any Borgia. The party was in a whitewashed hall in the Governor's Headquarters, with magnificent carved tables and chairs set around the walls. A two- or three-inch layer of fresh long pine needles covered the floor, and gave off a pungent fragrance as we trampled it. At the buffet, laden with American liquor and Chinese food, I found myself next to a little old lady with an elfin expression, an official's or general's wife to judge by her quilted silk robe and jade jewelry. She was cuddling a Siamese cat. Although it was cross-eyed and looked sick or very sleepy,

I complimented her on its beauty. She gave me a wicked grin.

"It is a special cat," she said, flipping it over. She undid a zipper in its stomach and took out a red rubber hot water bottle. It was a job of taxidermy, lined with red plaid.

"I'm always cold in this barn," she winked. "My old cat killed many mice, and when it died I thought it might as well go on being useful."

She loved Siamese cats, she said, and for months had been trying to find a new live one. She was overcome at hearing I wanted to give two away. She came around to the hostel in a chauffeured limousine early next morning and haled the beasts off to a life which must have been better than they deserved.

During this settled time in Kunming, the dissolution of the AVG was approaching. Our year's contracts would end soon, and few intended to go right into the regular Air Force, as Chennault and the Air Force wished. Brass arrived from Washington to push enlistments, but had the opposite effect when they threatened that all who refused would get draft notices on return home.

We had been out of step with our complacent, isolationist country the year before, when we volunteered. Now we were out of step again, when the conventional thing was to rush to the colors. We all had more money than ever before, and wanted some leave to enjoy ourselves and see our families before enlisting for the duration. It was finally agreed that everyone would stay until July 4, then the AVG would be formally disbanded.

Chennault called me in and asked if I would like to be chaplain of the regular Air Force which he expected to command. He thought it would be a wing of the 10th Air Force in India. I would start with the rank of first lieutenant. If I had understood then what I believe I do now of his state of mind, I might have accepted, for I respected him as a great man.

With the unexpected Burma sideshow finished, the AVG was approaching the job for which he formed it: the defense of Chungking and other cities of free China and the harassment of the Japanese in occupied China. But the group was already falling apart, slipping away. He must have felt that after the one great year he was sliding back into the frustration which dogged so much of his career. In the mess hall his manner became perfunctory, his jokes mechanical. In working hours at the airfield he looked even more like a man "eating bitterness," as the Chinese had it. We thought it was just bronchitis.

One reason I declined his offer was that I was dubious about continuing as a chaplain anywhere. In a regular Army unit with troubled draftees there might be real work for a chaplain, but the tough volunteers of the AVG came to me only when they had gotten into a scrape and wanted me to intercede with Chennault. My church services Sundays were attended by a hard core consisting of Chennault and two or three of his staff, the two nurses, occasionally some pilots and ground crewmen. For the rest I was mainly an errand boy and administrative odd-job man. I wanted to go home and think things out a bit, then decide what to do for the duration. I already knew whom I wanted to marry, and I hoped to make that definite too.

On June 5, Chennault took two Squadrons and moved his headquarters to Pei-shih-yi, a field in the outer suburbs of Chungking. The months which brought monsoon clouds elsewhere lifted the winter cloud-cover from Chungking. For the past three summers the Japanese had bombed the capital brutally, often with more than a hundred planes a day, against little or no opposition from the remains of the Chinese Air Force. Until the London blitz began, Chungking was the most bombed city in the world.

Chennault immediately sent the P-40's out on "morale missions" over Chungking and its satellite towns, and the appear-

ance of the shark-nosed planes did galvanize the city people
who avidly followed AVG exploits in the news and had suffered
so much from bombing. Chungking was built on a high rock
between the Yangtze and the tributary Kialing. The flanks of
this crowded peninsula were a tumbled mass of ruins and tenements, with a few patches of solid prewar building surviving
among them. A friend later told me that on June 6 he was
working in his hotel room high on the spine of the city, with a
view all the way down to the Kialing. When the air began to
tremble with a smooth new thunder, he looked out in time to
see six P-40's in perfect V formation rounding the tip of the
peninsula, just above the masts of the junks.

They came up the Kialing, then climbed steeply and in pairs
erupted all over the sky in a stunning display of acrobatic flying. Up and down the steep slopes, blue-coated crowds flowed
into the staircase streets or out on flat roofs, waving and shouting, loud with exultation. The planes performed for an hour
or more, and the human roar went on through every moment.
The people of Chungking had good reason to cheer, for they
were never bombed again.

After three days Chennault left four P-40's to keep on showing themselves over Chungking, reinforced by a dozen bamboo
and paper dummies for Japanese reconnaissance to see on the
field at Pei-shih-yi. He took the rest of the planes down to the
Kweilin-Lingling-Hengyang area in south-central China. These
cities were about halfway between Hankow and Canton, and
not much farther from Nanking and Shanghai.

More than a year earlier, when only China was at war with
Japan, Chennault had picked the area as his base for attacks on
occupied territory and the Chinese built gravel-surfaced airstrips for him, big enough for four-engined American bombers.
Japanese conquest in the six months after Pearl Harbor had
given these fields new importance, as an approach to Japan itself. In mid-1942 they were more than a thousand miles closer

to Tokyo than any other free territory, about as far as Manila, Guam, or Saipan, which were not to be recaptured until two years later.

For less than one tantalizing month, Chennault operated the AVG out of these fields. On June 13, nine Japanese bombers and twelve fighters came to Kweilin. They were met by ten AVG planes, well-warned and flying in three layers above 15,000 feet. Eleven Japanese planes were shot down at the cost of two American ships wrecked in emergency landings. Both pilots, Wright and Allison, escaped. The bombers made dozens of holes in the Kweilin field, but they were filled up before dark.

After a spell of bad weather, the P-40's from Hengyang made a dawn patrol up the Yangtze where they caught a Japanese supply fleet and sank one gunboat and three transports. That afternoon fourteen Japanese fighters strafed the Hengyang field and four were shot down. On the same day, six Mitchell B-25 bombers from the 10th Air Force in India arrived in Kweilin, but were kept out of action by another week of clouds.

On June 29 they flew to Hengyang, where seventeen P-40's were assembled. This was the largest force the AVG ever had together on one field, less than a week before its dissolution. On July 1, five bombers and six fighters attacked Hankow with no Japanese opposition. Unfortunately the novice bombardiers did not hit their target, the Yangtze docks, but bombed the city instead. On July 2, with clearer weather, they did hit the docks. Japanese fighters were seen, but did not try to intercept. On July 3, four B-25 bombers escorted by four P-40's bombed the Hankow airfield. Japanese fighters rose to attack but the light bombers quickly outdistanced them and their escorts shot one down. One AVG plane was damaged by ground fire, but its pilot, Bolster, parachuted down and was able to get back to the Chinese lines. That afternoon seven Zeros came to Hengyang through clouds which confused the warning net. One P-40 failed to get off the ground and was strafed and burned.

During these final days of combat, Chennault toured all the fields with Army and Navy induction officers, offering a last chance to sign up, indeed insisting upon it. But of some two hundred and fifty men still in the AVG, only five staff members, five pilots, and twenty-nine crew members agreed.

On Chennault's plea that crowded cities would be undefended if they left before enough regular Air Force personnel replaced them, nineteen pilots, and enough ground crewmen to keep them going, did sign temporary contracts for two to four more weeks. In a dive-bombing raid on a Japanese airfield on July 10, one of these pilots, Shamblin, was shot down and captured. Another, Petach, died when ground fire touched off his rack of bombs. In January he had married one of our nurses, Emma Foster, and had signed up for extra duty to make a little more for the baby they already expected.

The Japanese undoubtedly knew July 4 was the AVG's last official day, but their attempt to celebrate it was a fiasco. Five bombers from Hankow made holes in the Lingling field at dawn, and twelve more later bombed the Hengyang field. When their escort of twelve Zeros was attacked, they made the mistake of trying to defend themselves by flying in a big circle and five were shot down from above. Japanese fighter patrols roamed over southeastern China all day but the Mitchell B-25 bombers were not discovered as they made a first raid on the Canton airfield.

I was at Pei-shih-yi on July 4 but passed up the farewell party for the AVG which the Generalissimo and Madame Chiang gave in Chungking that evening. Summer in Szechwan province was a steam bath always, and that night it was raining. The idea of getting into dress uniform, even to attend a "historic" event, was not appealing. I had been to the Chiangs' receptions in Kunming, and their curious mixture of Chinese opulence, Methodist austerity, and YMCA heartiness supplied by Colonel "Fatty" Huang, was somehow embarrassing. It seemed more sensible to spend the evening in shorts at Pei-shih-yi drinking beer in an electric-fanned office where a couple of staff officers were pulling together some of the statistics on the AVG.

The official tally of Japanese planes destroyed was 397. Perhaps this was high, since so many had gone down in sea, mountain, or jungle where they could not be verified. Many planes were bombers, so a thousand or more Japanese were probably killed. Important ground installations were destroyed. The cost in American lives was twenty-two: four in aerial combat, four while strafing or bombing ground targets, three killed on the ground by enemy bombs, ten lost in accidents, four prisoners of war. Seventy-three P-40's were lost, twelve in aerial combat, and sixty-one on the ground, including the twenty-two burned at Loiwing. In its year of operation, the AVG cost the Chinese Government roughly $8,000,000 — about $3,000,000 for salaries and operating expenses, the rest for planes, gas, and ammunition. The total was less than a single big bombing plane costs today, twenty-five years later.

At eleven o'clock the other men came back from Chungking, sweating and subdued. The party had featured soft drinks and parlor games like musical chairs. Chennault was given a gold sword and an oil painting of himself with the Chiangs. Madame Chiang made a speech, coy but a little waspish, for news of AVG shenanigans on the ground must have reached her disapproving ears. "The Flying Tigers will always be known as the Flying Angels of China," she said. "Flying Angels, some of them a little naughty at times, naughty angels, but still our Flying Angels. . . ."

So that was it. There was a little more drinking and everyone went to bed by twelve. I am sure we all realized an important and unforgettable part of our lives was over.

Combat Intelligence Officer

CHAPTER IX

The Siege of Changteh 1942-43

IN THE STEAMY LIGHT of morning, sentiment could not compete with the big problem most of us had: how to get home as fast as possible. We were flown to Kunming on AVG transports, then were on our own. Because I spoke Chinese I may have been the first to get over the Hump, through a deal with a freight pilot for the China National Aviation Company.

He was taking a load of hog bristles to India and I was his only passenger. We flew at night through violent thunderstorms. Air currents made the plane drop thousands of feet, then jerk up like a crazy elevator. We took the shortest route, far north of the Burma Road, closer to the Himalayas. The lightning snapped awesome flash-pictures of mountain ridges and peaks soaring higher than 20,000 feet. Beyond the storms everything was so black — not a star nor any light on the ground — I couldn't tell up from down and had a wild delusion that the plane was turning over. I scrambled to the cockpit and beat on the door until the alarmed co-pilot opened it. The moment I saw the lighted instrument panel I realized everything was all right and sheepishly went back to my nest in the bristles.

At Indian airfields in the next few days I ran into other AVG

men and we found that if we were together in a recognizable
Flying Tiger group, we had a better chance for lifts on American planes. With three pilots and about ten ground crewmen I
reached Karachi, where friendly Air Transport Command officers arranged to send us all the way to Miami, across Africa and
the South Atlantic — right away, and completely free. We were
the first to get so far, and very lucky. The 10th Air Force brass,
annoyed because so few of the AVG had enlisted, ordered that
no more of us should get free rides or high priorities. Some of
our friends spent weeks and pots of money trying to get home
from India.

We stopped overnight in Natal, Brazil, and at the hotel the
first person we saw was Orson Welles. He seemed amused by
us, and we spent pleasant hours in the bar. By then we were
beginning to have some idea of the Flying Tiger publicity in
America, but not enough, according to this old master and vic-
tim of publicity.

"Just wait till you see what you're in for," he said sardoni-
cally as we left.

At the Miami airport, the Mayor was waiting, surrounded by
civic leaders with flowers, troops of Girl and Boy Scouts, several
bands. Reporters and photographers swarmed over us. Only
three of us were pilots, but to the press we all were heroic Flying Tigers, the first to return to home soil. The papers blos-
somed with pictures and imaginative stories; in one, I was the
killer chaplain who had shot down five Zeros while standing
on the wing of a P-40. We were applauded in restaurants and
people on the street stopped us to shake our hands.

An impulsive girl I had known in Hankow was then living in
Miami. She was astonished to see the pictures and stories
about me, for she thought I was still a missionary. She had no
conventional way to get in touch with me, so she called the
police.

"The newspapers have pictures of Paul Frillmann, the chap-

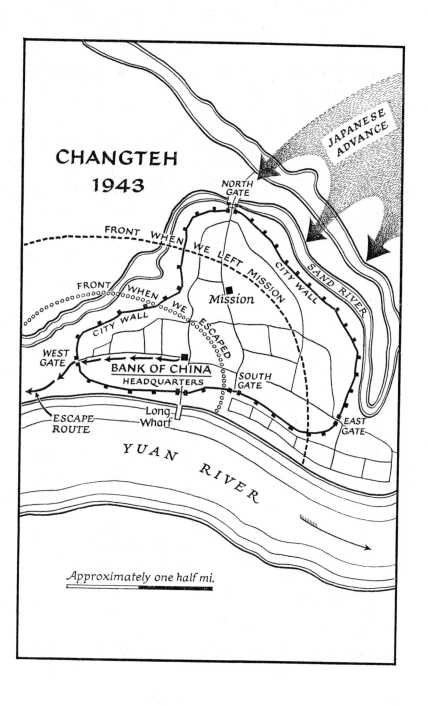

CHANGTEH
1943

JAPANESE ADVANCE

NORTH GATE

FRONT WHEN WE LEFT MISSION

CITY WALL

SAND RIVER

FRONT WHEN WE ESCAPED

CITY WALL

Mission

WEST GATE

BANK OF CHINA
HEADQUARTERS

SOUTH GATE

EAST GATE

ESCAPE ROUTE

Long Wharf

YUAN RIVER

Approximately one half mi.

lain of the Flying Tigers," she told them. "I want you to pick that man up. I have charges to bring against him."

Two burly policemen nabbed me at my hotel, refusing to say why. Judging from the rough way they shut me up, they thought something was seriously wrong. So did I. When my friend opened her apartment door and saw us hulking there, she burst into peals of laughter. When I grasped what had happened, I began laughing too, though less happily. The police were quite miffed but were finally persuaded not to haul us both to jail.

Two days later I flew to Chicago where I found the local papers had picked up the nonsense from the Miami press. Reporters and photographers waylaid me at the airport and another gang was waiting on the porch of my brother's home. My conservative father and brothers and sisters were not pleased. At the age of thirty-one, I was made to feel as if I were ten and had gone out in my best clothes to play in the coalyards across the tracks.

I found a "hero" in the press lasts about ten days and I soon had time to keep a promise I made to Chennault. I wrote the families of all men killed in the AVG, told them I was home, and would be glad to write further or see them. This led to long correspondence, some of it very sad. Several parents came to Chicago in the few weeks I was there. Most were learning to live with the facts, but one mother in the deep South, with whom I corresponded day after day after day, simply would not believe her son was dead. Sooner or later, she wrote, he would "come home and go squirrel-shooting with me like he did as a boy."

In mid-summer I had a telegram from the Air Force in Washington, signed by General F. Trubee Davison, head of A-1, Air Force Personnel. He asked me to come to Washington as a War Department consultant, salary $50 a day. It appeared that every branch of the Air Force had questions about the AVG. I wired back that I knew little of the military history, just administrative work and the Chinese setting, but the offer still stood, so I flew to Washington.

Every morning a secretary at A-1 would call my hotel and give me the day's appointments. I spoke to groups in the Fighter and Bomber Commands and the Supply Division. I lunched or had interviews with high-powered men like McCloy, Lovett, Davison himself, plus a series of Air Force generals. Evidently a full-fledged air force for China was being planned, not just a wing of the 10th in India. I answered questions about Chinese roads, railways, and airstrips, the availability of personnel, food, gas, and other supplies. Some queries about general conditions in China could have been answered by any encyclopedia in a free public library.

By the end of August my appointments tapered off and some days I had none. I went to General Davison and said my job seemed finished so I thought I would go home. He was an affable wealthy man from Oyster Bay, Long Island, who later became head of the American Museum of Natural History.

"Why don't you stay a while longer?" he asked pleasantly. "I'm sure we'll think of something else to ask you."

I said $50 a day for nothing made me uneasy. He laughed, then asked if I would like a commission as a first lieutenant in the Air Force. This was the same as Chennault's offer, and I must confess I hoped for something better, but I said yes, provided I would be sent back to China. I also wanted some Army training. I had seen enough men who had been commissioned for special reasons but had no military training and floundered in Army life.

I had a few days at home, then was sent to Officers Training School in Miami Beach. The six-week course included much that I didn't want to know — how to march, make coffee, and so on — but I did get a grounding in Army terminology, meth-

ods, and discipline. Most of my classmates seemed to be lawyers, who made the sorriest of soldiers, but this was Florida and
it wasn't a bad time.

More weeks at a Combat Intelligence School in Harrisburg,
Pennsylvania, followed. Here everything taught was useful. I
was certain my Chinese qualified me as a forward intelligence
and liaison officer, and I made a formal request to be sent to
Chennault. At the end of the course I learned I was being
posted to a Japanese Language School in Minneapolis, for
fourteen months' instruction in Japanese.

I couldn't believe it. I was fluent in German as well as Chinese and could be used immediately in either Europe or Asia.
I stormed into a public phone booth and called General Davison.

"Look, General!" I said, when by some fluke I got through.
"You promised I would go back to China. Now I have to spend
more than a year learning Japanese."

"Oh no, Frillmann," he said. "With your skill in Chinese
you can pick up Japanese quickly."

I suppose I was impertinent, but I tried to explain that while
written Japanese and Chinese used some of the same ideographs, they were no more alike than European languages —
say Spanish and German — which used the same alphabet. It
would be a full fourteen months out of my life.

"Sorry, lieutenant. You're in the Air Force now," he said,
affably, hanging up. Next day I was on a train to Minneapolis.

The Language School was new and chaotic, run by an Army
colonel who didn't know Japanese, and taught by young Ameri-
can-born Japanese who didn't know the Army or schoolroom
discipline. Two of my classmates who had China experience
and spoke Chinese resented being there as much as I, so we
planned to escape.

Knowing the Chinese pronunciation of ideographs used in
both languages gave us one way to bedevil our instructors.

When a lesson was written on the blackboard in Japanese, we could read parts of it in Chinese. We found other smart-aleck tricks to create amusement and confusion, and the instructors, whose authority was shaky at best, soon asked for our removal. Luckily the colonel in charge had no wish to keep rubbing our noses in Japanese, or even to punish us. After the customary military delays he arranged to have us sent off in the general direction of China.

As I recall, I was at the Language School less than two months, leaving in February 1943. Minneapolis was not too far from Chicago, and I succeeded in getting engaged to the girl I had long hoped to marry, a friend since childhood.

My next stop was Hawaii, where I was put into A-2 — Intelligence — and assigned to the interrogation of Japanese prisoners-of-war. I couldn't speak Japanese, but it didn't matter because there were no prisoners. When I managed to get this double nullity noticed, I was transferred to "R and R" — Rest and Recreation — where I was supposed to advise and guide airmen on leave from the South Pacific. This was utter nullity. Nobody on leave needed help in wide open Honolulu.

In March the newspapers announced that Chennault now commanded his own Air Force in China, designated the 14th. After months of frustration I was assigned to the China-Burma-India Theater and boarded a troop transport which took fifty-five days to reach Bombay by way of the farthest South Pacific, New Zealand, and Australia. It was a little like traveling on a slave ship, for the hold was packed full of severely segregated Negro engineering troops, on their way to build the road from India to China. We crossed the equator twice and were in the tropics most of the way, but they were allowed above decks for only a few hours a day.

In Bombay I got orders to the 14th Air Force Headquarters in Kunming, then flew to Assam, at the foot of the Hump, where I had to wait more days for a place on a plane to China. The monsoon rains were pouring down, and Assam was one great bog. Stretching through the jungles and tea plantations was a staggering disorder of felled trees, half-finished roads and airfields churned up by hordes of GI's busy with trucks and bulldozers. Long lines of warehouses were full of hundreds of thousands of tons of supplies for China. Only about two hundred cargo planes had arrived, and little more than five thousand tons a month could be flown over the Hump. Much of it was gas for return trips. A sizable tonnage also had to be Chinese banknotes, made in America so they couldn't be counterfeited in China; inflation was a growing problem, and big bundles of notes were needed for quite ordinary purchases. A few months earlier, when the total tonnage was smaller, nearly 10 percent of all Hump cargo was paper money.

When at last I reached Kunming and walked into Chennault's office — a new one, out near the airfield — he looked up from his desk, as matter of fact as ever.

"Hello, Frillmann. I thought you would be back," he said.

After the usual pleasantries, he shuffled through some maps and spread one on his desk.

"You've come just in time," he said. "The Japanese are starting something around Tungting Lake and I need a Chinese-speaking officer to send up there."

I didn't need a map to locate the lake, for it was only about 150 miles southwest of Hankow. Perhaps 50 miles long by 30 miles wide, it lay not far south of the Yangtze, whose flood waters filled it in summer and drained out in winter.

"How soon do you want me to go?" I asked.

"Right away," he replied. "A-2 will brief you tomorrow."

As I went out, his leather face cracked in a smile. "I see you're still a first lieutenant," he said. "You would have been a captain now if you had stayed here. If we knew you wanted it, we could have shifted you into intelligence in a few days."

He didn't have to rub it in. I could see what a dunce I had

been. But I was engaged to be married, and still think that was worth any amount of time. Aside from that, I had been around the world in a dull way and had knocked more than a year out of my life in China.

Next morning in the A-2 offices, I met the corporal who was going with me, Sven Liljestrand, about twenty, son of American missionaries in Chengtu, who spoke perfect Szechwanese Chinese. He was trained to operate and repair a radio, and could send code on a key.

We were given a ninety-pound field radio powered by a generator to be cranked by hand or by a bicycle on a rack. With it came a little brass code gadget dating from the First World War. Twenty-six disks, one for each letter, were fixed on a central core. By re-aligning them each day in a system prearranged with headquarters we could scramble messages. We were given a schedule of times to call in, and received formal papers of introduction in Chinese and English, signed by Chennault and stamped with his official chop.

American ground intelligence at the fronts was rudimentary in 1943. Near Tungting Lake another ex-missionary, Lieutenant John Birch, was stationed at Changsha, to the east, but for the rest, A-2 had to rely on air reconnaissance and what Chinese intelligence chose to reveal. It was believed that some 40,000 Japanese troops and 20,000 Korean, Mongolian, and Chinese puppets were massing north of the lake for a strike at Changteh, to the west.

Weather made us wait for a plane to Kweilin, and after getting maps, concentrated rations, and other supplies, I had time to see some of the changes since the Tigers flew the coop. The chiefs of Intelligence and Communications were former staff members of the AVG, and I found a few other familiar faces, but headquarters was a sprawl of new one-story buildings staffed by hundreds, perhaps twice the total of the whole AVG.

For miles around, American supply dumps, repair shops, and hostels stood among the adobe farm villages. The 14th Air Force was getting more than half the tonnage flown over the Hump, but in those days of scarcities everywhere, it had only about 130 fighter planes, 15 medium bombers, 35 heavy bombers, and 15 other planes.

I was billeted with some men from the offices — clerks and typists — and found the faceless mass war of wasted time and frustrating jobs had also reached Kunming. These men were so bored they drank much more than the AVG, and Chinese rot-gut instead of champagne. Around midnight, when enough bottles were empty, they would use them as pins for bowling in the hall, guffawing drunkenly as the broken glass flew up.

About three air-hours east of Kunming, Kweilin was famous for mountains like those in Chinese paintings, and the airfield was rimmed by limestone spires green with bushes and vines. The field was being enlarged by thousands of weary peasant men, women, and children in blue and black rags. In slow motion they beat rocks into gravel and flattened this with stone rollers so huge it took two or three hundred laborers, straining at long ropes, to move one.

From Kweilin we traveled to Lingling and Hengyang by train, on one of the few railways left in free territory, then switched to the old Canton-Hankow line and went north to a little town called Siangtan, where the tracks disappeared into a ricefield. Farther on we could see a former railway bridge across a wide river, now nothing but blasted piers. This was the edge of the "Roadless Area" the Chinese had created when the big Japanese conquest stopped in 1938. It was a protective strip anywhere from ten to a hundred miles deep on their side of all fronts. All railways, major roads, and bridges in it were destroyed.

By protocol we should have gone to Changsha, some fifty

miles north, to pay a courtesy call on General Hsueh Yueh, commander of this 5th War Area, but we heard the Japanese above Changteh were stirring, so we went directly there. In a week we covered a little more than a hundred miles, moving laboriously northwest on foot or by horse, mule, wheelbarrow, rickshaw, litter, boat, or whatever else the terrain demanded. Sometimes we had to change transport every few miles.

This was October, so the autumn harvest was in, and the dry ricefields stretched golden-brown under high blue skies. The trees were turning red and yellow. Sometimes we skirted Tungting Lake, an enormous expanse of glittering blue shallows striped with sandbars, dark reed beds and low islands. Migrating ducks and geese honked overhead. As we neared Changteh, I had some fears of being trapped there, but relief at my escape from the do-nothing war helped modify them.

Fifteen or twenty miles from the city, we began passing villages where urban refugees were boarding with the farmers. Farther in, soldiers were billeted in most farmhouses. Changteh itself was a close-packed walled city perhaps a mile square. Its old-fashioned gray houses were crowded with more than 12,000 soldiers, one complete division plus 2,000 service troops. Most civilians had fled or were in hiding. We called on the Division Commander, General Yu Ch'ien-wan, who seemed a little mystified by our purpose but welcomed us politely and gave us quarters in an abandoned mission compound, a small one with three American-style houses in a walled garden.

By now the Japanese push was definitely on, eighty to a hundred miles away, but it took a couple of days of liaison with Chinese intelligence before I could call in air strikes. We had to have long talks about maps and troop dispositions. In explaining what air power could do, I had to be most deliberate and polite, to avoid any appearance of teaching or interfering.

I soon learned good targets were hard to find, for this was

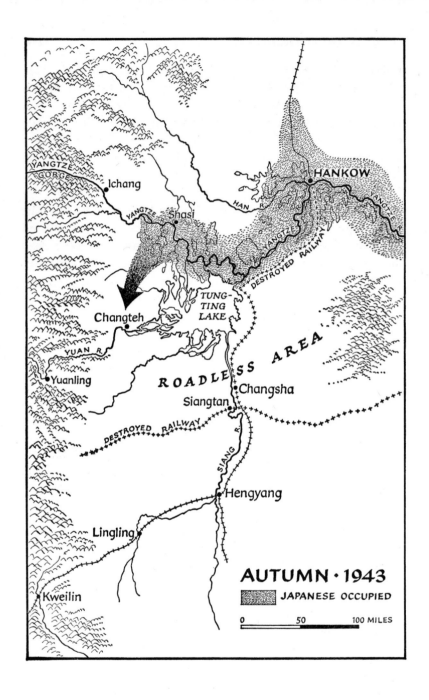

YANGTZE GORGE

Ichang

YANGTZE

Shasi

HAN R.

HANKOW

YANGTZE

YANGTZE

DESTROYED RAILWAY

Changteh

TUNG-TING LAKE

YUAN R.

R O A D L E S S   A R E A

Yuanling

Siangtan

Changsha

DESTROYED RAILWAY

SIANG R.

Hengyang

Lingling

AUTUMN · 1943

JAPANESE OCCUPIED

Kweilin

0   50   100 MILES

mobile guerrilla-style attack similar to that in Burma. It had to be, because of the "Roadless Area." The Japanese could not use trucks, tanks, and big columns of troops, easy to find from the air. The small units of cavalry and infantry which they did use — and especially their bands of puppet plainclothesmen — infiltrated the countryside and could vanish under trees when they heard planes. In a week they came within a few miles of Changteh.

As they converged they became a little more vulnerable, and Liljestrand and I began going out on bicycles to check on targets. When we thought we had a good one we would hurry back, twist the disks, and send the information to Kunming. Liljestrand was a quiet and rather withdrawn young man. I suspect he felt that his Chinese was better than mine, and if he were a lieutenant he alone could have handled the job we both were doing. He always wore a little smile during the message-sending sessions, for now the corporal was boss and tapped out the code, while the lieutenant puffed and pedaled on a stationary bike, grinding out the electricity.

At dawn the following day we always felt like Aladdins with a whole case of genie-filled lamps, as 14th Air Force planes thundered in from Hengyang, Lingling, and Kweilin. They would check in on voice radio, calling our signal, Peter William Fox — a call sign with my initials. Then I would describe the target in detail, and they bombed or strafed. Unfortunately the Japanese were still not visible enough. In a few days they encircled Changteh, breached the walls with mortar fire, and settled down to a slow but steady conquest of the city.

This was rich rice-growing country, and in the eighteenth and nineteenth centuries, when most of the town was built, good solid construction could be afforded. Each old courtyard house, built of brick sheathed with gray plaster, was a fortress. The battle became slow and rather low-pressure, with both sides dug in behind walls, invisible to one another unless a sniper edged into view or some small foray was made. Except for an occasional mortar shell, this was a battle with rifles and machine guns. The Chinese kept falling back, and the Japanese seemed to be allowing them to do so without maximum losses. Escape routes were left open, and the number of defenders noticeably dwindled.

With the enemy in the town, we only had to be sure where the front was to point out air targets. Our planes came nearly every clear day. Since both sides were at such close quarters I had the pilots repeat all directions back to me on the voice radio before giving them the go-ahead. I talked to some pilots so much we felt we knew one another, and they began warning us.

"You guys better get out of there," they would say. "You can't see what's around you, but we can see some of it." Of the 60,000 enemy troops in the campaign, a third to half were believed to be in the siege of Changteh.

About the middle of November, the Japanese lines came dangerously close to the mission compound, and General Yu invited us to move to his headquarters in the Bank of China, one of the few modern cement buildings in town. His staff and bodyguard were billeted there, and piles of bedding and charcoal stoves littered the lobby floor. The general's quarters were behind a half-partition cut by tellers' windows. Noise and movement were constant day and night, but this was welcome. The deserted mission houses with their comfortably over-furnished American rooms, cold and unlighted, silent, except when the noise of battle echoed through, had begun to depress us badly.

The defenders began to run short of ammunition and food, so I asked Chennault for supply by air. Someone in Kunming had invented wing tanks of bamboo and the P-40's began dropping them to us, packed with pork, rice, and bullets. On their first runs they released them too soon. Bamboo is bouncy, so

the tanks hit in our area, then bounded over the front and supplied the Japanese. With more practice the pilots were able to
make them hit both times in our territory, or else hit a Japanese area and bounce over the front to us.

By the last week of November, Liljestrand and I were per-
petually worried. No word of a Chinese counteroffensive came
in, and we felt like rats in a trap, waiting for the exterminators.
We tried to devise escapes but none was practical. We thought
of rigging up a vertical ladder on which one of us would stand
while a plane with a hook flew down and snatched it away. We
laughed ourselves out of that one. There wasn't a single helicopter in China in 1943.

One day General Yu told me the Japanese were experimenting with poison gas. His soldiers were successfully using the
simple gas masks devised at Ypres where gas was first tried —
urine-soaked rags fastened over nose and mouth. I reported
this to Chennault.

"Get proof of gas," he radioed back.

"What proof?" I queried.

"Smell it," he answered.

I just dropped the subject, and luckily he seemed to forget it
too. To my relief the Japanese used no more gas.

Though it seemed an academic question, I next asked Chennault for permission to leave. I got no reply. I think now that
he had such a romanticized idea of what Chinese troops could
do that he thought of Changteh in terms of a battle like Gettys-
burg, with great charges and counter-charges, hand-to-hand
fighting, and always the hope of victory against odds. I could
never have twisted enough disks to explain this inexorably closing hopeless trap.

General Yu had troubles too. One day I passed near his desk
while he was at his radio-telephone. He beckoned to me and
held out the earpiece.

"Just listen to this," he said.

Far away, amid the crackles and pops of worn-out equipment, I could hear a tiny high voice, apparently delivering a patriotic oration.

". . . Every last man . . . honored to die . . ." and so forth.

"Who was it?" I asked General Yu when he finished the call.

"Chiang Kai-shek, of course." He laughed wryly. "He's up there in Chungking, reminding us to die for China."

As we slid closer to disaster, Chiang called Yu more frequently, following his old habit of destroying his own subordinates' authority — in this case Hsueh Yueh of the 5th War Area — by getting directly in touch with their subordinates. According to General Yu, Chiang was even trying to bypass him, asking for details of the house-to-house fighting — hardly comprehensible to anyone not on the spot — and then giving Yu orders to relay to his subordinates.

By December 1 the end was clearly at hand. The Chinese perimeter was so small and every house and sheltered street inside it so clogged with soldiers, active or wounded, that the simplest logistics were becoming impossible. As our lines contracted, the 14th Air Force had found it harder to drop wing tanks, and supplies were short again. Liljestrand and I decided we might as well be killed escaping. Before dawn on the 2nd we destroyed our radio and went to the riverbank. A few Japanese on the opposite shore began sniping at us, provoking a fusillade from the Chinese on the city wall behind, so we returned to headquarters for another twenty-four hours.

There was less shooting that day, but great confusion and restlessness. I made a formal farewell to General Yu, forgotten the day before, and asked what he planned to do.

"We are staying to die for China," he said with an inscrutable smile. Changteh fell on December 4, and it was later reported that General Yu fought his way out with the last two hundred of his men. Then he was jailed by Chiang Kai-shek who had lost face by announcing Yu would perish with the city, and when it fell awarded his supposed widow a bonus of $200,000 — about U.S. $1,000.

Next morning we found the riverbank unaccountably deserted. In eerie silence we crept upstream for about a mile, keeping under the shelter of high banks, and there by some miracle discovered a small boat, a sampan, half hidden in dry grass. Suddenly in a panic, we heaved it into the water, poled it across with loud splashing, and plunged into hiding among trees on the south shore.

A ruddy sun came up in the frosty blue sky and we began walking south, with great caution at first. We wore U.S. Army uniforms and carried American rifles. Both of us were blond and blue-eyed, and Liljestrand was six feet tall. We could never pass as anything but what we were, so we dodged back and forth, avoiding big open spaces and trying always to keep within quick running distance of trees or underbrush. The autumn coloring had faded, but the country was still beautiful. Dark evergreens stood among the silvery leafless trees, and the pale brownish fields were laced with water shining in ponds and irrigation canals.

We walked through the morning without sight of any human. Big villages stood in groves every half-mile or so, but we went around them. We ate C-rations at noon and with full stomachs trudged on more carelessly, daring to whistle at times.

In midafternoon we climbed the steep side of a head-high dike and in horror discovered right below us more than a dozen Japanese soldiers lounging in a circle of sandbags, while food cooked over a campfire. A big black machine gun stood among them and other weapons were stacked at hand.

Together they and we all sent up a great screeching gasp of surprise and for a moment were transfixed in a motionless tableau. Then Liljestrand raised his rifle to take aim.

"Don't be a damn fool!" I shouted, wheeling him around and pushing him back down the dike. I jumped after him, and I was the fool then. He was wearing high boots but I had low shoes. As the edge of this ricefield happened to be muddy, I sank in and lost them immediately.

We ran for our lives, and in a few seconds some Japanese were on the dike firing after us with rifles. Luckily the others were so startled, or the big machine gun so heavy, they couldn't get it up on the dike until we were out of range.

When we paused to look back, we saw four or five Japanese starting after us. We ran again. This went on until dusk, more and more slowly as everyone tired. Our longer legs let us out-distance them easily, but they were dogged. We would think we had shaken them and sit down to catch our breath. In a minute or two we could see them again, tiny figures twinkling in the distance. So we got up and ran some more.

"They can't get away with this!" Liljestrand kept muttering. "We've got to stop and ambush them." I went on slogging prudently away in my stocking feet, and eventually he would follow. It wasn't until darkness was so thick we couldn't see to run that we felt safe. We found a clay threshing floor about a hundred yards from a village and partly sheltered by evergreen shrubs. We lay down on the bare clay and fell into deep sleep.

Through four more nights and five days we were in techni-cally occupied territory, though it was sketchily held. We began to meet farmers in the fields on the second day, and they said they had seen or heard little fighting. The Chinese soldiers simply went away and the Japanese came to stay in the villages.

These peasants whose own future was so uncertain couldn't have been more friendly to us. They brought us balls of cold gluey rice, and heavy wool socks and straw sandals for me, a great help since my feet were a painful mess. They advised us to hide during the day and walk at night, then hid us in a ruined outbuilding. At dusk a farmer came and guided us three or four miles, until another appeared and took us a simi-lar distance before turning us over to a third. This went on all night, and for the next three. Each morning we were shown a good hiding place, and fed cold rice during the day. Within a safe distance we usually could find a field of winter turnips which we would pull up and eat raw.

All our guides were simple peasants, their ages anywhere from ten or less to over seventy. As far as we could learn, their help wasn't the result of any government propaganda or Communist organization. The Japanese were here and hated; if we were their enemies, the farmers were our friends.

On the fifth morning our last guide pointed to a village on the horizon and said Chinese troops were there. We hastened across the fields and went in among the houses without seeing anything resembling a front. In the alleys many shivering soldiers were leaning against the walls on the sunny side. Nobody seemed surprised to see us, or interested. We found a little restaurant, pulled a table into the sun, and ordered a huge platter of *Huo Tsai Tai Mao* — a mound of bean sprouts, onions and greens crowned with a steaming blanket of scrambled eggs. It was the best meal of my life.

After some luxurious days of travel in wheelbarrows and the like, feasting and sleeping in village inns at night, we returned to Siangtan, the railhead. There we took passage on a coal-carrying junk north to Changsha to make the delayed protocol visit to General Hsueh Yueh. We found the general was elsewhere but we stayed a few days — the Christmas holidays, in fact — with my colleague, Lieutenant Birch. He was the John Birch whose name, long after his death, was appropriated by American rightists for their Society.

He had a little headquarters in the fields outside the massive city walls — Changsha had been a great city of nearly half a million until it was burned to "scorched earth" by the Chinese in 1938. Birch's place was a Western-style red brick building. apparently built before the war as a radio or telephone transmission station, but with roughly carpentered bunks and desks it made comfortable living and working quarters for Birch and his staff of two American GI's, three Chinese technicians, and three or four "Kung-yos" or "Working Friends," young coolie soldiers supplied by the Chinese Army to cook and do other menial tasks.

I remember Birch as a lean, hearty, enthusiastic young man of about twenty-five, an attractive character. He came from Macon, Georgia, and had started as a Baptist missionary near Hangchow, south of Shanghai. He was in Japanese territory through a couple of years of American neutrality, and saw or heard enough of atrocities to become implacably anti-Japanese. He moved into free territory before Pearl Harbor, and a few months later many of the Doolittle Tokyo raiders parachuted near his mission. He escorted them to Kunming, where Chennault recruited him into the Air Force.

It seemed to me that he was most conscientious and knowledgeable in his work. His headquarters was well-run, though with a sterner discipline than such a small outfit may have needed. It was the only non-drinking American outpost I ever visited in China. I never heard he had banned drink, but his men respected him and knew he didn't approve, so they either did their drinking in town or very much on the Q.T.

He had resigned from his mission when he entered the Air Force but every Sunday went out to preach to some village congregation. He seemed a paragon, and a likable one, except for times when we would be batting the breeze in a relaxed way and his passionate anti-Japanese feelings suddenly made everything tense. I certainly wanted this war won; but I regarded it as a man-made disaster and could remember individual Japanese I had liked. Birch thought it was God's war and our side was all good, the Japanese all bad. It was God's will for Americans to kill Japanese. I soon learned not to argue, just listen.

During most of the war Birch and I were stationed hundreds of miles apart, so I never knew him well. He was shot in confused circumstances in Communist territory on August 25,

1945, the first American killed in a clash with Communists after the Japanese surrender, and that was why his name was taken by the John Birch Society.

Later his mother wrote Chennault and asked if there weren't someone with whom she could correspond to learn more about her son's life in China. Chennault suggested me. In the course of our correspondence, Mrs. Birch sent me a copy of John's last letter to her, dated August 13, 1945, the day of the Japanese surrender and twelve days before his death. He was still violently anti-Japanese, all knotted up in rancors he had felt for years. Again, no mention of Communists. I have no way of knowing that he did not turn burningly anti-Communist in his last twelve days, but he was a frank and forthright man, and even if he did, I suspect he would now be disgusted with what has happened to his name.

In another letter Mrs. Birch mentioned that John had stopped remitting his army pay home to buy war bonds, and she wondered if he were investing money in China to help with mission work after the war. In earlier letters he had said he would like to establish some demonstration cattle farms, also mission-sponsored co-ops, an odd fact for the violently anti-Socialist Birchites to reconcile.

Birch apparently informed Chennault in Kunming of our safe arrival in Changsha, but not A-2 in Kweilin, the office out of which we were technically operating. When we reached Kweilin a few days later, we were a great surprise. Everyone thought we had been killed at Changteh. A certain air of embarrassment was noticeable, and we learned the Colonel in charge had put in for the Legion of Merit for himself, because Liljestrand and I were supposed to be casualties. After some backing and filling, quite Chinese in its indirection, our names were also put in for the decoration and eventually we received it.

CHAPTER X

Castles in the Air 1944

IN 1943 THE BATTLE OF CHANGTEH seemed more routine than crucial. Through previous years of stalemate and static fronts, the Japanese had launched many harvest-time campaigns to steal or destroy the crops, train new troops, perhaps take one or two limited strategic goals. Planned withdrawals followed.

Changteh apparently fitted the pattern. The Japanese occupied the town a few days then took the rice reserves and went back north. The Chinese fought them on the way out as they had on the way in, desperately when necessary, prudently when possible. The chronic shortage of arms, ammunition, and well-trained troops made any Chinese commander think twice before committing his men to all-out battle. If he couldn't get replacements, even a victory could be a setback for him.

The postwar publication of secret American and Japanese material has shown that the obscure Battle of Changteh, routine in itself, was a key to crucial events. It helped bring disaster to China and change America's basic plans for the Pacific War.

When the Burma campaign ended in 1942, American strategy for China had become the subject of violent dispute between groups centering around the rival generals, Stilwell and Chennault. Stilwell returned from Burma with plans to re-form and re-arm a Chinese force to take north Burma and open a land route from India. Then he wanted to recondition enough Chinese armies to start pushing the Japanese out of China. In Washington he was backed by General George C. Marshall, then Chief of Staff, Henry L. Stimson, then Secretary of War, and the China-experienced officers in the War Department.

Chennault maintained a small U.S. Air Force was all China needed. He accepted Chiang Kai-shek's optimistic claims for the strength of his ground forces. He was backed by the Generalissimo and Madame Chiang and, in Washington, T. V. Soong, plus such White House favorites as Harry Hopkins, Thomas Corcoran, and — after his repatriation — Joseph Alsop.

For months the controversy was academic, so few American supplies could be brought into China. In the autumn of 1942, the enmity between Stilwell and Chennault increased when Wendell Willkie visited China and Chennault gave him a letter to take directly to President Roosevelt, bypassing his superior, Stilwell. He wrote Roosevelt that with a force of 105 fighters, 30 medium bombers, and 12 heavy bombers, plus replacements, he could "accomplish the downfall of Japan within six months to a year." This claim was to be disproved in China within that year, and became absurd later when thousands of our planes from the Pacific began bombing Japan without accomplishing its downfall.

In the winter of 1942-43, it was enough to convince Chiang Kai-shek that the spring offensive Stilwell planned for North Burma was not needed. He became so reluctant to assign troops to it that the offensive had to be postponed a full year. This did not improve Stilwell-Chennault relations.

In April of 1943, the two generals were called to Washington to confer with Roosevelt during the so-called Trident Conference. From friends who were there I have heard that Stilwell's stiff military appearance and manner, and his rather school-teacherish attitude toward the Chinese, insisting on reforms in return for supplies, did not please the President. Chennault's Flying Tiger glamour, his warm admiration for his former employers, the Chiangs, and his assurance that great victory could be achieved easily, were more palatable. Chennault had already upped his requirements — 150 instead of 105 fighters, for example — but they were still small. The Generalissimo radioed promises that his armies could protect Chennault's bases.

The President decided on air power instead of army reform, over strong objections from Stilwell's supporters who warned that as soon as air attacks from bases in China hurt the Japanese, they would invade on the ground and capture them, just as they took the fields they thought had been used by the Doolittle raiders. Chennault replied that except when the Japanese advanced along a railway or navigable river they had never invaded more than a hundred miles at a time. Presumably the bases from which he intended to destroy Japan were safe.

Hump tonnage was the deciding factor. The President ruled that for a trial four months starting in July, the first 4,700 tons of cargo every month be given the 14th Air Force. The next 2,000 would be for all other American and Chinese uses — Stilwell's army training programs would get 500. Then the 14th would get another 300 and the remainder, if any, would be allocated each month. When the decision was made, monthly Hump tonnage was around 3,000. In July it neared 6,000 and four months later, the October total approached 9,000.

By the time the two generals returned to China in late May, the Japanese were midway in a harvest-time campaign along the Yangtze around Ichang, about a hundred miles northwest of Changteh. In the Gorges above Ichang they had an extra objective — some 20,000 tons of shipping from Hankow, stuck below the rapids. The invading force numbered about 60,000 Japanese, plus 10,000 puppets, and they were opposed by more than 100,000 Chinese plus the 14th and Chinese Air Forces. There was heavy fighting in spots, and much air activity, but by early June the Japanese had the ships and rice they wanted, and were pulling out. Planned withdrawals after seasonal raids were customarily hailed by Chungking as Chinese victories, and this one was called the greatest of the war.

Chennault must have been greatly stimulated by his visit to the heights of global strategy. Roosevelt had made much of him, and asked him to keep on reporting directly to the White House, outside regular channels. The aura of great power, in which wishes could so easily be taken as facts, could not but fascinate a forceful, subjective man like Chennault.

U.S. Army historians have quoted one of his early reports to Roosevelt in which he repeated the official Chinese version of the Ichang battle, calling it a great Japanese defeat in which the enemy lost a third of its force. Soon after writing Roosevelt, Chennault apparently received more realistic news of Ichang, for he wrote Harry Hopkins that it could not be considered a great Japanese defeat because the front was much the same as before the campaign. The two letters were carried to Washington together, but Chennault did not modify his letter to Roosevelt, saying he "did not want to add to the President's worries."

The battle of Changteh was the next big engagement, and years later I found some surprising things about it and myself in Chennault's autobiography, *Way of a Fighter*. I am sorry I didn't read the book before his death, because I would have had questions.

He claimed 15,000 Japanese casualties at Changteh, half by planes. I would have said one quarter of this figure might still have been an overestimate. On page 260 he said I filtered through the siege and escaped after a running fight with a Japa-

.l. This was complimentary but I was simply running
.fe. On page 264 he said: "Paul Frillmann, returning
.gteh with the Chinese armies, reported evidence of
.ighting in and around the city, with the Japanese aban-
doi.. g much equipment and many documents. Frillmann reported large quantities of Chinese and Japanese bodies strewn
through the charred ruins and rotting on the hillsides where
isolated Chinese units fought to the last man." The next two
sentences, not directly attributed to me, said: "By the end of
December the Japanese had been pushed back to their original
positions. It was evident to all concerned that only an all-out
Japanese offensive could dislodge the 14th Air Force from its
eastern bases."

I never returned to Changteh and did not write the report
quoted above. One of my colleagues in intelligence, Malcolm
Rosholt, did visit Changteh in late December and reported
great devastation. He had not been there during the battle,
however, and had no way of knowing how much had been destroyed by our own planes, how much by ground fighting.
His report may have been recast to supply the sentences quoted
above, then mistakenly attributed to me. Since these sentences
supported the dogma Chennault wanted to establish in the
face of much contradictory evidence, however, I have never
shaken the suspicion that while A-2 in Kweilin thought I was
dead in Changteh, a wishful report may somehow have acquired
my name.

According to U.S. Army historians who also used Japanese
sources captured after the war, Chennault and his staff's mis-
understanding of Changteh was a third and final reason why
they began overestimating their air support of Chinese troops.
The battles of Ichang and the Salween Gorge had been the
earlier two. Both had been interpreted as unqualified victories
by the 14th, while the Japanese regarded them as limited cam-

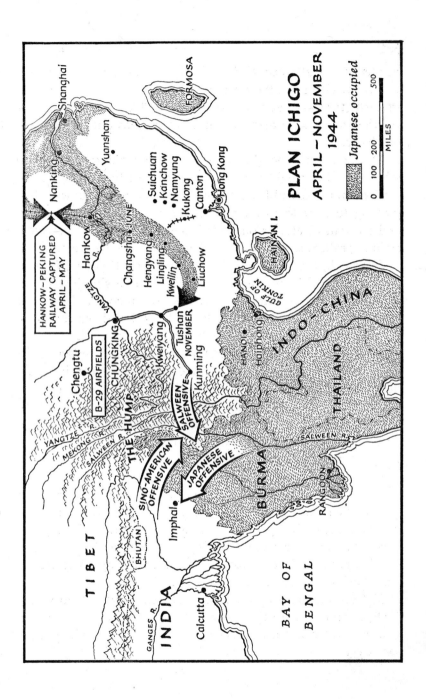

PLAN ICHIGO
APRIL – NOVEMBER
1944

Japanese occupied

0 100 200 500
MILES

paigns which attained their objectives. Chennault's ideas of imminent victory in the air were literally castles up there, but in early 1944 — after Changteh — his staff optimistically busied themselves with plans for larger operations out of the eastern bases.

At the same time the Japanese were making their own schemes. They might not have great respect for the 14th's effectiveness in ground battles, but the American planes were beginning to hurt them away from the battlefields. A summer and autumn of attacks on their Yangtze shipping had created serious problems. On Thanksgiving Day, just before the fall of Changteh, the 14th made its first attack on Formosa, from a new base at Suichuan, the farthest east of all. Flying just above the waves, the American planes arrived over the great Formosan base at Shinchiku without warning. They shot down six fighters and burned forty or more bombers on the ground.

With their own assessment of Chinese ground resistance at Changteh, Ichang, and the Salween, the Japanese immediately started planning the destruction of the 14th's eastern bases. The code name for this was ICHIGO, and the paperwork began before the Changteh campaign finished. The first orders for it were issued in January 1944, and the first troop movements began a month later.

In early January I returned to Kunming for re-assignment and learned I was going to the 3rd War Area, on the southeastern coast below Shanghai. This was on the far side of the provinces the Japanese were planning to attack, and despite the 14th's optimism I remember Chennault's telling me I might be cut off and should plan accordingly.

My job was to set up a net of intelligence outposts to watch Yangtze and coastal shipping, and locate other targets — troop concentrations and the like — if possible. Ku Chu-t'ung, a famously wealthy and conservative general, ruled the 3rd War

Area from a little farm village, Yuanshan or "Lead Mountain," where he had fled when the Japanese took the big coastal cities in his bailiwick. His armies had not staged an offensive in years and I was supposed to use the promise of air support to get renewed action.

As the U.S. Army expanded into out-of-the-way places, it seemed that the men to do a job always arrived months before their equipment, or vice versa. I could have taken a dozen American radiomen to Yuanshan, with only one radio for them to crowd around. Instead I managed to have one bright young Chinese, Corporal Yen from the Chinese Air Force Signal Corps, assigned to me. We were given a hundred-and-fifty-pound radio, again powered by a crank because it was not known if Yuanshan had electricity. We had a more modern disk-coding device, with another crank. This time we were to send most of our messages in Chinese, so we used a Chinese character number code, bought in a public bookstore.

Identical code-books were sold all over China, in enemy and free territory alike. They gave a different four-digit cipher for every one of about 15,000 Chinese ideographs. *"Wo"* (I) might be 2247, for example, while *"ni"* (you) was 3916. To make this public secret your own, you just added or subtracted a certain number of digits to or from all ciphers, in a combination prearranged with the receiver of your messages. For greater security you could change your combination every day. You might add 17 to all ciphers on Monday, for instance, subtract 313 on Tuesdays, add 278 on Wednesdays, and so on. The great number of ideographs made the code quite impossible to break.

Later, at General Ku's headquarters I found all departments used the same code, each with its own arrangement to make it secret. I was told that banks and private merchants used it, for the numbers could be sent through the public telegraph service. Smugglers and enemy agents undoubtedly used it, and

the Japanese themselves probably did. I liked to think of the
people all over China who wanted to send secrets and reached
for their own well-worn copies of the same popular book.

Corporal Yen and I flew to Kweilin, entrained for Hengyang,
and went down the Hankow-Canton Line to the southern railhead at Kukong. The trip on to Yuanshan was roughly a week
by public bus. It was seven or eight hundred miles as a plane
flew, but must have been more than fifteen hundred on the single narrow dirt highway which snaked up and down and
around the thousands of little green mountains and hills.

In Kunming I had been disagreeably surprised to find so
many Americans loose on the town with savage gripes and primitive prejudices; Sino-American relations had soured badly on
the everyday level. Yen spoke no English but obviously had
sensed the arrogance, and was sullen and shy on the plane and
trains. When we got into the rough-and-tumble of bus travel
and Chinese country life, he cheered up, and after a day or two
saw that I wanted to be a friend and equal.

In the near-tropical climate of southern China, February was
early spring, and under a pearly overcast the valley ricefields
glistened with water where men and women in shaggy brown
palm-fiber rain capes were setting out bright green seedlings.
Along the rivers tall bamboo waterwheels creaked as they
turned with the current, lifting bamboo canisters of water to
bamboo troughs spilling into irrigation ditches. Some farmers
raised the water to their fields with chains of buckets hitched
to a horizontal wheel turned by water buffalo. Others had their
wives laboring on contraptions like rickety bamboo bicycles,
raising smaller buckets. Over the uneven landscape of earth
and water big flocks of white ducks were herded by boys with
long bamboo wands. The birds pressed so close together,
whether waddling or swimming, that they moved forward like
undulating carpets of feathers.

Chinese New Year's was near, and many passengers were already celebrating, dressed-up or drunk or both. They were prosperous peasants or small-time merchants and money lenders, making holiday trips to collect or pay debts, visit relatives, make pilgrimages. As usual, conversation was general, and all day the careening bus rang with the shouts and laughter of new acquaintances who wanted to amuse one another — or outrage, antagonize, or mystify, whichever made for maximum human contact. In a country without radio, movies, or TV, the most had to be made of a trip.

Except in 1939 and the following years of Japanese terror bombings of provincial cities, war had not yet deeply affected these people, presumably safe among mountains. They seldom mentioned it, then tended to be cynical or humorous. I was kidded because my American uniform was better than a Chinese general's, yet I rode in a dirty bus with them, instead of a private car with a chauffeur. Several passengers had New Year's gifts in big bags of loose straw mesh. Cigarettes, liquor, sweets, and luxuries from enemy territory were conspicuous, but this was a joke too. "Guerrilla goods" they were called with laughter.

At least twice the bus crawled past a huge airfield being built for the 14th Air Force. Tens of thousands of farmers guarded by soldiers tottered along the road with carrying-poles or wheelbarrows overloaded with gravel. Their luckier compatriots in the bus would stare at them impassively, then turn to me with elusively mocking compliments on America's wealth and strength.

On the second night out of Kukong we reached Kanchow, the capital of a district ruled by Chiang Ching-kuo, elder son of Chiang Kai-shek and his deceased first wife. As we drove into the town at dusk, I could see it was unusually clean, with many whitewashed buildings. War monuments and triumphal arches decorated the main corners. An official messenger came to my hotel before I finished a bath, bringing an invitation from Chiang Ching-kuo for a party that evening at 10 P.M.

Remembering the stiff entertainments of his father and step-mother, I got into my dress uniform. The Chiangs' Western-style villa on the edge of town was imposingly official, but the moment I went inside I could see this party would be different. Young Chiang and his wife hastened to greet me warmly. He was a genial boyish-looking man in his late thirties, solidly built. She was an attractive Russian woman. Beyond them a dozen sophisticated-looking young Chinese couples chattered near a buffet covered with drinks and Russian piroshki. I later learned many wealthy Shanghai families had taken refuge in Kanchow. Dancing was strictly banned by the rules of the second Madame Chiang Kai-shek's "New Life Movement," but several couples were breaking her law around a record-player belting out "Deep in the Heart of Texas" or some such favorite. Quite a few U.S. Air Force officers were among them, for the 14th had recently occupied the Kanchow airfield and hostel originally built for Russians.

Chiang brought big whiskeys for both of us. Before they were empty, he whipped off his military tunic and T-shirt, showing well-muscled shoulders and torso. His father had sent him to study in Russia during the Nationalist-Communist coalition of the 1920's, and by his own will he stayed until 1937, working manually as well as studying and holding an office job in a factory.

Two servants came up with strong chairs. Chiang lay with the back of his head on one chair, his heels on the other, no support between. He patted his stomach and grinned.

"Sit there," he said, so I did.

"Now, stand on it," he said, and I warily got to my feet.

"Now, jump." I tried to make the smallest acceptable jump before getting back to the floor.

Indian wrestling between Chiang and the Americans followed. He won every match; his opponents evidently knew this had to be. Lively dancing and drinking went on until after midnight. For a while the Chiangs led a mad follow-the-leader chase, up on chairs then tables, on chairs again and under the tables. Later Mrs. Chiang danced with an American lieutenant who might better have been home in bed. Everyone stopped to watch as he led her into a dizzy twirl, faster and faster. Then he crashed down, helplessly snatched at her hand, and they ended sitting side by side on the floor, laughing at the applause.

Now in 1967 Chiang Ching-kuo is with his father on Formosa and is considered the heir apparent. He no longer mixes informally with foreigners and has become a man of some mystery, rather a sinister figure because of jobs with the secret police and the army's political commissars. Nobody knows how serious an effect his years in Russia still have on him, so the speculation on Formosa's future under him can be lurid. All I know is that in 1944 he was most hospitable and helpful to Americans. For months the airfield there was a main source of my supplies from Kunming, and whenever I came down from Yuanshan, a messenger would mysteriously appear with an invitation for a meal at the Chiangs'. Even when the Japanese were rapidly approaching Kanchow and young Chiang was trying to evacuate his government, he did what he could to help me salvage everything I needed.

For five or six days our bus traveled from Kanchow to Yuanshan through beautiful scenery. At the end of a hot dusty afternoon we got off at a tiny village whose name I have forgotten and were met by some soldiers with a dilapidated prewar Japanese staff car. We rattled up through pine-covered hills into a lush valley invisible from the main road, and parked in an empty lot with many footpaths spreading away through the farmland. Ahead was a big village, about five hundred houses with gray stucco walls and thatched roofs.

In the fields I was greeted by a six-foot, Mongol-looking general followed by many underlings. He introduced himself in fair English as General Wen, Ku Chu-t'ung's Chief of Staff. Almost in the next breath, he boasted that he was a graduate of the Command and Staff School in Leavenworth, Kansas. Rather brusquely he said General Ku was too busy to see me for two or three days, though the only bustle I could see around this headquarters were magpies squabbling in the dust. General Wen said he was busy too, but he would take me to the army guest house.

Accustomed to the turbulent commercial and family life of ordinary villages, I found the streets of Yuanshan quite spooky. The vividly blue-clothed and lively villagers had been driven away — where, I never learned — and soldiers in pale yellow cotton summer uniforms, like big thin bugs, occupied the houses. They seemed pleasant enough, but dimmed and sad compared to men living at home with their families. The painted shop fronts, the walls with bright advertisements, all the other signs of colorful civilian life, had been white or gray-washed, giving the house fronts a bleached, ghostly look.

The guest house was a hollow square of earth-floored barracks around a courtyard holding a great clump of bamboo. Yen and I were the only guests, and we had three primitive but adequate rooms. As we learned at our first meal that night, the food was going to be awful because this cook, too, was determined to make everything Western-style for me. About once a week in the months I later lived there, I implored him to cook me simple Chinese meals, but without success. I supposed his face depended on dreadful food, since he had been hired as a Western-style cook.

On the second day, General Wen invited me to ride in the afternoon, then have dinner with him and General Wang,

Ku's Chief of Intelligence. Wen rode a huge Australian stallion captured from the Japanese, but provided me with a hairy little Chinese pony so squat and swaybacked that I had to pull up my knees to keep my feet from dragging. As we rode he waved his arm with imperial gestures far above my head, and steadily patronized me in his loud rough voice. The Chinese had fought for seven years, he said, but Americans were ignorant novices at war. China had the oldest civilization known, while America had been a nation for little more than a century and a half. And so on and on.

Dinner was delicious Chinese home-cooking supervised by Mrs. Wen, a quiet, beaten-down woman, in an apparent farmhouse secreting a few comfortable upper-class rooms. Wang, the Chief of Intelligence, was a thin, sly-looking man whose politeness was so exaggerated it seemed sarcasm. With flourishing bows he gave me a roll of intelligence maps, unaware that I read Chinese. I saw that they were six to eight months out of date, and bowed deeply in return.

Next afternoon Wen took me to call on General Ku. We walked out of the village through vegetable gardens where soldiers in yellow shorts were cultivating cabbages and giant radishes for their mess. A cluster of big apparent farmhouses in a walled compound proved to be the headquarters — modern gray-washed offices with thatch-colored tile roofs. Ku's own residence had polished wooden floors and fresh white plaster walls, setting off some ugly, fancy, Western-style furniture, no doubt smuggled from Shanghai.

Ku was a dapper little man with a hairline mustache, who gave me an acute impression of deadliness. He had a wide smile of dingy teeth, flashed on and off with no other flicker of expression. As we went through the rituals, praising Sino-American friendship and expressing hopes for early victory, I couldn't help noticing his staring at me with a contemptuous lidded gaze as if to say, "You great big foreign idiot." I was relieved when his vivacious young wife came in with their twin four-year-old daughters, cute little bundles of lard in red knitted suits. Mrs. Ku was full of small talk, and soon swept me into another room to show me the twin pianos she had smuggled from Shanghai for her daughters.

I stayed in the 3rd War Area for more than a year, but was never sure about the games of Wen, Wang, and Ku — the Wolf, the Fox, and the Snake, as I found myself thinking of them. They were rumored to have a non-aggression pact with the nearest Japanese, and little appeared to disprove this. Yuanshan certainly seemed less of a command post than a hide-out where men were keeping out of the way — it was more than a hundred miles from any front. Later, when I began traveling afield, I found the fronts were usually silent and deserted, crossed by roads where a busy traffic in enemy goods was managed by officers of the 3rd War Area.

After the Japanese surrender, the rush for the rich coastal cities was to uncover a maze of intrigues between many Chinese and Japanese armies. A deal between Ku and the enemy then seemed more likely, and reasonable enough by his standards. In the middle years of the war he had had the Japanese on three sides, while Chungking and other sources of support were many days' travel away. A deal could have seemed the only way to survive. His later help to Americans like me would be part of the same picture. By the time I arrived in 1944, our advances in the Pacific made Japan's prospects poorer, and some collaboration with Americans might help further survival.

My first weeks in Yuanshan showed me that I would be tolerated and sometimes reluctantly aided, but was probably an embarrassment and annoyance. I wasted scores of hours in barren waiting rooms, followed by tea and smiling digressions, thus learning how slim my chances were for fresh, exact intelligence through formal channels — there was little news any-

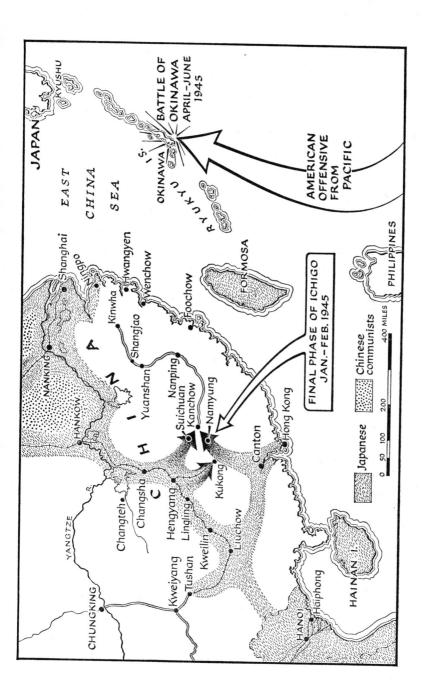

JAPAN

KYUSHU

EAST CHINA SEA

BATTLE OF OKINAWA APRIL–JUNE 1945

OKINAWA

RYUKYU IS.

AMERICAN OFFENSIVE FROM PACIFIC

Shanghai

Ningpo

Kinwha

Hwangyen

Shangjao

Wenchow

NANKING

CHINA

HANKOW

Yuanshan

Nanping

Kanchow

Suichuan

Namyung

Foochow

FORMOSA

PHILIPPINES

FINAL PHASE OF ICHIGO JAN.–FEB. 1945

Japanese

Chinese communists

0 50 100   200   400 MILES

Changteh

Changsha

Hengyang

Lingling

Kukong

Canton

Hong Kong

YANGTZE R.

CHUNGKING

Kweiyang

Tushan

Kweilin

Liuchow

HAINAN I.

HANOI

Haiphong

way, because the fronts were so inactive. I asked for radio operators to train as agents to send into enemy territory, and was
promised them, but they did not appear. Similar evasions
blocked other projects.

In April I insisted on going north toward the front, to find
a place for another outpost. Ku loaned me a truck, the guest-
house cook, half a dozen guards, and an intelligence officer
whose job seemed to be to keep me from learning too much. He
kept me away from the front on that trip, but in the remote
countryside the ills which were overtaking Nationalist China
could not be disguised, and I returned with disturbing impressions of decay. Inflation — and the hoarding of goods and raw
materials it encouraged — were bringing productive effort to a
standstill. The city people were utterly bored with their war
and were turning away from it, believing that America would
win for them and solve all their problems. Meanwhile the burden of the war was borne by peasants and soldiers of peasant
birth, and the latter often used the threat of their guns to
treat the former abominably, stealing food, clothing, bedding,
beating conscripted carriers like beasts of burden.

General Ku undoubtedly knew what I had seen on my trip.
To keep me busy inside Yuanshan, he soon produced a first
batch of radio operators.

At about this time, the 3rd War Area began to seem even
more of a backwater, for the Japanese launched Plan ICHIGO,
and a grim drama unfolded on the plains of central China.
From our radio we got only ragged reports and it was months
or years before I could fill in all the story. In a preliminary
campaign in late April and May, Japanese from North China
captured the remaining two-hundred-mile stretch of the Pe-
king-Hankow Railway. When I was a missionary in Hankow,
this line had been successfully defended in great battles with
tens of thousands of Japanese and Chinese casualties. In 1944

it was won in a light three-week thrust, costing the Japanese —
by their estimate — less than a thousand dead and little more
than two thousand wounded. I never saw numbers for Chinese
casualties, but they were probably not much higher, since most
commanders were reported to have withdrawn, perhaps to fight
again some other day.

An omen of the coming civil war lay in the news of skir-
mishes here between Chinese troops and armed peasant bands.
These counties had been through two years of drought and fam-
ine, and so much grain had been requisitioned by the government and armies that the farmers decided they were enemies.

In late May there was a lull while the Japanese improved
communications through their new conquests. The railway
track had been removed years before, but roads could be
quickly rebuilt in this dry flat country. At least 200,000 enemy
troops, and perhaps as many as 400,000, were now committed
to ICHIGO. In early June a large force advanced south from
Hankow toward Changsha, so rapidly that several provinces
panicked.

A Sino-American Infantry Training Center, part of Stilwell's
army reform program, was newly established in Kweilin, and
out of his own meager stocks its American commander sent a
chartered train with arms for General Hsueh Yueh and the defenders of Changsha. Anti-tank guns and rifles, machine guns
and Bren guns were freighted as far as Hengyang, but before
they could be put to use Changsha fell with little resistance, on
June 18. The Generalissimo's office in Kweilin complained
against the shipment of American arms directly to General
Hsueh, saying they might fall into the hands of "bandits."
This was taken to mean Chiang Kai-shek was no longer sure of
Hsueh's loyalty.

The Japanese pressed south of Changsha against spotty opposition, covering the hundred miles to Hengyang in less than two
weeks. They took the Hengyang airfield on June 26, then sur-

rounded the semi-walled city, which was held by about 10,000 troops as tough as Changteh's defenders. When they were surrounded, their commander, General Fang Hsien-chueh, rallied them into a dogged defense. The 14th began dropping supplies in bamboo belly tanks, plus parachutes, since this was a larger city than Changteh.

For a while the Japanese were slowed by supply problems. Summer floods stalled repairs to the roads and railway in the old "Roadless Area" south of Hankow. Intensive 14th Air Force attacks prevented daytime use of the newly-captured roads and waterways closer to the front. The attack on Hengyang came to a standstill on July 2, and on July 7 an imminent Japanese withdrawal was celebrated in Kweilin and other threatened cities. By the 11th the enemy had enough supplies to attack again. Reinforcements brought their number near 40,000.

At least 1,000,000 Chinese troops garrisoned the provinces threatened by ICHIGO, and an array of armies collected in a half-circle around the Japanese encircling Hengyang. Their efforts to relieve the beseiged city seemed to give prudence the edge over desperation, however, and the bloodiest counterattack came no closer than five miles. The Generalissimo was reported again at his telephone in Chungking, bypassing Hsueh Yueh, sending conflicting orders to his subordinates.

The troops inside Hengyang resisted tenaciously, and the 14th's planes nobly tried to substitute for ground reinforcements, strafing and bombing so constantly that the Japanese were confined to their trenches by daylight. After only a week, though, pilot fatigue and a fuel shortage grounded the 14th for two weeks; the problem of the Hump was beginning to ease, but transport to the eastern bases had been neglected. By the time the planes rejoined the battle, the defense inside the city had crumbled too far to be saved. Hengyang fell on August 8.

Classified material published since the war has described Chennault's alarm at the first successes of ICHIGO. In May he began radioing Roosevelt, Marshall, and Stilwell, telling them what the latter two men had told him a year earlier — that without massive help the Chinese could not prevent the enemy from taking anything they wanted. Because the Japanese were believed to have about 200 planes in North China, Chennault still thought the main attack would be in the air and must be repelled there. His Hump tonnage had risen to 6,700 a month, and he promised that with 10,000 he would stop the attack.

In early spring, the 20th Air Force of B-29 strategic bombers, then our largest and farthest-ranging planes, had begun moving into China. They were to bomb Japan itself from gigantic new airstrips handmade by hundreds of thousands of peasants near Chengtu, northwest of Chungking. Chennault asked permission to use the B-29's for tactical missions against Hankow and its supply lines. He wanted control of the gas and other supplies stockpiled for the B-29's in Chengtu.

Perhaps at Chennault's behest, Chiang Kai-shek radioed Roosevelt asking that the 14th be given the B-29 supplies, and that further Hump flights of arms and ammunition for Stilwell's ground forces be suspended. He called Stilwell in and told him this was his wish. After bargaining, Stilwell agreed to raise Chennault's Hump tonnage to 8,500 and give him 1,500 of the monthly supplies for the B-29's. This would provide the 10,000 a month with which Chennault said he could stop the Japanese. Stilwell refused to hand over the B-29 supplies stockpiled in Chengtu, or have the great strategic bombers diverted to tactical use in China. Both decisions were later confirmed in Washington.

Even without the B-29's, when Hengyang was attacked Chennault had about 340 fighters, 80 medium bombers, and 40 heavy bombers, a force at least three times bigger than the one which was to "accomplish the downfall of Japan." Beset by his other

problems and duties — defense of the B-29 bases, support of
Chinese troops on the Burma border — he could not prevent
the capture of one medium-sized Chinese city. It seemed tragic
that the same traits which had led him to heroic success only
two years earlier — aggressiveness, willfulness, the refusal to
admit anything he wanted was impossible — should reduce him
so close to failure in this more complex time.

In Yuanshan that summer, hearing the thundery echo of
great battles far away, I felt like a toy soldier. Though nobody
thought to inform me until weeks afterward, 14th Air Force
Intelligence had been taken over by OSS — Office of Strategic
Services, the spy outfit — and I had become a captain. My army
was the half-dozen very young radio operators first assigned me
by General Ku.

They were adept at the four-digit code, and I had received
some radios which could be hidden in small suitcases. My problem was to train them to be specific, not easy in a country where
a certain vagueness was customary. I had some flash cards from
Kunming identifying enemy plane and boat silhouettes. Using
arrangements of pebbles or nuts, I tried to teach rapid estima-
tion of numbers. I received some English-language material
from OSS which I translated for a course on security, escape
methods, and other spy crafts. We had daily memory drills until I was reasonably sure each man knew by heart his times of
day to call in, his position signals, and daily combinations of
numbers to alter the four-digit code.

One point I tried to hammer home every day was that in
calling in they must never, ever, stay on the air more than two
minutes. We knew the Japanese in Shanghai had direction-
finders mounted on trucks, and even one extra minute might be
fatal. They were supposed to change hotels every day or two,
in case the Japanese were beginning to get a fix on them.

As I recall, I sent about thirty agents into Shanghai in the
following year, training them in batches of five or six. Some

disappeared without ever calling in, and I never knew whether they were caught by the Japanese, or just sold their radios and returned to civilian life. They were not supposed to meet one another in enemy territory, and were on their own when they left Yuanshan in their new civilian clothes with pockets full of OSS cash. A few almost certainly were caught because they stayed on the air longer than two minutes. Corporal Yen would repeatedly order them off, then in impotent rage begin cursing in the four digits — 7543, 7543, 7543, "Pig! Pig! Pig!" At last the weak little signal from Shanghai would abruptly cut off.

Even the best agents, who reported in regularly for several weeks, tended to exaggerate. More than once I had news of a hundred or more planes on the Shanghai airfield, thirty warships along the docks. When I alerted Kunming and a reconnaissance plane was sent, only a fraction of the number could be found. But if only sixteen, say, of an imaginary hundred planes could be found and five later destroyed, it was a small victory.

For nearly a month after the fall of Hengyang, the Japanese were quiet, waiting for more supplies to trickle down the routes which the 14th's planes were again making quite unusable by daylight. Then they attacked to the southwest, down the railway toward the airfield cities of Lingling and Kweilin. A new Japanese force from Canton attacked northwest, up the West River, evidently planning to join forces at Liuchow, another airfield town.

Nowhere did they meet such stiff resistance as at Hengyang, for a new factor was corrupting the Chinese will to fight. Rumors told that certain War Area Commanders, local generals, and provincial governors, convinced that Japanese advances would cut them off from Chungking, were discussing a separatist movement to break with Chiang and form a coalition government in the south, possibly to include Communists.

The leader was Marshall Li Chi-shen in Kweilin. As he had

no troops he was technically powerless, but he was a figure of great influence and many connections. He had been the Generalissimo's Chief of Staff in the early years of the Nationalists' coalition government, and in 1944 was President of the Military Advisory Council in Chungking.

Later he became one of three claimedly non-Communist Vice Chairmen of the Communist government. Japanese generals interviewed after the war have said he was in touch with them in 1944, negotiating for their neutrality toward his separatists. It can be argued that Li was always a villain and his movement treachery. But anyone who knew provincial China in 1944 could see the growth of genuine popular feeling against Chiang's monopoly of power. Through the American Consulate in Kweilin, Li's supporters informed the American government of their plans one day after the fall of Hengyang. While discreetly withholding encouragement, the American officials did not ask not to be told more. Even the State Department could see a breaking point might be near.

The prospect of separatism had immediate military results. The regional commanders whom the Japanese pressed against after Hengyang became more prudent than ever. Sacrifices for Chiang — of their best troops or equipment — did not appeal when they might add their strength to a coalition where their own voices could be heard. More than a dozen U.S. Army ground liaison teams had been placed with the defending armies and their reports suggested this atmosphere might have made Stilwell's army reforms no more of a cure-all than Chennault's air war. Commanders who had received American arms from Kweilin were sending only token quantities to the front, keeping the rest safely in the rear. Chiang himself was doing much the same on a more massive scale. Throughout the campaign, his very best Nationalist armies, his own personal troops, were kept in the safety of the western mountains.

With no more pockets of resistance to concentrate around,

the Japanese flowed over the countryside in one of their classic guerrilla invasions, so hard to attack from the air. In August Chennault was dismayed enough to backtrack on earlier claims of air invincibility, and ask that 1,000 tons of monthly Hump tonnage be taken from the 14th and be put into arms for the ground defenders of the airfields. Though his request showed he knew Hsueh Yueh was implicated with the separatists, he suggested him as the chief recipient. John Birch used to extol Hsueh Yueh to me as a general eager to kill Japanese, and I believe his reports may have caused Chennault to single out Hsueh.

Stilwell disapproved Chennault's request, thinking the plan too little and too late, and the arms now more useful elsewhere. The Generalissimo also refused permission. Apparently no longer trusting any of his own generals in South China, he wanted all Hump tonnage channeled to his loyal American Air Force.

Lingling fell in early September. In another week the enemy came within thirty miles of Kweilin, then stopped for six weeks while they built up communications back to Hengyang. Kweilin fell in early November, Liuchow soon after. In the next three weeks small enemy units, mainly cavalry, raced up the refugee-clogged road toward Chungking, and the capital was thrown into a panic. Ground resistance had evaporated, and the 14th could not effectively attack the units threading among thousands of refugees. Some Chinese troops had become so demoralized they were looting villages. The Japanese seemed only to be exploiting an unexpected opportunity, however. The advance units wore summer uniforms and when bitter winter struck them in the mountains they turned back at a small town called Tushan, nearly a thousand miles from the start of their invasion in April.

CHAPTER XI

The "Roosevelt Incident" 1944

THE THREE BIG AIRFIELDS south of Yuanshan — at Kan-chow, Suichuan, and Namyung — remained in American hands through 1944, and in the summer and fall my operation rapidly swelled with newcomers flown in from Kunming. A dozen enlisted men with radios and a big generator came to set up a radio station. Several OSS officers from the Navy, Army, or Air Force, each with his own group of enlisted men, arrived and went on into the field to work more or less on his own — I never did know what some were doing. A bottleneck had evidently unclogged, because I kept getting queries from Head-quarters, asking how many more men I needed, with what rank and what equipment. The simple days when Corporal Yen and I just minded our business in the guest house began to seem like the good old ones.

When I heard of the pending arrivals I asked General Ku to help me rent a headquarters, and after some delay he assigned me a beautiful little Buddhist temple outside the village — re-cently emptied, it seemed, though I never knew what became of the priests. It was built of weathered wood with a heavy roof of russet tiles, and stood on a slope beside a large mountain stream of clean water coiling and splashing among moss-cov-

ered boulders. Pines and tufts of bamboo shaded it. Ku Chu-
t'ung let me hire some soldiers who had been carpenters and
masons, and I was able to get them to work before I took the
bus to Kanchow to meet the first batch of communications men.
I couldn't help feeling sorry for the newcomers when I found
them at the airfield. They were not much younger than the
AVG men had been, but most of them seemed so. The 14th
had agreed to release an old truck to me and the men were
huddled in it as if it were a fort. There were no Japanese soldiers within hundreds of miles but they had flown over the
front that morning, thus were technically behind enemy lines.
They kept glancing about as if expecting Banzai attackers with
beheading swords.

I am afraid the first day of travel convinced them China was
unfit for American habitation. Rain turned the steep zigzag
road into slippery mud, and the truck broke down. I hailed a
Chinese army truck and bribed the driver to dump his illegal
passengers and illegally tow us. He was in a hurry and went
around the hairpin turns without pause, making the long tow-
line whip through the bushes inside the turn. Going downhill
it was hard to keep him from towing us right off the road. Ferocious howls and offers to shoot the bastard came from my
passengers.

Repairs forced us to spend the first night in a village inn instead of a town hotel. I ordered a supper of scrambled eggs,
telling the men that newly-opened eggs had to be sanitary, but
the light from a kerosene lamp was so dim they couldn't be
sure the plates weren't dirty, and most ate only a few mouth-
fuls. A commotion broke out at dawn when a man with a horror of rats woke up to find eight in his room, and tried to shoot
them with his carbine. After several days of this, we reached
Yuanshan at night and in pouring rain. I found the carpenters
and masons must have quit the day after I left, for nothing was
finished.

I will say that when the men reached a place where they had work, their griping dropped by half and they efficiently got the radio station going. The housekeeping necessary to make them comfortable in a roughly American style was most tedious, however, especially since I preferred to live in Chinese style myself. I got the carpenters back and in the main temple room where we put the radios I had them build clean new wooden walls to seal off the crumbling old clay idols. They put bunks into one side building, and built a big round table and some sturdy chairs for the dining- and common-room across the courtyard. I had an open fireplace built here, but it always smoked and stank. Ku declined to make any long-term loan of the guest-house cook — I think his Western-style food, however bad, was part of the general's face as well as the cook's — but eventually I found a former servant of a mission who could prepare pass-able if tasteless Western meals. For a while I tried a cook who could fix superlative Chinese food, family style, but the men voted overwhelmingly against him.

I still pride myself on the Sino-American friendliness which developed in that little headquarters. The American radiomen had professional respect for Corporal Yen and were awed by the young Chinese nonchalantly training to be spies in Shang-hai. Many evenings, groups of Chinese and Americans would sit together, trying to teach one another their languages or lis-tening to the entertainment our powerful radios picked up — old jazz from Shanghai, blandishments by Tokyo Rose, GI broadcasts from the Pacific. We laid out a volleyball court on the flat space in front of the temple and had games several afternoons a week — mixed teams, otherwise the agile Chinese would win too often. Among the odder supplies sent by OSS were inflatable Navy survival rafts of bright yellow rubber, and in hot weather it was great sport for everyone to hike up-hill along the stream, then shoot back through the rapids.

*

I have no idea how many Americans were tangled in China's war by 1944, but it must have been tens of thousands. Starting with tiny groups like mine, scattered in the eastern provinces, the concentrations grew bigger and thicker farther west. Thousands of Americans manned the surviving airbases in the west, and smaller groups were spotted all over the countryside, repairing roads, buying supplies, training troops, holding liaison jobs, or manning field hospitals in the Chinese armies; these were thickest along the Burma border where the American-supported Salween campaign was expected.

More thousands of men kept the Hump airline running. A few American combat troops were in Burma, fighting toward China, and a multitude of support troops worked in the jungles, building the new road from India. Other Americans were on railways, waterways, and airfields in India, the sole purpose of their jobs being to support China.

Few of us had the foggiest idea what was happening on high policy levels in 1944, but later years have revealed that as the debacle of the eastern bases reached its climax, strategic decisions affecting all our futures were made. In early 1944, for example, sizable American landings for the southeastern coast of China had been planned. Every man in our group at Yuan-shan would probably have been dead or imprisoned by 1945, since the threatened Japanese could hardly have allowed us to survive behind their lines. As I learned the details of what had happened, it seemed like the world of Greek myth, where the fate of lowly mortals was decided by the soap operas played on Olympus.

The stage for 1944 was set at the Sextant Conference between America, Britain, and China, held in Cairo in November 1943. The Chinese cast for the conference was drastically altered on its eve, by intrigues inside Chiang Kai-shek's family. T. V. Soong, formerly a supporter of Stilwell's, had tried to persuade his brother-in-law Chiang to remove Stilwell, evidently in the hope of getting a freer hand for his friend Chennault, and obtaining for himself control of the enormously valuable Lend-Lease aid, then administered by Stilwell.

For reasons unknown outside the family, perhaps just because they thought their little brother was getting too big for his britches, his sisters Mei-ling (Madame Chiang) and Ai-ling (Madame H. H. Kung) — May and Ella, as Stilwell's knack for nicknames dubbed them — joined forces against T.V. By the time of the conference, the two strong-willed women had won the Generalissimo over, at least partly, making him temporarily less committed to Chennault, more open-minded about Stilwell. Instead of taking T.V. to Cairo, Chiang ordered him to stay in his Chungking house and play sick, a form of arrest or exile which was to hobble this ambitious man for nearly a year.

Because of excessive security, Roosevelt and Churchill were not warned of the Chiangs' arrival at Cairo, and their absence at the airfield was a resented blow to Chinese pride. The next few days must have mollified the Chiangs, however. Roosevelt still seemed determined that China would end the war as one of the Four Great Powers, and in meetings the Chinese were treated most deferentially — not always easy. With T. V. Soong left behind, Chiang was aided mainly by "household generals" — courtiers, really — and important military questions had to be answered by Stilwell and his staff.

While the top echelon continued to treat China as a great power, the lower echelon of American planners who were doing the spadework had taken full notice of Chinese inaction on the Salween throughout 1943. They were also impressed by the growing speed of our aircraft-carrier and amphibious-assault advances in the Pacific. They began to abandon earlier ideas of a great American land campaign in China — something on the scale of Europe. Major aid to China was still in the books, however, and re-arming of sixty, even ninety, Chinese divisions was contemplated. The commitment of at least a dozen American divisions to southeastern China was suggested, as soon as the U.S. Navy could take the ports of Canton and Hong Kong.

Re-opening a land route came first, and a three-pronged attack on Burma was set for the spring of 1944. The Sino-American force from India and the American-aided Chinese armies on the Salween were to make a pincer attack on North Burma, while an Anglo-American amphibious force landed in the south and took Rangoon. Chiang blew hot and cold on these plans so capriciously, alternating every few days, that he may here have ended Roosevelt's notion of him as a great leader of a Great Power. Madame Chiang, a shrewd aggressive woman, consistently blew hot, and when they left for Chungking Chiang was agreeing with her.

Then Roosevelt and Churchill flew to Teheran, Iran, where they met Stalin. He said he would go to war with Japan when Germany was defeated. He wanted a cross-channel invasion of France and landings in southern France as soon as possible. He had first promised action against Japan months earlier, but Churchill — never enthusiastic about a campaign which would put the Chinese into the former British colony of Burma — persuaded Roosevelt this was an important change in Russian policy, and the amphibious attack on Burma must be shelved to provide more landing craft for the invasion of France.

When Roosevelt and Churchill returned to Cairo for final meetings, a radio message was sent to Chiang Kai-shek telling him the amphibious assault on Rangoon was off, but his allies still hoped he would advance across the Salween. Chiang, whose youth had been spent as a broker and trader in the hard exchanges of Shanghai's business world, replied that China would probably drop out of the war unless the number of planes already allocated the 14th and Chinese Air Forces be doubled, Hump tonnage be increased to 20,000 tons a month, and he be given one billion dollars in gold.

*

The posthumous book *The Stilwell Papers* has shown that at Cairo Stilwell feared the President was continuing a dangerous complaisance toward Chiang. Less than a year earlier Roosevelt had in effect reprimanded Stilwell, Marshall, and the War Department for attempts to bargain with Chiang. A Presidential letter in February 1943 had stated that Chiang came up the hard way, was undisputed leader of 400,000,000 Chinese, and in a short time had created a national unity which took America two centuries to achieve. One could not speak sternly to him, or exact commitments from him as might be done with someone like the Sultan of Morocco. This had been the background of Roosevelt's 1943 decision to approve Chennault's air offensive, already endorsed by Chiang. In his private meetings with the President at Cairo, Stilwell found little reason to hope for any change. Almost immediately after Cairo, however, especially when Chiang so nakedly displayed his own wish to bargain, Roosevelt showed he had listened to Stilwell. His later dealings with the Generalissimo became increasingly hard-headed.

In the early months of 1944, Stilwell's small Sino-American offensive from India into Burma began to show that Chinese troops could take the offensive. The alarmed Japanese in Burma made a counter-offensive into India, repelled by the British after heavy fighting. Meanwhile, quiet ruled the Salween front where some 11,000 Japanese with 36 cannon faced 72,000 Chinese with 244 new American howitzers, tons of other American supplies, plus American advisers and technicians.

Roosevelt began sending stern notes to Chiang, calling for action on the Salween. Despite the postponement of the amphibious assault on Rangoon, he felt the great amount of Lend-Lease aid already received by China obligated some return. He warned that Lend-Lease would have to stop unless it was used.

Chiang finally ordered his troops to cross the Salween in mid-April, a few days before the Japanese began their invasion against the 14th's eastern bases, and about a month before the monsoon rains must slow or stop operations in Burma. The American advisers on the Salween wanted the Chinese to exploit the enemy's thin dispersal by flowing around the strong points and pressing on as the Japanese themselves would have done. The Chinese cautiously preferred to besiege and destroy the strong points one by one. Chiang was at his long distance phone again, issuing orders which confused and paralyzed his subordinates. The Chinese advance on Burma slowed to a tortoise crawl, while the Japanese in eastern China were racing like hares to Hengyang.

Roosevelt's dissatisfaction with Chiang increased that spring because of the bargaining over money. Chiang's initial demand for a billion dollars gold was poorly received and left unanswered, since it seemed to put a demeaning price-tag on China's part in a war for its own survival. Chiang next suggested the Chinese would stop building bases for the 14th Air Force, or providing supplies, unless America built the Chengtu bases for the B-29's at our own expense, and at the official exchange rate of twenty Chinese dollars to one U.S. dollar. The black market rate, roughly equal to real values, had already spiraled up past 250 to 1 and was climbing with increasing speed. This meant America would have to pay at least $12 to the Chinese government to get $1 of construction value at Chengtu; the other $11 would be squeeze. The B-29 fields would cost hundreds of millions of U.S. dollars, and if we stuck to the official exchange rate as requested, while the uncontrolled inflation rocketed higher, we could end up paying billions of U.S. dollars just to meet the housekeeping expenses of a tiny American force in China.

Roosevelt toughly replied that the United States could not afford to spend more than U.S. $25,000,000 a month on China, and any projects which could not be included in this budget would have to be cut. The practical-minded Dr. H. H. Kung, Chiang's other brother-in-law and then Minister of Finance, agreed, apparently on his own authority, to advance the U.S. Army fifteen billion Chinese dollars — roughly U.S. $60,000,-000 on the black market — for three months' expenses, with five hundred million Chinese dollars to go to the B-29 fields.

The hitch here was that the Chinese currency, handsomely manufactured in America, was in India and had to be flown over the Hump, taking up military cargo space. Even with bills of the highest denominations, a ton of Chinese currency was worth only one hundred million dollars, and with lesser bills could be as low as seven million. It was not long before the American government and U.S. Army accepted the inevitable and began to fly much less bulky U.S. currency over the Hump, selling it on the black market.

By late June, when the Japanese reached Hengyang, Roosevelt and other top men in Washington were having most serious second thoughts about China. General Marshall was convinced Chennault's air offensive and the great supply effort behind it were a waste, doing little for China and slowing the war in Europe. Allied advances north of Rome and General Patton's push across France were both curtailed because so many pilots and transports were flying the Hump, to support a relatively small and failing defensive action.

Alarmed by the Chinese performance on both the Salween and eastern fronts, the Joint Chiefs of Staff in early July made the drastic proposal that Stilwell be made Field Commander of all Chinese and American forces in China, not just the Generalissimo's figurehead Chief of Staff. To keep some face for Chiang, Stilwell would be made a four-star general. Roosevelt agreed, and on July 6 radioed the request to the Generalissimo. Chiang acceded "in principle," then began hedging. There the matter rested all summer, while China teetered on the brink of dissolution.

Chiang's spokesmen later claimed the summer's negotiations failed because Stilwell wanted to have the Chinese Communist troops under his command, along with Chiang's elite National-ist troops from the anti-Communist blockade. Coalition was in-deed an aim of Roosevelt and the Joint Chiefs of Staff, since it had been a success in Yugoslavia, but the Chinese Communists were always a side issue. Discussions about them had barely started before all talks collapsed. The central issue seemed to be that Chiang's national power was squarely based on his ar-mies, and there it was preserved by a precarious balance of loyal-ties and rivalries he had created through two decades in power. If an outsider like Stilwell should start shifting generals and armies about, with no thought but the best combinations against the Japanese, Chiang could be out of a job.

In mid-September, Stilwell informed Washington of an ulti-matum from Chiang. The Sino-American force from India had invaded about two-thirds of the way across Burma and was exhausted. Chiang's trans-Salween forces were under Japanese counterattack, and he wanted the Sino-American force to ad-vance another hundred miles in a week and attack the Japanese from the rear. Otherwise he would pull his American-supplied troops back across the Salween. In other words he expected the blockade of China to be broken with minimum help from him.

Roosevelt was provoked into writing a harsh note to Chiang, received in Chungking September 19. The President pointed out that the other Allies were winning victories all over the world, and if Chiang invited his defeat by insufficient action on the Salween, it would be his own responsibility. He must act.

As far back as April, U.S. Army headquarters in Chungking had reason to think stiff notes from the President either disap-peared in Chiang's household or were so softened in translation that Chiang thought they were polite greetings. Roosevelt therefore ordered that all his messages be delivered to Chiang by a ranking American officer, but Stilwell was usually in Burma and the men in Chungking apparently could not resist the dim-pling Madame Chiang — the chief interceptor — when she daintily but firmly pulled a state paper out of their hands. Madame had shown she wanted action in Burma, but may have feared her husband's reaction to Roosevelt's stiffening attitude.

Stilwell happened to be in Chungking when the September 19 message arrived. He could have had it delivered by Patrick Hurley, the new Special Emissary from Washington, but he decided to follow presidential orders to the letter and pass it right from his own hand to Chiang's. He had a Chinese translation made and drove to Chiang's residence. After years of frustration it was a natural decision, but it proved to be his fatal error.

Chiang was conferring with several Chinese dignitaries and Hurley. Stilwell asked Chiang for permission to speak to Hurley on the veranda, and showed him the message. Hurley recognized it as an ultimatum, and suggested that he paraphrase it, making it less direct. Stilwell said he felt under orders to deliver it in full, so they went back into the conference room where Stilwell announced he had a message from the President to the Generalissimo, and prepared to read it. Hurley quickly took the note and handed it to Chiang, who read the translation silently.

"I understand," he said mildly, and ended the conference.

Word soon seeped out that as soon as Stilwell left, Chiang flew into a spitting fury and raged for days. Quite possibly he had never before heard a word from Roosevelt which suggested the President was anything but his doting friend. He called in T. V. Soong — back in favor by now — and said the insult canceled any promise to give Stilwell command. He felt Stilwell's delivery of the message showed this American already regarded him as a subordinate. Soong, or someone else anxious to see him feel he was getting face back, suggested that Stilwell concocted the message himself, then made it look as if it came from the President.

Negotiations on command were deadlocked for two weeks, then on October 1 Soong had a radio from H. H. Kung in Washington. He reported that at a dinner party Harry Hopkins told him that if Chiang insisted on Stilwell's recall, Roosevelt would simply withdraw pressure and appoint another American general for China. Hopkins later denied he said this, but it was believed in Chungking. Next day Chiang told the Central Executive Committee of his Kuomintang Party that Stilwell would have to go. He would accept any other American general as commander, he said.

After half a month of diplomatic chess Roosevelt recalled Stilwell on October 18, and the China-Burma-India Theater was split. American forces in India and Burma were put under General Daniel Sultan, while General Albert Wedemeyer was sent to Chungking as Chiang's new Chief of Staff. Chiang offered to make him Commander, too, but Roosevelt and his advisers now cagily declined. They had decided China was in such a precarious state that Chiang would take an American Commander only to get a scapegoat for future defeats.

These events have come to be known as the "Stilwell Incident," but they might better be called the "Roosevelt Incident." Stilwell was the man in the middle, and his crankiness, his tactlessness, his widely-quoted derisive nicknames — Chiang was "Peanut" — poured no oil on waves. The "Incident" nevertheless marked Chiang's collision with America's highest policymaker.

In the following weeks, China was drastically demoted in American plans. The 14th Air Force was still to be built up, but the B-29's would be moved to fields on the Pacific islands. There would still be landings in southern China, but minor ones, aiming to open supply routes for the 14th rather than start an American ground offensive. The Burma campaign would be finished and the road from India opened, but again mainly for supply of the 14th. The retraining and re-arming of

Chinese troops would continue, but pressure for reforms in the higher echelons was relaxed. Face would be maintained, but China as a major ally was written off.

In early winter the active war briefly moved closer to Yuanshan. Chennault brought a task force into Suichuan and the two other airfields south of us, and began attacking Hankow, Nanking, Hong Kong, the Yangtze, and the enemy railways. While his more convenient fields were lost, his planes and supplies had increased so much he could use these more distant ones to nearly the same effect. He had about 500 fighters, 100 medium bombers, 50 heavy bombers, and was getting nearly 10,000 monthly Hump tonnage of gas and oil alone. Until the B-29's left for the Pacific, he had permission to use them on some missions. With ground fighting at a standstill, he no longer had to divert planes to the support of Chinese armies. The Japanese had sent so many planes to the Pacific, they had only an estimated 50 fighters and 35 bombers to oppose him over the mainland.

His biggest raid was on December 18, when 77 B-29's and 200 fighters and bombers of the 14th attacked Hankow, leaving what was hoped to be great damage under a pall of smoke and dust. Along with the lesser raids, this provoked the Japanese into repeating what they did with the other bases which had hurt them. In January, after the winter overcast settled in and air support of the ground defense was rarely possible, they launched two rapid invasions, one toward Suichuan and the other down the last stretch of the Hankow-Canton railway.

General Hsueh Yueh was again in charge of the defense, and Chiang Kai-shek's ban on arms for him was still in effect. Intercession by Chennault and Wedemeyer finally persuaded Hsueh to promise enough allegiance to Chiang to get arms, but none were made available until late February, when the campaign was over. The Suichuan, Namyung, and Kanchow airfields were by then in enemy hands, so was the railway. The Japanese had raiding parties speed ahead of the main force and capture the railway bridges and tunnels before the Chinese could destroy them, so the trains were soon running again.

One airfield, at Changting in the coastal province of Fukien, was so small and remote the Japanese never tried to take it. We Americans in the southeast were never completely cut off, but as the three big bases were captured we felt our last reliable sources of supply were being destroyed. We didn't know if our isolation would last for months or years. As the Japanese approached each base and the U.S. Army engineers began blowing it up, teams from the backwoods — Navy, Army, OWI, as well as OSS — would flock in from the other direction like vultures, hoping to fill our trucks and jeeps with salvage before everything was destroyed.

These bases at the farthest end of all supply lines might be short of everything, but from anyone coming from a medieval village like Yuanshan they had the fascination of great abandoned department stores with their goods free for the taking. It was the Rangoon docks all over again. More fuel, generators, and radios were what my group officially needed, but we coveted more vehicles, typewriters, clothes and shoes, bedding, canned food and cooking equipment, books, liquor, an endless list.

I was amused to find what squirrels some of the newcomers were when it came to weapons and ammunition. Fearing that enemies might pop out of any bush, they hid carbines, pistols, and cases of bullets in their trucks. As I learned months later, on the way back to Yuanshan they got their interpreters to help cache most of the arms along the road, in the safekeeping of mystified mayors or garrison commanders. No telling when and where a man might need a gun.

For someone like me, accustomed to a drowsily peaceful War

Area Headquarters, an air base in the throes of destruction was like a sudden bad dream. The gigantic waste of American wealth — with planes, equipment, and ground installations vanishing in explosions and sheets of flame — was surrounded by a sea of Chinese misery. All roads were thronged with frightened families of refugees on foot, everyone struggling under bundles of food and bedding for an unforeseeable future. The number of refugees displaced by all the Japanese campaigns of that year was incalculable, but probably exceeded three million in China south of the Yangtze. Before the winter was over, several hundred thousand must have died of hunger, exposure, and disease. This could not but help the Communists' postwar conquests.

No doubt because I was an ex-missionary, the story I remember most clearly from this tragic helter-skelter was told me by a transport pilot waiting impatiently to have the bombs unloaded from his plane before returning to Kunming. That runway was slated for demolition later in the afternoon.

While evacuating another airfield earlier in the year, he said, he flew out a party of elderly missionaries, members of a fundamentalist sect. They had lived in China for decades without any home leave, and men and women both wore dark obsolete clothes in stiff styles of the First World War. They were most unwilling to leave their mission, saying God would protect and provide for them. It nearly took bodily force to get them out of their houses, into a truck, then into the plane.

Halfway to Kunming, both the plane's motors went dead and a crash was inevitable. The crewmen offered to help the missionaries into their parachute harnesses but were imperturbably refused.

"God will provide," they were told.

The plane began curving steeply down, so the panicky crewmen simply seized the old ladies and gentlemen like sacks of potatoes, stuffed them into the harnesses, jammed the release cords into their hands with hasty instructions, then heaved them into thin air. After a frantic scramble everyone else got out before the crash.

Pilots and crew assembled and apprehensively set off on what they feared was a search for bits and pieces of missionary, but they found the whole group intact, already untangled from their parachutes and kneeling in prayer.

"God provided," their leader explained.

CHAPTER XII

Behind Japanese Lines 1944–45

THE ONLY BOOK I know to have been published about Americans in the Japanese-surrounded provinces of southeastern China was written by a man who spent rather a short time there. He called the place "The Dark World," and painted it full of mysterious villains hiding in the shadows — bandits and pirates, smugglers, assassins, beautiful girl spies. Except for the Americans he didn't like, we were "intrepid kids" or "a swell bunch of boys," outwitting and outbraving "the dwarfs," as he called the Japanese.

I don't remember it that way. There was plenty of wickedness around, but of a peculiarly Chinese kind, sunny and pragmatic. If the negotiations were discreet, almost everything was for sale — secrets, loyalties, perhaps even lives though I doubt that since the tendency was to keep things tidy and unemotional. When the campaign for Suichuan ended, violence disappeared and we relapsed into an almost bucolic calm.

As Ku Chu-t'ung appeared to have done, other generals may have made deals with the Japanese or puppets, ensuring their own neutrality. Our safety might have been a by-product, for if anything happened to us, American reprisals and Japanese counter-reprisals could disturb the local peace. By the end of the war several of us, including myself, had headquarters con- spicuous from the air, marked by tall radio antennae. With the fronts so open to agents, our presence could not have been unknown to the Japanese, but we were never bombed. All of us were sometimes good targets for assassins. Nobody was killed.

Our preserve was about six hundred miles long, from north to south, and perhaps three hundred miles across at its widest. The Yangtze bounded it to the north, the Hankow-Canton rail- way to the west, and the curving coastline of the China Seas and Formosa Straits to the south and east. Except for the cities with big garrisons and fronts guarding enough land to support them, the Japanese held its periphery quite lightly, relying on speedy armored launches, trucks, or trains, to patrol areas they didn't actually occupy.

Inside the enemy lines, our country was almost all hills or mountains, with villages in the valleys and a small town every fifty to a hundred miles. Until the war, it had been backwoods, isolated and primitive, seldom visited even by city Chinese from the coast.

The "intrepid kids" were widely scattered, and I couldn't estimate how many there were — three hundred, perhaps, with our small number divided into several alphabet agencies. No co-ordination had been set on higher levels, so we had to work out our own. After the war, some of us found we had been buy- ing the same dubious intelligence from the same sources, or had even been working against one another.

The biggest and most secret group was SACO, the Sino- American Co-operative Organization, less formally known as the "Rice-paddy Navy." It was sponsored by OSS, though not my branch, and was staffed with Navy men who trained guer- rillas to go behind the Japanese lines. They worked with Chiang Kai-shek's secret police under General Tai Li — the dreaded force formally known as "The Bureau of Investigation

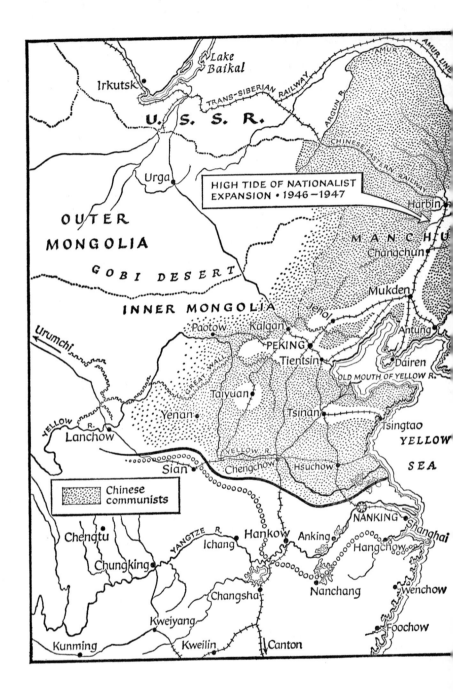

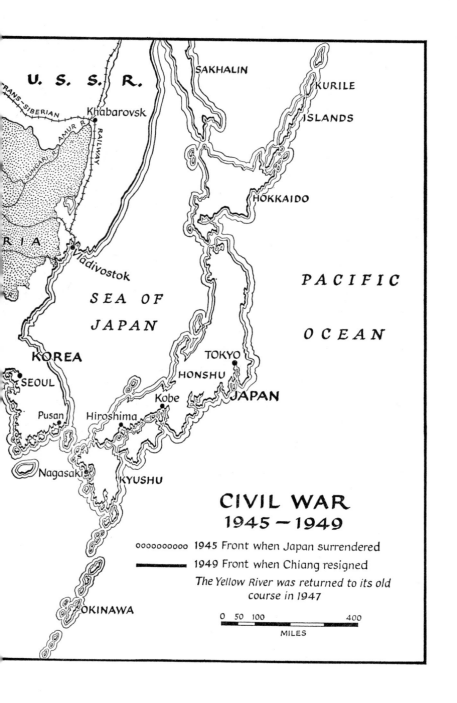

U. S. S. R.

SAKHALIN

KURILE

ISLANDS

TRANS-SIBERIAN RAILWAY

Khabarovsk

AMUR R.

SUNGARI R.

HOKKAIDO

RIA

Vladivostok

SEA OF

JAPAN

PACIFIC

OCEAN

KOREA

TOKYO

SEOUL

HONSHU

Kobe

JAPAN

Pusan

Hiroshima

Nagasaki

KYUSHU

CIVIL WAR
1945 – 1949

ooooooooooo 1945 Front when Japan surrendered

1949 Front when Chiang resigned

*The Yellow River was returned to its old
course in 1947*

0   50   100   400

MILES

OKINAWA

and Statistics." SACO operated throughout China on such a scale that it had its own Hump allocation; the peak was 200 tons monthly, as I recall.

We others didn't see much of the SACO men, because their camps were remote and they seemed reluctant to mingle with people whose security might be less perfect than their own. Most of us were happy not to mix, for General Tai Li had an unsavory name as a persecutor of all critics of Chiang, not just Japanese and Communists. The OSS-Tai Li link had been arranged soon after Pearl Harbor, by a naval officer who came to China with no knowledge of the country, and it certainly contributed to the anti-Americanism which later helped the Communists.

We had an example of an agency's getting so secret its right hand didn't know what its left was doing, and vice versa, when SACO was called on the carpet by U.S. Army Headquarters in Chungking, and charged with giving arms to anti-Communist guerrillas, at a time when we were not officially hostile to the Communists and were getting their help in the rescue of downed U.S. fliers. Investigation showed that SACO at the very least had been lax in demanding assurances that its aid be used against Japanese instead of Chinese. At about this time a colonel from still another branch of OSS flew to Yenan, the Communist capital, with a proposal that OSS arm twenty-five thousand Communist guerrillas.

AGAS, or Air Ground Aid Service, was much smaller and more efficient than SACO. It sent agents into occupied territory to help downed fliers, and tried to aid the prisoners of war in internment camps in Shanghai and elsewhere. Before the Japanese surrendered it was in touch with General Wainright of the Philippines, then interned in Manchuria.

AGFRTS, or Air Ground Forces Resources Technical Staff (!), was the 14th Air Force intelligence net. Although I had been transferred to OSS, most of my work was with it.

OWI, or Office of War Information, was a civilian agency with two outposts. One handled the routine of a propaganda bureau — news services, translations, picture exhibits. The other was a radio-monitoring outpost, the only American station close enough to Japan to pick up the weak long-wave broadcasts of propaganda for home consumption, often quite different from the short-wave broadcasts Japan wanted the world to hear.

Other small outposts watched the weather or shipping for various agencies. Through the one airfield, at Changting, we were visited by a floating population of men from the Army and Navy and other alphabet agencies, ostensibly inspecting the smuggling, the roads, the refugees and many other things. Some were serious and hard-working, but news soon spread of this area which had the glamour of being behind enemy lines without being especially dangerous to reach or travel in. We had mysterious visitors on missions so secret they couldn't confide in anyone below the highest ranks. The more secret they were, the more conspicuous they tended to make themselves. General Ku had to deport two from the 3rd War Area because they traveled near the front and upset the townspeople wherever they went, by carelessly shooting off guns, drinking with whores in the biggest restaurants, and generally making themselves known to the dimmest enemy agents.

Captain Preston Schoyer, head of AGAS, a former teacher at Yale in China, was the colleague who lived closest to me, in a larger town called Shangjao, about fifty miles to the northeast. We saw one another often, driving back and forth to swap information, equipment, or supplies, and sometimes kept in touch by Chinese telephone. Since food was always a problem — not the quantity, but the kinds our men liked — we sometimes talked about it on the phone after our other business.

"I have two extra bushels of potatoes," Schoyer might say. "What can you give me for them?"

"Plenty of onions on the market here," I could reply. "I'll send you a sackful."

We would hear clicks and mumbles, suggesting our calls were monitored. While the Japanese didn't seem very interested in us, we knew the Chinese kept close surveillance. At a later dinner-party of General Ku's, celebrated with many bottoms-up toasts of strong Tiger Bone liquor, one of his aides became loose-witted enough to question me about the secret vegetable code he said Schoyer and I were using.

I remember this as typical of our life. We might be working on strange war jobs, under a few cloaks of secrecy or mystification, but we were also prosaically trying to live as well as possible from day to day. We didn't do badly at it either.

The weather was in our favor, mildly subtropical in the lowlands, pleasantly temperate in the higher valleys. Except for monsoon-like rainy spells in summer and occasional cold depressing periods of overcast in winter, it was always comfortable to be outdoors. The long slow autumns were wonderful.

The enlisted men never stopped the traditional army griping, but I think some began having a very good time. All officers were quite junior, and as long as everybody did his work, few of us bothered with military regulations. High brass was unlikely to inspect. There was no saluting, and the men could dress as they pleased. Some began to enjoy the picturesqueness of lurking behind enemy lines and dressed for the part. Exotic fur facings appeared on uniform collars, and big buccaneerish boots were ordered from the leather stores. Some men let their hair and beards grow, others favored long walrus mustaches and shaved skulls.

For recreation there was good hunting in the hills, partridge and pheasant chiefly. A few bigger hunts for deer, boar, or tiger were set up, but without much success, none at all in the last case. Despite sporadic New Life campaigns against superficials like permanent waves or red fingernails, girls were always available in hotels and bath-houses. Our food improved greatly when cooks and servants from the coast, trained by foreigners now interned, heard about Americans in the interior and came through the lines looking for jobs; our salaries in American dollars made us nabobs. Christopher Rand's OWI office at Nanping near Foochow, the old treaty port which was a principal source of sophisticated help, was the most civilized, with a chef who had French, Russian, and American specialties, a former valet to launder, and an amah to iron and mend.

The men in my own office gradually became more tolerant of Chinese fare, first relishing the wonderful fruit; peaches from Anhwei, the province north of us, were the best I have ever eaten. Next they found a local wine which tasted more like alcoholic grape juice than a French vintage, but was palatable. They learned to make fair hard liquor by taking Chinese schnapps — strong but foul, like bad moonshine — and steeping it with orange quarters for some weeks, then filtering it through charcoal. The best Chinese rice wine, of course, was as good as sherry.

One of the first solid foods they began to like, in sandwiches and for breakfast, was delicious but unusual-tasting ham from Anhwei. Once I happened to travel through the town where it was made, and found it was parboiled in huge vats before smoking. For every fifty hams one dog was added. I never had the heart to tell the men.

We heads of offices realized how poisonous it could be if our small groups were cooped up within themselves, so we tried to see that every man went on a trip whenever possible. Travel was necessary to get gas and other supplies, from the Changting airfield or points near the coast where we bought from smugglers. A trip would be a social event because the going was slow, and the journey back and forth might take days. The nights were spent at other American outposts housing a whole new group with whom to drink and talk. I think medieval travel was a little like this, with wayfarers feasting while their hosts had their mounts fixed up and filled — free repairs and gas, in this case, all on Uncle Sugar. There may have been medieval precedent for our custom that if the hosts' men could find precious spare parts or tools not locked up or hidden, they took them in formalized burglary.

One of my office's two casualties, Charles Annell, was on a trip by himself to bring back gasoline. The weather had turned rainy, the bridges began washing out, and one collapsed under him, dropping his truck into a gulley. The full fifty-gallon gas drums tumbled forward and crushed the cab, injuring him badly. Chinese road officials telephoned me, but it was many hours before I could reach him by jeep. He was still in the cab and unconscious. Luckily an emergency landing strip was five miles away and I could get a small plane to fetch him to Changting. He was flown to the base hospital at Kunming next day, and became fully mobile again after several years of therapy.

The other casualty was a young White Russian, Sergei Bourlin. I had heard rumors of Chinese Communist forces with Red Russian advisers, up near the Yangtze, and thought I should have a Russian interpreter, just in case. On a trip back to Kunming I found Sergei, who had walked out of Shanghai and made his way more than a thousand miles overland to get a job with the U.S. Army; he hoped it would be a first step toward American citizenship. We returned the thousand miles to Yuanshan, bringing along a heavier transmitter, and Sergei was fatally wounded the next afternoon when the whole staff turned out to rig a taller aerial for it.

We were hauling up a heavy length of bamboo to top our older tripod when it slipped out of the ropes and fell straight down, striking Sergei squarely on the top of his head. He was knocked unconscious instantly and died twelve hours later, choked on blood from his concussion. The long travels back and forth which brought him to that exact spot at that moment made a deep, almost superstitious, impression on us. As far as I could learn, the presence of Red Russian advisers along the Yangtze was never verified, though some young White Russians from Shanghai, exhilarated by Stalingrad and other victories in Russia, were believed to have left the city to work with the Chinese Communists and probably gave rise to the rumor of Red Russians. Sergei's presence in Yuanshan could have been caused by kids like himself, perhaps even some he knew.

Another disaster was narrowly averted when a Kung-yo or "working friend" — one of the orderlies loaned us by Ku's headquarters — was getting my jeep ready for a trip. We had twelve fifty-gallon drums of high-octane gas, and because it was so valuable I got permission to keep it in the walled and guarded compound of General Wen, Ku's chief of staff. We had used less than one drum, and to find the opened one the Kung-yo started lighting matches and peering into them until the great explosion. He wasn't killed and the drums were far enough apart so not all went up, but we spent a couple of hours frantically running with mud from the paddy-fields to stifle the fire before it could reach General Wen's house.

Some Americans at outposts farther south, nearer the coast, had close calls when U.S. Navy pilots from the newly-reconquered Philippines, strafing Japanese shipping in the Formosa Straits, began to crash-land in their neighborhood. The briefing officers in the Philippines seemed to know nothing about China, and the pilots who survived crashing were sure they were in enemy country. They would hide in the bushes and shoot at any Chinese who came near. When Americans were called in, the pilots thought they were cleverly-disguised Japanese, and kept sniping as they shouted questions like: "If you're a real American who won the World Series?", or "What's Lana's latest movie?" Our isolated men weren't always up on this kind of news and had to stay under cover until the pilot ran out of

bullets and could be dragged away to be convinced over a bottle
of hoarded Coke.

This problem was bad enough for the 14th Air Force to send
a liaison officer flying from Kunming to India and Australia,
then up to MacArthur's headquarters, to explain who we were,
and how we could help pilots. He got nowhere, and after waiting a couple of futile weeks to see anyone on MacArthur's staff,
flew back to Kunming. It has since become known that when
Hengyang was falling the summer before, and Chennault was
crying for more planes to save it, he sent a reconnaissance ship
over Manila, easily interpreted as a step toward a token raid
which would skim the cream off the publicity expected for the
imminent reconquest of the Philippines. No more co-operation
from MacArthur could be expected.

Some OSS officers in my branch, sent out to work in the field
but vaguely affiliated with me, were far from regulation issue.
I'm afraid Washington was running short of men with useful
experience of China.

I had an eccentric captain whose sole qualification was having
been the first white man to hike through Hainan Island off the
coast of China, years before the war. He couldn't speak Chinese
and didn't seem to care about the country except as the scene of
his great walk. While the problem of Hump cargo was still
acute, he managed to fly in with a heavy duffel bag of old *National Geographic*s featuring his article about it. When he met
someone new, he would get the talk around to his feat, then
say casually:

"By the way. Here's a *Geographic* with that article. It's an
extra copy you can have."

His walk had been hazardous, but it must have used up his
daring. He thought he saw Japanese everywhere, and wanted
a gun always within reach. His post was near enemy garrisons
on the Yangtze and this may have disturbed him, for his reports

kept getting stranger. Once he raised an alarm about a battle at a certain place, with eight hundred casualties. Cross-checking showed it had taken place in the Ming Dynasty. He reported a new Japanese railway, but I found it had been planned by the Chinese before the war, never built. Not long before V-J Day, he began warning that Japan planned another attack on Pearl Harbor. He stayed on in coastal China after the war and was mysteriously mixed up in the shooting of the husband of a famous White Russian belle; apparently one of his ever-ready guns had gone off. Eventually he died in a plane crash.

Another OSS type was academic, for example a naval officer who had been an instructor in Chinese studies, and knew the language well. He was irked by his college's shortage of funds for his department, and with a pile of OSS money set up a regular research institute in our backwoods, employing several Americans and a couple of dozen Chinese. They turned out beautiful detailed reports on many subjects of long-range importance, but the group was supposed to be in combat intelligence and it produced nothing that aided combat missions.

A few men sent out with little or no China experience and no knowledge of the language nevertheless took to the country right away and did very well. One was Lieutenant Commander Henry Shoemaker, known as Shoe, on loan to OSS from the Navy. Whenever he checked in at Yuanshan with tales of his travels, I felt quite rueful that seniority in China now tied me so closely to a base headquarters, while others went to more interesting places.

Shoe arrived a couple of months after I did, and his first experience was something of a farce because his "cover" was as an air-ground liaison officer for the 14th Air Force, specializing in air support of infantry in combat; he had come from this kind of work in Sicily and Italy. As a naval officer his real interests were on the coast, but the 3rd War Area refused to allow Americans to be stationed there, with good reason as we later

learned. Air support was greatly desired by all Chinese commanders, however, for prestige as well as military reasons, and
Shoe's cover ensured him a warm welcome in Yuanshan.

A few weeks later, at spring harvest time, the Japanese
launched a small invasion from the coast, toward Kinwha, a
couple of hundred miles northeast of us. After a flurry of conferences General Wen, the chief of staff, took Shoe off toward
the front at the head of a musical comedy retinue of elite
guards, flag-carriers, bugle-blowers, and high-speed four-bearer
sedan chairs. For parades he was taking along his big Japanese
horse and, for Shoe, the little one on which he had once tried
to humiliate me; Shoe said he felt he should carry it around
like a prayer book. Shoe also told me privately he expected no
results from the trip. The airfield at Suichuan was still open
at that time, but it took twelve gallons of gas to fly one gallon
from India to Suichuan and the invasion was another five hundred miles farther on. A target would have to be extremely
big and stationary to make it worthwhile.

A week or two later Wen returned inconspicuously, without
Shoe; he declined to see me when I tried to call. Shoe came in
a few days afterward in a dilapidated country rickshaw. He
said the trip out had been a triumph, with parades, reviews,
and feasts at all garrisons. Great excitement and expectation
attended their arrival at the "front," a stretch of peaceful country with a few new trenches. Sometimes faraway gunfire could
be heard, and a couple of enemy planes floated about in the
distance. The frontline commander said the Japanese were
near, but he didn't know exactly where. This was the target.

A few days of rain and trouble with his radio gave Shoe excuses for not "unleashing" the 14th Air Force, but Wen
fumed and sulked. It was hard to guess his motives. If the
3rd War Area did have a deal with the Japanese, perhaps this
whole show was a kind of publicity stunt. The bombing planes
and their great explosions would be a display, like fireworks,

prestigious for Wen and Ku, but relatively harmless, blasting an indefinite target, manned — again, perhaps — by expendable puppets.

In a few days the Japanese took the Kinwha airfield, then seemed to busy themselves with maneuvers. The gunfire tapered off. One morning Shoe awoke to find Wen and his retinue had whisked away without him.

His Chinese radioman-interpreter hired coolies, and they walked most of the way back, in tropically hot wet weather. "I just stripped to my drawers, changed my GI boots for a pair of straw sandals, bought a waxed-paper umbrella, and pushed my big stomach into the slashing rain," he said. One day he was able to hire a big Missouri mule which had inexplicably found its way into the interior of China, and another day traveled luxuriously on twenty miles of railroad which had somehow been overlooked when this "Roadless Area" was created.

Shoe found Wen was not at home to him for weeks, but he moved closer to his real purpose when he went as liaison officer to a British Military Mission group at Pucheng, to the southeast on the way to the coast. These men had been sent out to do the groundwork for a Sino-British guerrilla force to be led by General Orde Wingate, organizer of the Chindit guerrillas in Burma. When Wingate was killed they were trapped in frustration and a waste of skills, preparing for nothing and receiving hardly any supplies. They included specialists in commando tactics, veterans of the Dieppe raid, but the Chinese wanted presents of new weapons instead of training; they couldn't be interested in Molotov cocktails improvised from gasoline and old soy sauce bottles when they hoped for bazookas and plastic explosives from SACO.

The language and intelligence experts with BMM were equally frustrated, but had learned enough for Shoe to see that the information he wanted was tantalizingly easy to gather on the coast. He kept sending me messages asking that I tackle

General Wen for permission for him to go there, but Wen always blandly changed the subject.

While he was at Pucheng, Shoe told me later, he used to hunt deer and pheasant with the British, and once they found signs of a tiger. They stalked it for days with Browning and Sten guns, then found fresh pug marks and warm dung. They camped there with their sleeping bags, and were awakened by a shot in the middle of the night. A Chinese sentry who happened to be awake had seen the tiger drinking at a stream beside his post, and shot it dead.

Next day was declared holiday in Pucheng and peasants from miles around swarmed in to see the tiger paraded by soldiers, propped up in a ferocious pose on a big litter decorated with paper flowers. That night the beast was roasted and the garrison commander invited Shoe and a few of the British to the feast. Tiger meat was supposed to give to the eater the animal's strength, bravery, cunning, sagacity, and sexual prowess, and all qualities were tripled in its private parts. These were served sliced with gravy at the garrison commander's table, where Shoe sat.

"What did you do?" I asked him.

"I ate some, of course," he replied. "What could I lose? The Chinese might be right."

The Japanese made another small invasion at autumn harvest time, coming over the mountains to occupy the town of Lishui, east of Pucheng. This seemed mainly a training maneuver. Although the Chinese put on no pressure, and indeed were retreating before patrol activity, the Japanese suddenly packed up and withdrew down a narrow valley to the seaport of Wenchow. It was a perfect trap. No roads led out of the valley and the only exit from Wenchow was by sea. With his radio equipment and some officers from the BMM, Shoe followed, out of sight over the rim of the valley and he began alerting the 14th

Air Force. When four troop transports sailed into Wenchow and the invaders embarked, our planes arrived promptly and sank three ships, badly damaging the fourth.

This so impressed General Li Mo-an, commander of the coastal areas, that he gave permission for Shoe to set up a headquarters at Hwangyen, a smaller seaport north of Wenchow. Li not only agreed to keep news of this from his superiors, Generals Ku and Wen at 3rd War Area headquarters, but wrote many letters of introduction to officers and officials up and down the coast.

In the next few months I was able to send enough men and equipment to Hwangyen, by roundabout ways, for Shoe to set up a string of coast-watching and weather stations. American submarines had by then sunk so much enemy shipping that surviving boats, including some of the capital class, would creep up the coast within the ten-fathom line, where they could easily be identified and counted. Weather reports from Hwangyen were important because these stations were the farthest north on Far Eastern waters, and could aid in predicting patterns for the whole Pacific.

Hwangyen was a major port for the "smuggling" trade with occupied Shanghai, carried on openly and taxed by the Nationalist customs. Fruit, vegetables, and rice were shipped out, and drugs, textiles, cigarettes, small manufactured goods, and gimcrack luxuries came in. Scores of large ocean-going junks would be in its harbor at once, and this made another of Shoe's missions easier. He was supposed to get junks to rescue American pilots downed in the sea, and had $100,000 in American hundred-dollar bills for the purpose; it was a wad about the size of a brick.

He would buy up the junks at the going market rate, then give them back to the owners in return for a promise of aid. He gave them colored cloth panels to spread on their decks, showing American planes they were friendly. Most junk-owners were smugglers and some were probably pirates, but they had their own honor and a number of pilots were brought in to Hwangyen. No betrayals were ever reported. As a bonus Shoe was able to get the junk-owners to buy and bring him almost anything he wanted from Shanghai — gasoline, radio parts, canned goods, once three cases of Scotch for "political gifts."

With AGAS, he placed agents in Shanghai to help pilots parachuting above this city of about four million, the largest ever occupied by Axis forces and too big for the Japanese to patrol. Some rescues were melodramatic, with Japanese in cars speeding to the place they judged the pilot would float down, but being thwarted by Chinese who seized him, whisked him into houses, up and down alleys, through markets, passing him from hand to hand, until the enemy gave up the chase and the pilot was hidden while American agents were notified. At least one pilot was rescued from the river within sight of the skyscrapers of the famous Bund, in waters patrolled by Japanese launches but confusingly full of little wooden Chinese boats which would suddenly bob into the path of a launch.

Shoe was also supposed to evaluate the coast as a scene for American diversionary landings, and for this he traveled as far as the Ningpo peninsula. It was his most sensitive job, so he tried to be inconspicuous, walking all the way in a dark second-hand Chinese robe and a black felt hat, shading himself with a big black umbrella. The getup was so right for a Hwangyen merchant or smuggler, he said, most people passed him without noticing his foreigner's red face and big nose. He tried to mask his interest in tides and beaches by hunting for more junks for pilot rescue. He had what was left of the $100,000 bundled in greasy paper, and he tossed it among soiled clothes in his luggage-coolie's basket, figuring this was better security than any attempt to hide or guard it. He never lost a dollar.

When he returned to Hwangyen, he was unsettled to learn the Japanese in Shanghai had broadcast where he had been, and what he was doing. They offered a reward for his capture. He felt they couldn't have known without information from the Chinese officials he saw on his trip, so he complained to the magistrate in Hwangyen. The answer was surprisingly frank. "We must tell the Japanese, otherwise they would not trust us. We only tell them where you have been, not where you are going."

Shoe lived in an abandoned mission house in Hwangyen, gutted in a Japanese raid. "I always look for a place like that," he told me cheerfully. "Irish potatoes gone wild in the garden, and Walter Scott novels tossed around the house." For his radio station the garrison commander loaned a big Confucian tomb on a nearby hilltop, with excellent reception. It was a good lookout for planes, too, and although his orders did not include this, he and his radioman, Corporal Arthur Bichan, began keeping a log of the enemy planes they saw. Flights of bombers and fighters, low-flying seaplanes, sometimes transports, came over often. Some flew for miles overland and Shoe saw that if he could chart a schedule, the 14th Air Force might be able to shoot them down where the wreckage could be examined. Any transport flying along the coast regularly was likely to be a courier plane, carrying officers, mail, and military reports.

Not long before he left, summoned to Guam to report to high Navy brass, a new flight of two unescorted transports began appearing quite regularly in the late morning, flying overland from the north, then veering out to sea, probably enroute from Nanking to Formosa. He arranged with the 14th to have the gas brought forward and a P-40 sent to hit them, but because of urgent messages from Washington he had to leave two days before the scheduled attack. Both transports were shot down by an AVG veteran, Herbst, but landed in the water where nothing could be retrieved. A few months later the pattern Shoe set up was used to intercept a four-engined seaplane which the U.S. Navy in Kunming had tracked all the way from Singapore. It was forced into the sea off Hwangyen and a Japanese admiral was captured.

On his way back to Yuanshan, Shoe called on General Li Mo-an who had given him permission to go to the coast. This straightforward general said he had an impression the Americans might land near Ningpo. He asked Shoe to warn his superiors that no matter what rosy promises they had from Chinese of higher rank, he himself, right on the spot, could give a landing little or no help. His under-manned and under-supplied army was no longer a combat force, but a political weight which by its mere existence, it was hoped, would bar the spreading Communists. Most of his soldiers had no more than 40 rounds of ammunition for their obsolete rifles. On Guam Shoe reported this to Admiral Nimitz and his staff, and tentative plans for a Ningpo landing were shelved.

Before leaving Yuanshan, Shoe had drunk a final cup of tea with General Wen, all smiles and courtesy now. The general could not possibly have been ignorant of where Shoe had been for the last several months, or how large an operation he had left running in Hwangyen, but face had to be saved. Wen said how sorry he was he hadn't been able to let Shoe go to the coast. Perhaps it could be arranged another time. Shoe said he could see how impossible his request had been. When he came back from Guam and a short leave in the United States, he didn't even ask Wen for permission again. He went on liaison to the BMM, then seeped off to the coast.

In the spring of 1945, Japanese air activity over China all but disappeared. The airfields around Shanghai were briefly crowded with planes gathering for the battle of Okinawa, which began April 1, four hundred miles offshore, but the other fields emptied. In March the 14th Air Force met only forty-seven Japanese planes over the mainland, and in April only three — obsolete models at that. The unopposed 14th blasted railways and bridges up and down the central belt of occupied China.

This was out of my territory and at the end of April I applied for forty-five days' leave to get married. Louise and I had been engaged more than two years. I later heard Chennault helped me get prompt approval, and I flew back to Kunming, then over the Hump, in the middle of May.

The Japanese withdrawal from China, which I had been anticipating for years, began in late May. Enemy outposts around Liuchow, the last of the 14th's big eastern bases to be captured, moved back, then a general retreat from Liuchow, Kweilin, and all the other farther conquests began. In the ten weeks before V-J Day, the enemy quietly gave up more than half its China conquests of the year before. The 14th's attacks on supply routes and the outflanking victories in the Pacific were the obvious reasons.

Our wedding in Chicago was set for June 2, and by great good luck I flew in with three days to spare. We went to New Orleans for our honeymoon, and when my leave was over I was temporarily assigned to OSS headquarters in Washington.

Of the following month I have only dim impressions — glaring, stifling heat, worse than Yuanshan's, and shadowy air-conditioned offices where extremely well-tailored civilians and officers gravely discussed lethal toys like explosive pens, poisoned toiletries, or thin knife blades which could be hidden under the skin. They evidently thought of southeastern China in terms of "the Dark World," and treated me with deference, as if I were a super-desperado. Once I was taken to see a training school in Virginia, and I felt that if I had gone into OSS at the bottom and had to graduate from this school, I would never have reached Yuanshan.

It was on a big secluded estate, and the trainees lived in a rambling Tudor manor house. They were of all ages, from all ranks of every service, and civilian life as well. They wore GI uniforms without insignia, and weren't supposed to know one another by their real names, only nicknames assigned by OSS. They were taking written, spoken and acted tests invented by two Viennese psychiatrists, a man and a woman.

Because of the somewhat zany air of the school I may have the wrong recollection of this couple, but I retain a distinct picture of two small Marx brothers in white clothes, one with a mustache and one in a skirt, both wearing big white pith helmets and both conspiratorial. I had lunch in the general mess, where everyone could see me, but when the psychiatrists took me out into the grounds to watch a couple of tests, they wanted to keep me hidden from the trainees. There was much peering around corners, hushings and beckonings, then dashes across open spaces, hunched-down creepings behind hedges, and other movie-comedy bits.

One test, for leadership, seemed sensible. A dozen men were turned loose in a grassy field, cut in two by an artificial crevasse too wide to jump and too deep to climb out. They were told to get to the other side. Within minutes one of the youngest — an army sergeant, I later learned — organized the others into search parties to comb the field and surrounding woods for bridge materials. They soon found timbers and ropes and laced up a rough bridge. The sergeant won honors.

Another test was staged in the big cobbled Tudor stable-yard, surrounded by stalls for a dozen horses. The psychiatrists and I crept in by a back way and peered over the double door of a stall.

A tough-looking man, identified to me as a Marine major fresh from months of combat in the Pacific, came in with an instructor who showed him a heap of big round wooden joints, and a pile of dowels six or eight feet long, like a giant Tinker Toy set. The instructor told him to build something, anything, a shape, and left him on his own.

The major was obviously nonplussed, but began building a

sort of double box. Then two objectionable young men came out of a stall — raucous, zoot-suity, somewhat flitty, lurid examples of what a Marine veteran might think of as draft-dodging civilians. They jeered at him and got behind him to pull his construction apart as fast as he could build it. He began to look worried. He evidently saw they were part of the test, but thought everything so nonsensical that his judgment was weakened. He failed to drive them away and flunked the test. I was later told an agent behind enemy lines should have knocked them out and gone on playing with his Tinker Toy.

In China after the war I knew an OSS man who graduated from this school. He told me that at the end of the course all trainees were invited to a banquet where they were given unlimited drinks, with toasts of congratulation from their instructors. In the good fellowship nearly half told their names to their classmates. They all flunked.

My friend also said he had flown to China with a star graduate, an athletic ball-of-fire who did push-ups in the aisle and shadow-boxed constantly as the plane flew halfway around the world. Both men were parachuted behind the Japanese lines in North Vietnam, and the star was killed in his first contact with an enemy patrol. He panicked, and despite shouted warnings from the men with him ran straight toward a Japanese who sliced him up with machine-gun fire.

When the atom bombs fell in mid-August and war vanished like a pricked balloon, Washington seemed more than ever a prison. I enviously imagined what my friends in China were doing, for they were suddenly liberated, all barriers between them and the coast demolished. As I later heard, many piled into their trucks and jeeps and headed for Shanghai without waiting for orders. Out to the fronts they drove, over worse and worse roads, then jolted through roadless no-man's-land, past goggle-eyed Japanese sentries. Down the ever-better highways of enemy territory they sped. The Japanese troops ignored them or saluted. At last the skyscrapers and factory chimneys of the fabled metropolis showed over the treetops.

Other men, especially from SACO, rented launches and went to Shanghai by water. One party was victor in what must have been the last naval engagement of the war, about a week after the surrender. They had an old Chinese tub, but fitted it out with bazookas and other high-powered weapons, and flew a big American flag at the masthead. When an armed junk, Japanese or puppet, evidently without radio or any news of the end of the war, bore down on them and opened fire, they blasted it apart.

Days before this, Schoyer and Shoemaker had gone into Shanghai on the first American plane. Schoyer was head of the mission, a most risky one since it had not been possible to contact the Japanese garrison commander and the plans of the Nationalist and Communist armies around the city were not known. No more than twenty-five lightly-armed Americans came in that first plane, hoping to accept the surrender of at least one hundred thousand Japanese soldiers and take control of a city of four million, coveted by both Chinese factions.

They landed at the largest airfield without permission from the control tower, got out of the plane and waited. The Japanese commander of the field bustled up in a truck full of soldiers, and the Japanese-speaking Chinese whom Schoyer had brought as interpreter recognized him as a prewar classmate at Waseda University near Tokyo. They greeted one another warmly, and Schoyer was taken to call on the garrison commander. He proved most co-operative, and kept perfect order in Shanghai in the weeks before Nationalist authority was fully re-established.

Schoyer and Shoemaker and a few others opened an American headquarters and in the period of change-over it was virtually Shanghai's municipal government. They were supposed to keep the place in shape for the Nationalists, but soon found the Nationalists themselves were their chief problem. A great fleet of American planes began flying armies and government agencies in from western China, and many officers and officials proved to be voracious carpet-baggers, sometimes prevented from illegally "confiscating" property only when faced by an American or two, backed by Japanese army authority.

Shoe handled liaison with U.S. Navy forces preparing to come in from the Pacific, and he later told me of his special difficulties with some supply officers in the Philippines who couldn't believe the liberated people of Shanghai, particularly the former prisoners of war, were not dying for lack of Vitamin C. They sent Navy planes to bomb the city with big drums of fruit juices and preserved fruit. They didn't know how to harness them securely to the parachutes, and many would break loose, plummeting the rest of the way. This wasn't so bad for prisoners of war, who were surrounded by open spaces and could run away from them, but some landed in built-up areas where they caused damage and fury. After every mercy mission, at least one moist householder came to American headquarters to complain that a Navy drum had smashed through his roof and exploded, showering everything with, say, tomato juice or pineapple slices.

Consul of the United States

CHAPTER XIII

The Communist Tide 1945–49

I DIDN'T HAVE TO SPEND much time in Washington wishing I was in China. A few days after the surrender, I heard I was to take charge of the OSS office in Peking. Louise thought I was mad not to complain, but I promised to get her to China as soon as I could. No transports were flying all the way across the Pacific yet, so I went by the wartime route for the last time, over Africa, India, and the Hump.

At Kunming thousands of American soldiers from Burma and India, with long caravans of dusty trucks and heavy equipment, showed how completely the blockade of western China had been broken. Men and materiel were already being flown back across the Hump.

The big new American airfields around Kunming were soon to be abandoned, but hundreds of planes lined the runways or circled overhead. Air transports had been rushed in from India, the Pacific, even Europe, to help take the Nationalists down to the coastal cities before the Communists could get in. Here was American air strength thundering as never before above China, and I couldn't help remembering the days when the AVG had one obsolete transport plane and thought it a triumph to get half a dozen wobbly little P-40's into the air.

Acres of Chinese troops squatted patiently around the airfields, waiting their turn to climb into the huge multi-motored transports. Some were the American-trained-and-equipped crack troops, others were only semi-modernized. Some seemed to be old-fashioned warlord troops, as brutalized and pitiable as other tattered armies I had known in the southeast. Some half million Nationalist troops were moved by American planes and ships in the first six months after V-J Day; the government we had written off as an ally against Japan was now to be our champion against the Communists.

On the flight from Kunming to Peking, we landed a few Nationalist officers at Hankow, and as we circled in I could see the old Lutheran mission with painted American flags still fading on its roofs. It was such a clear flash from a dim past, I fancied that if I could look through the leaves on a certain tree I would see myself at twenty-six, quaking through my first bombing with a penny vase clutched in my hands.

We flew over Peking before landing, and although I had been enthralled as a young railway tourist from prewar Hankow, I now saw that the perfect approach was by air. The symmetrical city-plan, with wide streets and open spaces, gray walls within walls, was as logical and beautiful from a plane as it must have been when first ruled out on paper by its medieval architects. Cutting straight up through the gray mat of roofs from south to north stretched the white marble-paved avenue of the emperors. At its head stood the Forbidden City, a chess set of ceremonial halls, temples, and palaces, more than a mile square. Standing among white marble courtyards, all the red-walled buildings had glistening roofs of yellow tile.

I spent five mad months in Peking. Communist-occupied hills and mountains rimmed the western and northern horizons, and Communists ruled the plains for hundreds of miles to the south and east. They had not captured Peking because American Marines landed at Tientsin and came up the railway from the coast, peacefully taking over from the Japanese and puppet garrison. By the time I got there, tens of thousands of Nationalist troops were arriving in American planes, and puppet forces were being legitimized as Nationalists with a speed which suggested wartime deals. No Japanese were to be repatriated until enough Nationalists were on hand to keep the Communists out.

I'm afraid this isolated little patch of the free world was not much of a showcase for us. Its masters were Nationalists, as grasping and venal as those in Shanghai. Puppets and collaborators were bribing their way out of trial as war criminals, unless they happened to be relatives or old cronies of the new governing clique. Blackmail of lowly people who had betrayed their neighbors, or merely offended them, was a sport in corner police stations.

The OSS officers from whom I took over had come in from the northern backwoods and seemed to have assigned themselves to R and R — Rest and Recreation — the moment they hit Peking. They had been showered with offers of luxurious houses by Chinese who wanted protection, and chose the palace of an old mandarin family of puppets. This was a honeycomb of ten or more courtyards surrounded by red-pillared pavilions, almost on the scale of the domestic quarters in the Forbidden City. The largest courtyard led into a banquet- and ball-room with space for two hundred guests. Here the OSS men had parties for American officers and the handsomer European women — neutrals or enemy aliens — who had lived in Peking through the war. On party nights most of them left their husbands at home. Out in one of the back courtyards the ancient wife of the chief puppet sat in her web, offering bargains in jade which she hoped would be politically favorable for her husband.

My first assignment in Peking was to gather intelligence on

the Japanese Kwantung Army, the elite force which had garrisoned most of Manchuria and North China. This proved easy because so many Japanese wanted to surrender to OSS; they said they mistrusted the Nationalists and feared the Marines. Whole companies would march into the street in front of the OSS palace to stand at attention while the officers came inside, bowing and clicking heels as they offered up their swords. I told them they would have to surrender to Chinese, but suggested I might be able to speed their repatriation if they brought me their records and other intelligence. This resulted in bushels of material to send to Washington.

Among odd jobs, I was a number-one boy as I would be years later in Hong Kong. American generals and other big shots came flying in on high priority and wanted me to order shopkeepers to bring silks, jade, and furs to spread at their feet. Word had flashed over half the world that the Peking merchants, eager for the security of American dollars, would sell their treasures for bargain prices. The confusion of the first weeks after V-J Day made junkets easy.

I also found myself spending hours listening to Chinese who wanted to complain about high-handed behavior of the Nationalists or the Marines. I had no authority to interfere but I often did have time on my hands and the situation was disagreeable enough to make an outlet for complaints seem useful. Sometimes a word in the right ear could ease friction.

I was besieged by Germans, Italians, pro-Axis White Russians, and a whole menagerie of neutrals who had lived among the Japanese through the war and now wanted to explain it away. Several were husbands of women who came to OSS dances, and obviously thought a pair of horns a bargain if this helped their security. Others tried to advance themselves by tattling on their friends.

An American consul had arrived before I did. Since we were no longer at war, he should have been our top-ranking man, but the Marine general who had occupied the city quietly, by indirect arrangement with the enemy, nevertheless seemed to regard it as his bloodily-won conquest, to rule as he liked. We had an informal American committee which met every few days until the Nationalists were in full control, and the efforts of the rest of us — an Army colonel, the consul, and myself — were mainly to block the general from riding roughshod over the Pekingese.

He singled me out as his special enemy and would summon me to his headquarters where he sat in a T-shirt among clouds of stale cigar smoke. "Now listen here, Frillmann," he would bark. "I'm a General in the Marine Corps and no little pipsqueak of an Air Force Major is going to tell me what to do." I never could think of any way to explain to him the Chinese subtleties and divided loyalties which surrounded him, or how we might need future friends here instead of temporary subjects.

One autumn day a Japanese cavalry unit tried to surrender to me. I told the commanding officer to go to the Chinese, then he asked me to take his two hundred horses; he had seen how badly many Chinese treated animals. I hadn't ridden since Hankow and was eager to, so I went to his barracks and picked out four of the most beautiful animals I had ever seen. After I chose them, the commander told me the biggest, a black stallion about sixteen hands high, was out of Man o' War. He said I could have gear for all four, and he would loan me grooms as long as his outfit was in Peking. He would try to keep me supplied with fodder. Perhaps I could help him be repatriated sooner.

The French Embassy loaned me stable space, and every morning until I left China I found the four grooms grinning in a row there, each holding his saddled and bridled horse for my choice. In the first few days I took out the lesser animals and

trotted for half an hour or more in the parks around the nearby
Forbidden City, where elderly gentlemen aired their caged
birds in the dawn light or shadowboxed in slow motion.

The first morning I took out the black stallion — Din Din,
he was called — I allowed for extra time and slowly walked
him down through the crowded alleys of the lower city, until
we reached the big pine-filled park around the tiered white
marble Altar of Heaven and the conical purple roofs of the
Temple of Heaven. This park was empty early in the morning,
and I let Din Din out into a full gallop. A light dry snow, the
first of the year, had fallen the night before, and white plumes
flew up underfoot as we rushed below the black branches.

Din Din galloped into the more open northern end of the
park, and we came to a big empty parade-ground. Before I could
react, I saw the Japanese had built a crude clay wall, five or
more feet high, all across the center. There was nothing to do
but jump, and over we went. It was a magnificent ride.

I suppose it was the feelings of release given me by the greatest jump of my life which made me wake up a few mornings
later knowing I couldn't get out of the Air Force and the OSS
fast enough. It was like the morning in Illinois when I woke
up realizing I was through as a missionary. In Peking my work
on the Kwantung Army was finished and my other jobs were
trivial. I was tired of the corrupting influences in an occupying
force — having Din Din showed I was ripe for a fall.

I had more than enough points to get out of the service.
China might be heading for civil war, but the bigger cities were
temporarily peaceful and many American civilians were beginning to bring out their families. Louise and I planned to start
a family soon, and I wanted our first child to be born in China.
The director of the China office of the OWI — then changing
into the USIS or U.S. Information Service of the State Department—had promised to hire me as soon as I was demobilized.
I began tugging at the red tape which separated me from civilian life.

In December I flew from Shanghai back to Washington, over the Pacific for the first time. In those same days General George Marshall was flying the Pacific in the opposite direction, ordered to China by President Truman in the hope of arranging peace between the Nationalists and the Communists. I later learned that on the day I left Shanghai, Marshall's headquarters had asked the OSS in Washington to find an interpreter for him, preferably an American field officer who had experience with Chinese armies and generals. The request was forwarded to Shanghai where my name was suggested, but luckily I had already gone and a Chinese-American officer was chosen.

The job would have been an honor, but I was glad to miss it. General Marshall needed an optimist, and I was already a pessimist. I was sure neither Chiang Kai-shek nor the Communists would settle for anything less than complete dominance.

I also suspected the Communists would win. The fronts around Peking had been as porous as they were static, and travelers with news often came in from the countryside. The Communists were reported to be strongly supported by peasants they had organized against the Japanese. They had set up an alarm system to warn of harvest-time invasions, recruited village militia, and led the guerrilla resistance. Anti-Communist travelers claimed some Japanese attacks had been provoked by Communists who wanted to strengthen their ties with the peasants by helping them fight off the Japanese, but almost all agreed the Communists had also gained popularity through tax-relief and some land reform.

Everywhere I had lived under the Nationalists, they seemed to regard the peasants as nothing but an endlessly exploitable source of money, food, and conscripts. They made no special effort to help the frontline villagers against the enemy. They exorbitantly increased taxes, and had done nothing to curb the growing land monopolies of the rich, including their own officials.

Since the Japanese surrender they had begun destroying

their formerly strong support in the urban middle and upper classes, who were anxious to have a stable commercial life re-established. This was prevented by carpet-bagging and the growing inflation. Nationalist officials and officers led in profit-eering from both evils.

Two special problems for General Marshall had been con-trived by Americans. The postwar plane-lift of Nationalist troops, which mixed the opposing forces higgledy-piggledy to-gether along the coast, creating artificial weaknesses and illu-sory strengths, made a lasting truce all but impossible. As far as I ever learned, the plane-lift was ordered by President Tru-man and his Chiefs of Staff.

Secondly, Roosevelt's policy of unqualified aid and praise for the Nationalists, though modified after the "Stilwell Incident," still persisted strongly enough to make the Nationalists quite intractable. They appeared sure that no matter how they squandered our aid, and destroyed their own strength through corruption and greed, we would still come to their rescue. They were right, too. Years afterward it was revealed that Mar-shall had secret orders to continue aid to the Nationalists, even if they refused to negotiate with the Communists.

Back in Washington after New Year's, I was disconcerted to learn I could not get out of OSS until I accounted for all the equipment assigned my command in the southeast, including what arrived after I left. Several hundreds of thousands of dol-lars were involved, more than I was likely to save in the rest of my life. Not only more jeeps, generators, and radios had been flown out, but fancy things like a helicopter — which I cer-tainly wished I'd had in besieged Changteh. I couldn't begin to locate materiel lost or expended in the exultant rush to the coast after the Japanese surrender.

Luckily the OSS interest in thrift was fleeting. When I

proved that I had been on leave, I was given an honorable discharge. In the spring of 1946 I joined USIS and sailed to China on the first troopship reconverted to civilian use. I was going to open a USIS office in Mukden, Manchuria.

After a decade of life in China, I had grown a bit blasé about its surprises, but for a while in 1946 I had a fresh eye. Louise joined me that summer in Mukden, and began seeing everything for the first time.

Her boat reached Shanghai during the annual floods, and as the wars had disrupted the system for sand-bag dikes, the downtown blocks were awash with a foot or two of dirty brown water. She knew she was supposed to ask about her plane ticket as soon as she disembarked. Transferring from an ocean liner to a landing launch to a sampan which took her up a city street and into a flooded hotel lobby where she found the ticket window, was the most irregular thing she had ever done in her life. She didn't like it when I met her in Peking and kidded her, saying that in China we always boated into hotel lobbies to get our plane tickets.

In Mukden we had rooms in the Japanese railway hotel, the Yamato, the best in town. It was a good imitation of an American hotel of the Statler grade, and was only a little worn and shabby after months of occupation by Russian officers, but like nearly every other building in town it had no utilities. The bathroom was luxuriously American, but in the American style it had no window and was lit only by one feeble candle. All water had to be brought in buckets by coolies who also carried away the wastes. I offered to hunt for a kerosene or magnesium lamp — in the gutted city this would have been a wild goose chase — but luckily Louise was toughening fast and said better not. She feared that if she had one well-lit look at the bathroom she could never bring herself to go into it again.

Mukden struck us as a stage set of a modern Western city

with nothing behind the painted facades and glassless windows
except barbaric poverty and deprivation. The Russians had
come in the previous August, at the end of their last-minute
campaign against the Japanese, and soon removed all machinery and raw materials from the factories, railway shops, and
arsenals, taking everything away from the Chinese Communists
as well as the Nationalists. They hauled off trains full of furnishings and supplies from Japanese and puppet government
offices and business firms. In the following months — which
grew savagely cold — Russian soldiers looted private houses,
Chinese as well as Japanese, taking household equipment for
their barracks, food and clothes to mail back to Russia. They
carried off furniture, doors, and woodwork to break up for their
stoves.

The last of them pulled out during my first spring weeks
there. Healthy dirty boys they seemed, and they were cheerfully loading their trucks and boxcars with weird loot, the
dregs of the city's debris. I remember filthy, torn mattresses,
bags of worn-out overshoes, garlands of frayed suspenders,
boxes of buttons. Then they were gone, leaving a grandiose
"Victory Monument" in front of the railway station, and an
"Observers' Group" of officers who lived at the Yamato and
used to glower at us few Americans in the dining room. At
about this time, American observers began hearing the Russian
withdrawal from farther north had been planned to let the
Chinese Communists rather than the Nationalists capture Japanese arms and ammunition left behind.

When Louise arrived, Mukden was firmly controlled by new
masters, crack Nationalist troops trained by Americans for the
Burma campaign and brought to Manchuria in U.S. Navy ships.
They were uniformed and armed like American GIs. They
didn't loot or rape as the Russians had, but their arrogance and
brutality made the Mukden Chinese fear them as conquerors
instead of welcoming them as liberators. Throughout the war

Louise had been reading indulgent news about the Nationalist armies in the American press — really fairy tales — and she was furious when she saw the real thing. Her coloring was so fair and her hair such a pale blond that a Chinese could easily mistake her for a White Russian refugee, and after she started venturing into the streets alone, she was several times pushed into the gutter by tipsy Chinese soldiers swaggering down the sidewalks in American uniforms.

When we were walking together, I could hear her murmuring if we saw plump American-fed-and-uniformed Chinese MP's gang up on an unfortunate rickshaw or wheelbarrow coolie, who could not understand these occupying soldiers who shouted in an unfamiliar provincial dialect. The MP's would pull off their belts and whip the half-starved wretch with the buckle-ends until he fell to the ground. This was a not uncommon incident.

At their barracks the Nationalists had sentries on the sidewalks to force everyone into the gutters, for no apparent reason except to show what big boys they were, and here Louise would start muttering again as we discreetly crossed to the other side. From her reading in America she seemed to have gotten the notion that China must be grateful to America for our aid, hence all Chinese would be polite to Americans. When she became noticeably pregnant, though, she found her weapon. She learned that sentries and even the tipsiest soldiers would defer to her. She began walking directly into them, regally straight-arming them into the gutters. Luckily it always worked.

General Marshall had promoted a truce within China proper in January of 1946, but Manchuria was too big and far away for enforcement, and open civil war began there in the summer, along the railway a couple of hundred miles north of Mukden. The Nationalists were full of confidence, for by then they had some three million regular soldiers all over the country, with much American armament, while the Communists had only about one million including militia and guerrilla units. In northern Manchuria, however, the Nationalists were dangerously over-extended, and the Communists doubtless tempted them into open warfare because they knew it. After a few weeks of bloody seesaw battle, the Nationalists began slowly falling back toward Mukden. The city was in such a state of postwar disorder that heavier troop movements were the only sign of the new conflict, and for months the civilians of Mukden seemed hardly to notice it.

Louise and I found that no hospital in the city had heat and complete windows, and since winter temperatures could drop to twenty below, Louise flew to Tientsin in late autumn to spend a few weeks with friends while waiting for the baby. Before she left we had the good luck to rent a small flat in the Hong Kong-Shanghai Bank Building, a big white relic of British imperial times, with water and lights as well as heat and windows. Louise had brought some American magazines with pictures of Swedish modern furniture and somehow found a Chinese cabinet-maker to start copying it in teak.

In Mukden I began keeping regular office hours for the first time in my life, but while I was alone that winter I had my last mildly adventuresome fling, when I went down to Antung on the Korean border to smuggle American propaganda into Communist North Korea. The branch railway line had been partly demolished by the Russians, semi-restored by the Nationalists. The broken glass in the passenger coaches was patched with boards, and the only heat came from close-packed bodies. When we slowly chugged over the many great swamps, the tracks slumped down in a noticeable wave motion. Closer to the border, tunnels and rickety timber bridges led across a washboard of mountain ridges and gorges. The longest bridge went straight from one tunnel-mouth to another, and as we crept across it I could feel the timbers buckling. The whole track seemed to sway back and forth several feet. "Hit that other hole!" I found myself fervently whispering to the engine. "Just hit that hole!"

As Mandalay had summed up for me the lush picturesqueness of warm southern Asia, Antung on the wide half-frozen border river, the Yalu, had all the non-picturesque fascination of the semi-Western, semi-Arctic, upper half of Asia. Grimy black and red nineteenth-century Russian buildings stood among Asian slums swarming with wolfish crowds in dark fur-lined rags and big shaggy fur hats. Over the bare purple mountains upriver, the empty sky was as icy a pale blue as if the North Pole were only a few miles farther on. The railway dominated this town which it had spawned on steppes inhabited by a few nomads only decades earlier. Many white stalks of smoke flowered over the freight yards, and a great shrilling of whistles broke out whenever a train edged across the long spindly bridge over the Yalu. This was the span whose bombing or non-bombing was to be so hotly argued in America five years later, when the Chinese Communists had Manchuria and American troops were deep in North Korea.

Through shopkeepers who openly sold Japanese goods, technically illegal, I soon found smugglers who were eager to take American propaganda — especially the big picture magazines — into Communist territory. They had fishing junks which mingled with the legitimate traffic, crossing in lightly-guarded stretches, and they were glad to take USIS material for a modest fee. Until the civil war cut the railway I made periodic shipments to them. The North Koreans must have been starved for outside news, and the magazines could have a wide underground circulation. On the other hand, Korea had a paper shortage, and the smugglers may have found it paid more to sell the magazines as raw material, for stiffening cloth shoes, lining luggage, and the many other uses to which paper was traditionally put in East Asia. I had no way of checking, and never knew.

The Antung trip was fun, and perhaps USIS in Washington could use the colorful smuggling angle to get money out of Congress, but when I settled into routine again in Mukden, I began to have my first misgivings about USIS work. I had opened a reading room with a rather limited stock of American books and magazines, ran a news service for the Chinese papers, and published a magazine of translations from American sources. Grandiosely, my mission was to get in touch with the Chinese of Manchuria, give them favorable ideas about America, and convince them American policy was to their best interests.

The great handicap, of course, was the unpopularity of America's Nationalist protégés. Next was the difficulty of communication in a land where the majority were illiterate, and movies and radio — never widely developed — had been knocked out by the war. The only Chinese I could realistically hope to reach were the students and intelligentsia — a tiny literate minority — in Mukden and a few other cities. Even with them, contact could seem strained and hypocritical because our conditions of life were so different.

Through the rest of that winter I taught English in a university with glassless windows. I had U.S. Army Arctic clothing but my kneecaps would get so frost-bitten I once fell on the stairs after class. I had a warm flat and consular office to escape to, but I knew many of my students could keep semi-warm only by getting in bed and staying there. It would have sounded hollow to claim we were allies fighting shoulder to shoulder for democracy.

When Louise and I came back with the baby, Julie, I began learning about formulas and other household chores. Some of the furniture was ready, and we had bought thick Chinese rugs and warm draw-curtains. After dark we shut ourselves away, as snug as a family of chipmunks under a stone wall, barely hearing the occasional shots and cries in the night. The war was still far away, but the Communists were infiltrating the Mukden area, getting ready to cut the railways. The countryside was in disorder and bandits sometimes raided the edges of town.

In January of 1947, General Marshall decided a truce was impossible and returned to America. Through that spring the fighting widened and spread southward. After the big conventional battles of the previous summer, the Manchurian war had settled into a special pattern, with the Nationalists entrenching themselves in cities or along the railways, giving the Communists the advantage of mobility. One by one the besieged garrisons surrendered — generals, crack troops, American arms, and all. Mukden was encircled, and although the Nationalists still controlled a sizable territory around it, starvation began in the city, overcrowded with destitute refugees from smaller towns. Along the rows of young trees lining the big avenues, strips of bark were torn away for boiling by the hungry. Corpses of starved babies were seen in the gutters.

Along with the fifteen or twenty other American families, Louise and Julie were evacuated in the late spring, on a U.S. Army plane to Peking and Shanghai. I made many trips to the airfield at that time, helping to get equipment and more evacuees off, and remember pathetic and terrible scenes. The last of the Mukden garrison did not in fact surrender for more than a year, but the feeling of being cut off encouraged panic. By now few believed the Communists could be kept from taking Mukden and the rest of Manchuria.

When news from the fronts was bad, thousands of refugees — Nationalist carpetbaggers, Mukden Chinese who had been too friendly with the Japanese, plain people who just wanted out — would camp around the airfield for days, hoping to get off on one of the Chinese commercial planes, their only hope. The planes simply weren't enough, and after panic news the refugees would swarm aboard one as soon as it came in, crushing the few incoming passengers backward and overloading the plane so badly it could not take off until the pilots had bullied half of them out again. Meanwhile other planes coming for refugees circled futilely overhead, waiting for a place to land.

Big officials commonly fled in chartered planes, empty except for relatives and courtiers, bodyguards, furniture and other valuables. Sometimes when panic swept the field, furious ordinary refugees would drive or push trucks out on the runways to keep the officials from taking off. Again, more arriving planes were kept from landing.

In the summer I was replaced in Mukden by a bachelor and transferred to Shanghai, where, for more than a year, I ran the USIS office of the Consulate-General. Louise and I found comfortable quarters on the seventh floor of Hamilton House, an American style apartment-hotel built in the 1930's. Our rooms were small, but we had a big terrace with a wall high enough to confine the baby. Whenever we needed a fresh garden, the roomboy would call in gardeners with a new one in pots, everything in full bloom. The war might be hundreds of miles away, and when we arrived, it still was.

The Hankow USIS office was a branch of the Shanghai headquarters, and in the fall of 1947 I flew up the Yangtze to inspect it. On my first morning there, a farmer came to the U.S. Consulate building shared by the USIS, and left a scrubbed pink piglet for me. Next morning I got up early and met two farmers I remembered well from Three Eye Bridge Village. They were bringing a hen and some eggs and a watermelon to me. They were smilingly mysterious about how they had learned of my arrival — I suppose someone in the Consulate or USIS had relatives in the village — but on every morning of my short stay, a gift of food was left for me.

I was on such tight bureaucratic schedule that I could visit Three Eye Bridge Village only once. I was delighted to find some of the Lao Po-pos alive, feeble and nearly blind but still enjoying life with tiny cackles and hoots, especially when lording it over their daughters-in-law. The sign "Brave as David" was still over the main entrance, but new American families, strangers to me, had moved into the compound. They were busy with their own affairs, mainly teaching, and contact between the mission and the village had subsided to its pre-Japanese level. I could hardly be sanctimonious, though, for by then I was preoccupied with my own need to survive and raise a family.

This was my last fleeting touch with peasant China, and it helped make the final hectic months in Shanghai specially unreal. The civil war steadily drew closer to the jammed metropolis, but Shanghai was so big, and so alien to the rest of China anyway, it seemed a country in itself. The American colony must have numbered two thousand, perhaps three, and it was a self-engrossed town within the detached country. The few remaining "Old China Hands" were submerged by crowds of younger Americans who regarded China as a strange but incidental background to their office work and their pleasures at parties, country clubs, or nightclubs. Against my better judgment I tangled in an amateur dramatic group of newcomers, as a stagehand, and I'm afraid I remember some of the Chinese civil war in terms of our production of *My Sister Eileen*. The new Americans were beginning to go as fast as they had come, and after every Communist victory some members of the cast would be ordered to evacuate. A general reshuffling of roles would follow, with many extra rehearsals. We never did get the play on.

Defeatism and cynical detachment were so strong among the Shanghai Chinese that our well-intentioned USIS projects could seem as superfluous as amateur theatricals. This was a sophisticated part of China, with radios in the villages, auditoriums and theaters even in the smaller towns. USIS had quite a bit of money, and enough personnel for some to seem permanently idle. But we could not make any meaningful approach to the general public, because so little meaning could be found in American policy.

Without criticizing the Nationalists we could do nothing about peasant opinion, which was bringing the Communists to power. Our Nationalist protégés wanted only munitions and money from Americans, not ideas, so there wasn't much to say to them. We continued to inform and entertain the detached or third-party literate minority, with reading room, lectures, concerts. In metropolitan Shanghai, they at least totaled some tens of thousands, though vastly outnumbered by the growing hordes of wretched refugees who lived and died on the streets.

In 1948 the inflation went wildly out of control. During the eight years of the Japanese war, prices had increased roughly 2,500 times. In the three years after the Japanese surrender they increased another 2,500 times. By 1948 they were doubling every few weeks, then every few days. Shoppers had to carry out a heaping basketful of paper money to come back with less than a full load of food. Productive effort and normal commercial life began to wither away, because workmen and small businessmen had to spend so much time in queues, trying to convert their Nationalist dollars into gold or foreign currencies, or hoping to speculate in goods. For a while we Americans, including the government-employed, were exempt from such worries because we were paid in American dollars we could sell on the black market.

In July, Chiang Ching-kuo, older son of Chiang Kai-shek — the jolly host on whose stomach I had jumped in Kanchow four years earlier — was appointed "Economic Czar" of Shanghai. He flew in from Nanking in a whirlwind of patriotic and portentous news releases. A new currency, the "Gold Yuan," equal to the American dollar, was to save the country. Speculation and black marketing must stop, and all loyal citizens were to surrender their hoards of precious metals and foreign currency as backing for the "Yuan." A harsh fate awaited evaders.

I did not see Chiang Ching-kuo that time, but like everyone in the apprehensive, rumor-ridden city I was uneasily aware of him. The sirens of his motorcycle guards and his limousine were often heard howling through the streets as he tracked down black-marketeers and their hoards. On August 8 he had eight of the worst offenders shot by a firing squad on lower Nanking Road — this was the equivalent of a public execution on Fifth Avenue at 42nd Street. Fearful crowds hastened to exchange their gold, silver, and foreign money for "Gold Yuan." Even the U.S. Government was alarmed enough to start paying its employees in "Yuan" and forbade us to use the black market.

For a few days the new money was stable, but Shanghai had become too cynical to believe the "Yuan" had real backing. Apparently it did not, and before the end of August was inflating. Like the Chinese, we Americans had to spend hours in queues as soon as we got our salaries, trying to beat the rise in prices by buying rice, oil, salt, soap, etc., for our own monthly needs and to pay our servants who no longer wanted any kind of Chinese money. Soon the new inflation was so steep that the U.S. Government cynically went back on the black market and began paying us in American dollars.

The only lasting result of young Chiang's "Economic Czardom" was that he had shaken down China's richest city for an unknown amount of treasure, and had it ready for removal to the island refuge of Formosa. This was the *coup de grâce* for what was left of the Nationalist economy, and the last straw for many well-to-do Chinese who until then had doggedly supported the Nationalists.

*

By the early autumn of 1948, the destruction or surrender of Nationalist troops had made the opposing armies roughly equal. In October the Nationalist garrisons of Mukden and other long-besieged Manchurian cities — some 350,000 men — surrendered.

In November and December the deciding battle of the civil war was fought. With a great booty of American arms, the victorious armies from Manchuria bypassed Peking, Tientsin, and other big cities of northern China and moved south toward the Yangtze. At Hsuchow, two hundred and fifty miles from Shanghai, Chiang Kai-shek concentrated more than a quarter of his remaining armies, including the best. This was against the advice of his staff and field commanders, but Chiang overrode them for one final time, perhaps because his single clear victory against the Japanese attacking Hankow in 1938 had been won at Taierhchwang near Hsuchow.

The Nationalists started the battle with superiority in American arms, and good lines of supply from their bases on the Yangtze. They had more than 500,000 men, the Communists had some 300,000. Again the Nationalists dug trenches and built forts and let themselves be encircled. The Communists harassed Nationalist supply lines while improving their own. One by one the static concentrations of government strength were isolated and reduced. By the time the Nationalists gave up on January 10, 1949, nearly all their soldiers were lost; the Communists claimed at least 300,000 by non-resistant surrender. With his "face" gone, Chiang Kai-shek resigned as President and went into "retirement," only to turn up on Formosa a few months later, President again by his own decree.

During the battle of Hsuchow, the people of Shanghai knew their future was being decided, but little fear of the Communists showed. Curiosity was more common, along with an intense desire to see the last of the Nationalists. Quite a few Americans and other foreigners were planning to stay, ready to be open-minded about the Communists, but most expected the capture of the city would cut ties with the outside world indefinitely. As the tide of battle turned, they crowded all departing ships and planes. Except for a few bachelors who would stay as test cases, American officials were ordered out. Louise and Julie were flown to the United States in November, and I followed in December.

After the defeat at Hsuchow, Nationalist China fell apart like a house of cards, but in slow motion because of the huge distances and multitudes involved. Encircled Peking and Tientsin surrendered peacefully in January. Through the winter the Nationalists fortified the south shore of the Yangtze, but when the Communists crossed in April the defenders left so hastily that Nanking was abandoned to looters before the victors could occupy it. Against little resistance, the Communists pressed on to Shanghai and took it in late May. As a final tribute to the Nationalist obsession with forts, the Shanghai garrison — perhaps 200,000 men — built a five- or six-foot fence of railway ties and stray timbers encircling the great modern city. The fence was not defended and most of the garrison surrendered peacefully.

For the rest of 1949, the Communists fanned out through southern and western China, where more and more regional generals and governors sought to join them. Chiang Kai-shek stayed in Formosa, pulling together his new web of drastically reduced power, but he kept a skeleton government on the mainland, hopping ahead of the Communists by plane, and sending off futile missions to try and persuade the provincial powers not to turn their coats. The capital at Canton fell in October, and its successor at Chungking in November. The last remains of Chiang's government on the mainland joined him in Formosan exile before the end of the year.

CHAPTER XIV

There but for John Birch   1953

WHEN I RETURNED in earlier years, Americans had been smug
in their ignorance of China, boasting of it with self-indulgent
chuckles. I was thought odd because I was so interested in a
foreign country. When I came back after the Communist victory, I found Americans were outraged, as if China had been
their personal property, like the family car. Now it had been
stolen by Russians and Chinese Communists. When they asked
how we "lost" China and I replied I doubted if we ever "had"
it, they were offended.

I was sent to the State Department in Washington for a few
months, and witnessed the rapid enlarging of the national
trauma which has dogged us to this day. Recalling what I
learned from columnists and commentators in 1949, or heard in
conversations and conferences, I remember America then as a
vain country which simply could not accept that it had been rejected by a China in which it tried to preserve an intolerable
government.

Scapegoats had to be found. The Russians were blamed,
though the bulk of the Japanese arms the Russians helped the
Chinese Communists capture in Manchuria had been exceeded
by the American arms the Communists took from surrendering

Nationalists. With a new campaign ahead, the Republicans were beginning to blame the Democrats, claiming Democratic presidents had not sent enough aid to the Nationalists — who never made effective use of the very considerable aid they did receive.

To anyone like myself, hoping to continue a career centered on China, the crucial news of 1949 was that the country had dwindled into an academic subject for Americans. By summer, most of the men who stayed in China as guinea pigs for Communist treatment were recalled or returned in discouragement. Those I knew felt it would be years, perhaps decades, before normal relations could resume.

In September the State Department sent me with two colleagues to Harvard, where special courses in advanced Chinese had been arranged for us. We studied "Documentary Chinese," the formal language used for state papers and diplomatic exchanges, and had a refresher course in "Newspaper Chinese." We learned "Grass Characters," a kind of shorthand used for informal notes and correspondence; its simplified, scriptlike ideographs could be scribbled faster than formal characters.

I was sent to the Hong Kong Consulate-General in the autumn of 1950, and two and a half pleasant, trifling years quickly followed. Louise and I made new friends and went to many parties. We had a comfortable house in a tropical garden near the top of the Peak — pink stucco, with a patio in California style, built by the American wife of the governor of the colony, and furnished largely with Chinese antiques Louise and I had gotten out of Peking before the Communists came. I was one of five American consuls, head of the U.S. Information Service, and half of my work was in "public affairs," the rest in publishing for Chinese readers in Hong Kong and Southeast Asia.

"Public affairs" included contact with many Chinese, British, and others in that great polyglot city. I had an entertainment allowance and was expected to know the people whose opinions could affect American interests. I also acted as welcomer, secretary, interpreter, and much else for the endless chain of American officials and distinguished private citizens who included Hong Kong in their round-the-world junkets. I'm afraid this sometimes made me feel like a number one roomboy, for impressive public figures would arrive with fighting statements about Democracy and Communism, then go limp at a suggestion that they inspect a refugee camp or missionary college, or call on officials. I was told to summon the twenty-four-hour tailors and dressmakers whose fame was spreading over the world, and was asked for lists of restaurants, night-clubs, and shops with the best buys in jade or silk.

The work with publications was more satisfying. I had a staff of about eighty Chinese and twelve Americans, four of whom could speak, read, and write Chinese as well as I. Aside from pamphlets and leaflets, we supplied a daily news service to the Hong Kong newspapers, published two magazines, and every year issued translations of twelve American books. We ran a reading-room and library in Hong Kong.

Our translated books aimed chiefly to show America had an interesting literature. Most were new novels; Hemingway's *Old Man and the Sea* was our great success. We tried to make the magazines propaganda only in that honest reporting was in our favor. One was a monthly patterned on *Life* and called *The Four Seas*. The other was a bimonthly newsmagazine, *The World Today*. Both were so popular in Southeast Asia that every month my office was able to send a check back to the Treasury Department, sometimes for more than HK $25,000. I believe this was the only place in the world at that time where foreign customers were paying so much of their own money to buy American propaganda.

The Communist-garrisoned border of China was less than twenty miles from my office, but my estrangement from China was complete. Like all non-British officials in the Crown Colony I had an "Exequator," a paper signed by Queen Elizabeth, recognizing me as an officer of the U.S.A. Collecting or spreading information on the mainland was prohibited on pain of banishment from Hong Kong.

Our second daughter, Kristin, was born in Hong Kong on December 30, 1952 — a sweet bundle of a baby and an additional, eleventh-hour tax exemption as well.

In the spring of 1953 I was given three months' home leave and in early summer we sailed for Honolulu. We needed a complete rest, so without telling anyone, even our families, we settled into a tiny flat in Waikiki and began several weeks of swimming and sunbathing. One morning I heard a knock on the door and in the hall found a U.S. Army major in full uniform, who handed me a telegram.

"You are to read this in my presence and reply immediately," he said stiffly.

"What is this?" I asked. "A joke?"

"I don't know," he said. "I'm just the messenger."

"A major, and just a messenger?" I smiled.

"Yes," he said without a trace of expression.

I found the telegram was from my boss in the State Department in Washington. "Proceed fastest to Tokyo, then to Chinese prison camps in Korea," it said.

I started to close the door but the major asked, "What reply?"

"Drop dead." I laughed. Still no expression.

"Are you sure you want to send this message?" he asked.

I said yes and closed the door. In the newspapers I had read of trouble in the prisoner-of-war camps in Korea. Former Chinese Nationalist troops, still anti-Communist but sent into battle by the Communists, had been put into prison camps with real Communist captives. Army censorship was strict, but rioting, fights, and murders were admitted to. It was a mess, crying for attention, but I was on an overdue leave and Hong Kong was my job.

Next morning the major came with a long telegram from Washington which said Communist propaganda was making capital of the prison story all through Asia; I was politely asked to interrupt my vacation, go to the camps, do what I could to improve conditions, then try to make a short movie refuting Communist lies. In Washington they always seemed to think that real tasks in foreign places were as easy as sending telegrams out of Washington, but I agreed to go.

After the major left, Louise said, "I didn't think of this yesterday, but how do you suppose he found our address?" We hadn't checked in with anyone in Hawaii, and it was unpleasant to realize we might be under surveillance.

Leaving my family in Waikiki, I flew to Tokyo where I found Army Headquarters so sensitive about the prison camps that they would not give me permission to go to Korea. After my request had bounced up through the ranks and was refused by General Mark Clark, I went to the American Embassy. Apparently Washington had not informed the Ambassador, and he said he could do nothing for me; everything was too irregular, too far out of channels. I went to a U.S. Air Force officers' club and began drinking with some transport pilots I found in the bar. When they learned that I had been chaplain of General Chennault's Flying Tigers, nothing was too good for me, and I easily hitched an unofficial lift to Korea.

The trouble at the prison camps proved to be simply one of communication. Most of the guards were Marines and if any of them, officers or enlisted men, spoke enough Chinese to handle the problems they faced, I did not meet them. They could not screen the prisoners and separate the ex-Nationalists from the real Communists. When violence broke out they felt all the prisoners alike were murderous idiots, and they ventured into the camps only in armed groups. As I later learned from the prisoners, ex-Nationalists had sometimes run up to the gates, imploring to be sent to a camp without Communists, even to be allowed to fight on our side. Several had been wounded or killed by young Americans who panicked at the approach of ragged foreigners shouting in an unknown tongue.

At each camp, I would first ask the Marine commandant to let me go inside myself. This caused disbelief or sardonic amusement.

"Good-bye, pal. This is the last we'll see of you," was one gibe of the grinning Marines who unbarred the gates. Inside I could see prisoners slowly coming out of their barracks, blinking in the sunlight.

"I am your friend," I called out in Chinese. "I have come to help you."

Incredulity inside the camp now, but for only a moment. Then the prisoners swarmed around me, plucking at my sleeves as they showered me with questions and requests.

Without many more men who spoke both English and Chinese, nothing could be done. I spent only two weeks in Korea, writing a scathing report which made some Marine generals furious. I heard hints that writing such critical stuff was unpatriotic, maybe worse. Because of my report, or those of others, Chinese-speaking Americans were later brought in, and several thousand prisoners were allowed to join the Nationalists on Formosa.

Back in Honolulu I found Louise had finished buying the clothing and other supplies she wanted for another long stint in the Orient. On one of our last afternoons in Waikiki we were visited by one of my staff from Hong Kong, on leave too. He had less than two hours between planes and stayed only a few minutes, with his taxi waiting in the street, but he said he must warn me. A Hong Kong girl who can be called Fifi Kwok had been passing word around town that she was going to "ruin Frillmann." Then our friend left so abruptly that neither Louise nor I thought to ask how he found our address.

Fifi was a bit of a mystery, and perhaps could harm. She was very pretty, with a fetching accent in English. She was supposed to be a reporter for a small Nationalist newspaper and did have a press card, but when I began to suspect her game and had my translation service check, I found nothing she wrote was ever published. Still, whenever I gave a press conference for a visiting American dignitary she would be in the front row with knees crossed high in her slit skirts, complexion freshly applied, and a pencil poised over a blank pad of paper. She was always in the group clustering around the dignitary afterward. If he didn't have a wife along, she often left with him or was seen with him later in his visit.

I checked with other Americans and found they also thought she was an agent but didn't know whose. As her cover was that of a Nationalist reporter she was probably working for that side, but Hong Kong was so complicated, with some Nationalists doing favors for Communists in case they took over, she could equally well be working for the Communists.

When one of our fireball junior congressmen came to Hong Kong he had me arrange a heavy schedule of visits and interviews, including one with the British Governor. Then he gave a press conference and met Fifi. Next day he sent a message telling me to cancel all appointments because he had left town. I later learned he and Fifi had shacked up in Macao, the Portuguese playground across the Pearl River estuary. I virtually had to wear sackcloth and ashes to apologize deeply enough to the Governor and others who were not used to having appointments broken without reason.

I barred Fifi from a few press conferences, saying she wasn't qualified because her stories weren't published. I telephoned her editor, who used our news service. He just laughed and said in Chinese slang, "She's a good kid. Why not give her a break?" Fifi must have seen I disliked barring her and she soon seeped back. No doubt she despised me. She already knew people in Washington, and was again in a position to meet more.

*

With only a few weeks of leave left, Louise and I stored our purchases for Hong Kong in the flat at Waikiki and flew to the mainland. I left Louise with her family in Chicago and went on to Washington for the standard five- or six-day briefing at the State Department. On the first day someone in my boss's department said, "The new security office telephoned and said they'd like to see you before you go back."

"Is it something special?" I asked.

"I think it's routine," he said. "Everyone who comes back from overseas seems to check in with them now."

I knew I had been through repeated security checks, for the U.S. Air Force and OSS as well as the State Department, but I had never been conscious of them because I wasn't questioned. I suppose people who knew me were, but I didn't hear about that either. The whole idea of security seemed rather abstract; and the notion of guilt by association simply had not occurred to me as an American precept.

In Hong Kong, for example, some Chinese Communist officials and journalists mingled socially with foreigners, including Americans. I had known a few for years before they or China turned Communist and would chat with them when we met at parties or on the street. Naturally I knew of McCarthy's rise to power on charges about Communists and fellow travelers in the State Department and of Eisenhower's endorsement of the McCarthy accusations in the presidential campaign of 1952, but I believed this did not concern me in Hong Kong because it was part of my job to know all kinds of people.

It took only a couple of days in Washington to learn how deeply the State Department was affected by the furor over security. At McCarthy's suggestion the new Secretary of State, John Foster Dulles, had accepted a former FBI man, Scott McLeod, as chief security officer, and by the time I arrived hundreds of men had been "released." Their numbers were well-publicized, and it was believed Dulles was trying to fight McCarthy's influence in his Department by making a maximum number of dismissals on his own. As Eisenhower had been elected on a platform which included charges of Communism in the Department, somebody had to be fired, Communist or not.

After a few busy days I telephoned the security office and made an appointment for ten the next morning. At the address I was given, near but not in the government district of Washington, I found a building which looked like a middle-class apartment house. There was no identification by the door, and in the white-painted lobby no directory of occupants, but many people were going up and down the elevators. Some were sharp-looking, conventionally dark-suited, youngish men — Madison Avenue operators, I would have said. Others were big thick-looking gents like funny-paper cops in mufti. A few were distinctly odd or exotic. Two who went up in the elevator with me were Japanese, but others just looked like international spies of no fixed nationality.

I reported to the receptionist on the floor to which I had been told to come, and in a few minutes two men approached and introduced themselves. One was a surly rough-looking character with a heavily-bandaged thumb. The other was younger, dudish, and quite bright-looking. Each carried a filing-cabinet folder bulging with papers. They ushered me down a corridor and into a former family apartment. A big committee table with heavy chairs filled the living room. Here they spread out their piles of papers and began questioning me. I suddenly realized this mass of paper was the dossier on Paul Frillmann, and I looked around the room wondering where the bugging devices were hidden.

The younger man efficiently led me through a quick biography, then asked about a Chinese who had headed my translation service in Mukden about five years earlier. I admitted helping him leave town secretly when Nationalist troops began looking for him because he was publishing satire against their general. I did not know whether he had been a Communist at that time, though he had come out as one in the years since the Communists took the mainland. I knew nothing about his past and had not hired him for the USIS. I said I would still have helped him leave Mukden since I knew something of brutality in Nationalist prisons in that period of collapse and demoralization.

The older man asked if I had seen anything of perversion in the State Department. In one of my posts, I said, I had learned a young American clerk was a homosexual and had been fired.

"How about yourself?" the cop asked. "Ever been a pervert?"

"What do you mean?" I asked incredulously.

"Ever play with yourself after the age of fourteen?"

He swore at my involuntary snort of laughter and the younger man took over again. "Tell us about your colleagues in Shanghai," he said quietly. "What were they like? What did they read, what magazines did they take? How much did they drink? What about parties, love affairs?"

Whatever the political reason for such questions, I could see their contempt for privacy and human dignity, their pressure for betrayal, were evil. I felt a growing fury that my government could handle such dirt.

"How about your own drinking?" the older man asked. "Ever take a few?"

"Of course," I said.

"Ever get drunk?"

"Certainly." I had been in army service for years and didn't think I needed to explain how an occasional binge with men you saw too much could relieve strained nerves. Anyone who didn't drink in the service was thought a bit of a nut. At the diplomatic and press parties I later attended as a civilian, drinking was standard, seldom excessive.

The younger man began inquiring about people and incidents quite unconnected with my life in government. "What about the night of June such-and-such 1950, in New York?"

he asked. "What were you doing between 9 P.M. and midnight?"

That was three years earlier, so I had to think for several minutes. Then I remembered I had been staying in the New York apartment of friends from China, and one night they mentioned that Agnes Smedley, whom I had known in Hankow in 1938, was visiting other China friends nearby.

Agnes, of course, was a controversial figure, and as a good little State Department boy I suppose I should have pretended not to hear what my hosts said, but to learn she was within walking distance made the idea of calling on her irresistible. I went, and we had a fine evening, sometimes uproarious, sometimes almost tearful, as we reminisced about the months when we had been fellow members of a tiny American community in a bombed and beleaguered Chinese city, square in the path of the Japanese invasion.

As a grown man fully aware of an old acquaintance's politics, I didn't see then why I shouldn't call on Agnes, and three years later I wasn't prepared to hide it, apologize for it, or even explain it. I did realize, however, that if my questioners were going to investigate things that had happened before I went into the State Department, my situation was probably hopeless. In my years in China I had held four very different jobs and had known thousands of people. I had never tried to know only the ones, or do only the things, that might be approved by a couple of spooks in a Washington of the far future. Now I wasn't going to try to placate them or lie for them, so I stopped answering their questions.

They dug out a paper and asked if I would sign an affidavit saying I was not and never had been a Communist. I said I would not sign anything. Instead, I would resign from the State Department. I had, of course, signed such affidavits before, as a matter of routine, but it seemed a point of honor not to be cowed and do it again for two men I despised.

I'm afraid the last minutes of our interview were noisy. The cop-type had become especially abusive and personal, so I made a rude surmise about why his thumb had to be bandaged. For one wild moment I thought I was going to exit from government by being thrown through a plate glass window and swan-diving to the pavement below.

Then I asked to see the head of their branch, to resign formally. He sat in a big office, looking like any executive with a good tailor.

"If that is the way you want it, that's the way it's going to be," he said briskly, waving me to the door.

I went to a phone booth in the street and telephoned my ex-boss. He was horrified. He asked me to go back, answer all questions, sign all papers, and he was sure everything would be all right. I said I had gone too far to turn back.

Then I telephoned Louise in Chicago. She was horrified too, naturally. I knew she was fascinated by our life in the Orient and hoped we were securely settled in it for a full career. I said I was sorry but I couldn't have acted any other way.

When I looked at my watch I was amazed; my whole life had been changed and it was still only a few minutes after twelve. I remembered a lunch date with a colleague from State, so I went to the restaurant and waited. Three quarters of an hour after he was supposed to join me, I miserably concluded he was afraid to be seen with me, and left without eating. He got in touch with me next day and apologized effusively, saying he simply forgot. I really believed him while we talked, but when I hung up I began to think, did I really? I had entered a new country.

I have never learned the specific reasons for this personal disaster. At the time, I thought I had been singled out, perhaps denounced by an irate Marine general, a Hong Kong party girl with a grudge, or a zealous CIA or FBI man, new to his job, who might have seen me talking to a Chinese Communist newspaperman on a Hong Kong street. Now I suppose it could have been a routine questioning, interrupted by my own quick temper.

In February 1954, after sixteen months of purge, Dulles and McLeod announced the total they had "released" for security reasons was 534 men. State Department officials later summoned to a secret hearing of a House Appropriations Subcommittee conceded only 11 were fired for questionable loyalty. No active Communists were found. I believe a fair number of the 534 had not been "released" but resigned like myself, appalled or infuriated by their questioners, unable to afford lawyers to steer them through a full-dress investigation in which the identity of their accusers could be kept secret.

It wasn't easy for someone newly out of the State Department to find another job in 1953, and I was lucky that Harold Oram, an American I had recently shown around Hong Kong as part of my work, was head of a large public relations and fund-raising organization in New York. Among its clients were some of the Negro colleges in the South, and various liberal causes like the NAACP. In Hong Kong Mr. Oram had told me that if I ever wanted to leave the State Department, I should get in touch with him. The day after my resignation I telephoned him and he offered me the job I have had ever since.

Louise and I found that for people detached from China, New York was probably the best place in the world to live, so many old friends kept coming through. At odd hours we would be telephoned by former missionaries, AVG pilots, redomesticated spies and the like, asking if we had a bed or a patch of floor where they might sleep. Hours and days of China talk usually followed.

In New York I began seeing Chennault again. He had been in Shanghai while I was there but I don't think I saw him more than twice for a brief lunch. He had organized a commercial airline and at the Chiangs' request, UNRRA, the international relief agency, procured him planes to fly relief supplies into the interior. When his bill for flying the supplies at high emergency rates equalled UNRRA's low charge for the war-surplus planes, they became his.

In New York such things were softened by time and distance, and at one of the annual AVG reunion banquets I had a long and amiable conversation with him. I think he may already have known he was dying. He liked to talk of old times in China. He used to come up from Louisiana for board meetings of the airline, and he fell into the habit of telephoning me to come to his hotel for several hours of reminiscing.

I saw him for the last time about a year before his death of lung cancer, when he came north to do a cigarette ad later featured on the back cover of many magazines. He called and asked if I could take time off to visit with him. We went to a loft where two skittish young photographers had assembled heaps of pseudo-Chinese junk, and stayed hours while they plunked the general up and down in arrangements of phony gongs, soapstone dragons, and other gimcracks.

They mauled the ailing Tiger around as if he were a bundle of rags. "Look there!" "Look here!" "Hold your hands this way!" "Blow the smoke that way!" they would order, then they touched up his cheeks with theatrical makeup. I had never seen that hawk face so full of concentrated hate. In the taxi on the way over, he had said he was doing the ad job only to get money for medical expenses. He also assured me that, despite popular opinion, he was not a wealthy man, but living on a salary which was not excessive.

When we finally went out into the drizzly afternoon, he seemed exhausted. He must have felt death close ahead. He settled his deaf ear into the corner of the taxi and sat silent for several blocks. Then he began talking about the death of John Birch, a subject he had never mentioned before.

He said he was telling me because he hoped I would someday

write a book about Birch and myself and the others in combat
intelligence in southeastern China. I remember replying that
perhaps my own story and Birch's, too, might better not be
publicized, since we had both been missionaries. The Communists were beginning to claim all missionaries were imperialist spies, and an admission that Birch and I had gone into
intelligence could be used to persecute other missionaries.
Chennault reminded me we had simply been in combat intelligence against the Japanese, whom the Communists were also
fighting.

Not long before the Japanese surrender, he went on, and only
a few days before he had to retire and leave China, he heard
one of his P-40's had shot down a new kind of Zero near Hsuchow, in country where Japanese, Nationalist and Communist
troops were entangled. He sent John Birch to examine it and
bring it back, if possible. Knowing how confused the situation
around Hsuchow was that summer, I couldn't help thinking
this was another of Chennault's unaccountably optimistic decisions, like asking me to test the poison gas at Changteh. There
might be a fifty-fifty chance of Birch's reaching Hsuchow, but
not one in a thousand that he could bring the plane back.
There was no reason, either, why Chennault could not have suggested to the Nationalists that they ask the Communists to help
get the plane; the two factions were negotiating then, and Mao
Tse-tung was in Chungking for talks with Chiang Kai-shek.

The roads and railways were so destroyed and the country so
cut up by little fronts that Birch could not get to Hsuchow until ten days after the Japanese surrender. The whole area was
under Communist control. By the ordinary rules of Chinese
protocol he should have gone into town, called on the ranking
officer, and after enough tea and small talk, politely asked for
permission to see the plane. With his usual single-mindedness
he went directly to the plane, which was guarded by soldiers
with orders to shoot anyone who came too close. As he

approached, they shouted their orders and asked him to turn back. He kept coming. Amid much shouting and scuffling the young soldiers — boys really — confusedly opened fire. One bullet went through John's forehead, killing him instantly. His Chinese assistant was wounded, played dead, and at length returned to Kunming with the story. When the Nationalists took Hsuchow after Birch's death, peasants showed them his shallow grave. A hasty effort to destroy the evidence had been made, for the body was covered with oil and partly burned.

"By the way, Frillmann," Chennault said reflectively, "if you hadn't been in America getting married, I would have sent you on that mission instead of Birch."

It took a while for this to sink in. Since then, it has come to seem the crowning irony of my years in China. Without my being at all different, an accident of time and place could have provided a different ending to my life in China. I hope I would have been smart enough at Hsuchow to avoid Birch's fate. Perhaps not, though. Then I could have been the first American killed by Communists after the Japanese surrender and instead of commemorating John Birch, many rightist idiots might now be members of "The Paul Frillmann Society."